MW01129702

Focus on
AFRICA

Edward Reynolds
Professor, Department of History
University of San Diego

D.C. Heath and Company
Lexington, Massachusetts / Toronto, Ontario

Editorial, photo research, design, and production
Book Production Systems, Inc.

Published simultaneously in Canada
Printed in the United States of America
International Standard Book Number: 0-669-40551-5

2 3 4 5 6 7 8 9 0 – BAW – 01 00 99 98 97 96

Contributing Authors

Robert Addo-Fening
Senior Lecturer
Department of History
University of Ghana
Legon, Ghana

Barbara Winston Blackmun
Professor of Art History
Mesa College
San Diego, California

Susan H. Broadhead
Associate Professor
Department of History
University of Louisville
Louisville, Kentucky

John Kofi Fynn
Chair, Department of History
University of Ghana
Legon, Ghana

Candice L. Goucher
Associate Professor
Department of Black Studies
Portland State University
Portland, Oregon

Paul S. Orogun
Assistant Professor, Political Science
DePaul University
Chicago, Illinois

Consulting Reviewers

Eren Giray
Outreach Director
Visiting Assistant Professor
Center for African Studies
University of Illinois at Urbana-Champaign

Ivy L. Murrain
Social Studies Teacher
Hoggard High School
Wilmington, North Carolina

K. Chaka K. Nantambu
Chair, History Department
Cody High School
Detroit, Michigan

Clarence G. Seckel, Jr.
Social Studies Coordinator
Department of Curriculum and Instruction
East St. Louis School District 189
East St. Louis, Illinois

Gloria Sesso
Supervisor of Social Studies
Half Hollow Hills School District
Dix Hills, New York

Contents

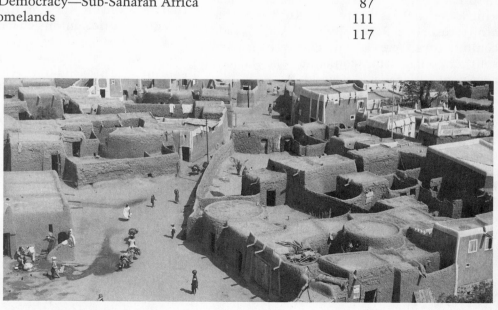

Introduction

Considering that several decades ago many Westerners were not even aware that Africa had a history, the fact that you are reading this textbook is a bit remarkable. You are about to learn that not only does Africa have a history, but it is a history that is both fascinating and filled with events that impact you. As you read, remember that while the history of Africa is mainly distinct from that of the United States, Africa is part of your history as well. The growing interdependence of our world demands that all its citizens gain awareness of its people and places. In many ways, we are all members of the same community.

Chapter 1

When Europeans began to explore the African continent, they were not aware of Africa's rich and diverse history. For centuries they looked at Africa through European eyes and did not realize that the cultures of Africa embody ancient traditions that stretch back in time many centuries. This ancient culture and history is the focus of Chapter 1.

One fact emerges immediately to those who study Africa; it is a continent with many diverse and distinct cultures. Even its geography is a panorama of landforms and climates. These different regions have been linked by the great rivers of the African continent: the Nile, Niger, Zaire, and Zambezi. Archaeological evidence shows that human beings originated in Africa. As the human race developed, ancient kingdoms such as Egypt and Kush emerged along the Nile River. By A.D. 1000, trade communities were developing in eastern and southern Africa that connected the African continent with the wider world.

Chapter 2

One sad aspect of Africa's past that most people are aware of is the slave trade. Slave trading has been part of Africa's history for centuries. The scope and impact of this trade increased dramatically, however, when Europeans began to trade with Africans for slaves in the 1400's. The Atlantic slave trade caused the forced migration of millions of Africans to the Americas. This migration was part of the triangular trade that shipped goods from Europe to Africa in exchange for slaves who were taken to the Americas. In this chapter, you will read about the inhuman suffering endured by Africans during the so-called Middle Passage from Africa to the Americas. The impact of this trade on Africa's economy and culture is long lasting. Many scholars trace present-day racism toward Africans and African Americans to this episode in world history. As you read this chapter, consider the factors that caused this shameful episode in world history to occur.

Chapter 3

Until the 1800's, Europeans were content to maintain trading posts along the African coast. After 1850, however, the African continent became involved in a European power struggle that resulted in the colonization and partitioning of Africa. In this chapter, you will read how European desire for power and money led to a drive to establish colonies on the African continent. This land-hungry drive was fueled in part by European missionaries who believed in the superiority of European religion and culture. The colonization of Africa was often brutal, and African resistance movements were forced to deal with the harsh reality of superior European weapons.

Colonization also resulted in the subjugation of African culture, for which Europeans had no regard or understanding. Colonization affected all aspects of African life, but probably none so much as Africa's economy. Colonial business enterprises drained African natural resources and labor. Africans today continue to struggle with this economic legacy.

Chapter 4

In Chapter 4, you will read about Africa's successful struggle to throw off the yoke of colonialism. A number of factors spurred African nationalist movements, including Western-style education and the ideas of Christian and Muslim religious movements. African soldiers returning home from fighting for colonial powers in World War II had gained a new sense of their own mission—to liberate their homelands from European domination. By the 1950's, European nations such as Britain and France began to acknowledge the growing nationalist movements. Many roads led to African independence: for some nations, the transition was peaceful. In others it was violent. As you read this chapter, consider how colonialism affected Africans' ability to govern themselves after independence.

Chapter 5

More than likely, your life has already been impacted in some way by African culture. In this chapter, you will learn about the traditions from which African cultures spring and how these traditions are evolving to affect the world today. African art can be traced back 20,000 years to rock paintings in the southwestern part of the continent. Ancient cultures in western Africa created intricate sculptures and pieces of art using techniques that were advanced even by today's standards. In the 1500's, the trade corridor of the Niger River allowed the development of an advanced art culture. The brilliant African civilizations that developed in the Nile River valley possessed unique and distinct cultures as well. In this chapter, you also will read also about present-day African artists who combine traditional art forms with contemporary techniques in sculpture, painting, and music.

Chapter 6

You probably have already read or heard about the problems facing Africa today: famine, AIDS, and political instability. In Chapter 6, you will read about these problems and the efforts being made to overcome them. A number of factors have contributed to instability in Africa today, including ethnic differences, government corruption, and economic decline. A recurring problem in Africa today is food shortages. Sadly, many African leaders continue to force farmers to grow cash crops to prop up their economies while their own people die from hunger.

While it is true that African countries have struggled with democracy and that many African governments are repressive, there are also glimmers of hope on Africa's horizon. In this chapter, you will read about a number of grass-roots movements that are trying to re-focus Africa's resources on its own people. You will also read about the ongoing struggle to establish human rights for South Africans.

Chapter 7

Perhaps more than any other country, Nigeria epitomizes the hopes and struggles of African nations. Nigeria seemed poised for a prosperous history when it gained independence from Britain in 1960. So far this dream has not been fully realized. Nigeria's independence has been characterized by instability and violence. Like many African nations, Nigeria contains a number of distinct ethnic and religious groups within its borders. This has caused political and social friction. In the late 1960's, Nigeria fought a costly civil war that debilitated the nation. Currently, Nigeria continues to struggle with democracy and determining how best to use its abundance of natural resources.

Chapter 1

Africa: The Land, Peoples, and Early Civilizations

Africa from space

Key Terms

oral tradition
griot
archaeology
botany
linguistics
savanna
desertification
oasis
trade language
sedentary
pharaoh
hieroglyph
syncretism
divine kingship

Read and Understand

1. Africa is a diverse continent.
2. Africa is the birthplace of humankind.
3. Trade communities arose in the east and south.
4. Trade empires flourished in the western Sudan.

In the beginning, according to the Yoruba, the world was a watery place. Olodumare, the Almighty, decided to make the marshy land into solid earth. He asked the chief of the gods, Orisha-nla, to make the ground solid. Olodumare gave Orisha-nla some loose dirt, a hen, and a pigeon and sent him on his way.

Orisha-nla climbed down a spider web that connected the heavens to the earth. He threw the dirt onto a watery place and at once the hen and pigeon began to spread it around, making solid ground. Orisha-nla went back to the heavens to report to Olodumare that he had been successful.

Olodumare then asked the chameleon to see if Orisha-nla had indeed been successful. On his first trip, the chameleon said the earth was wide but still not dry enough. On his second trip, the chameleon said the earth was both wide and dry enough.

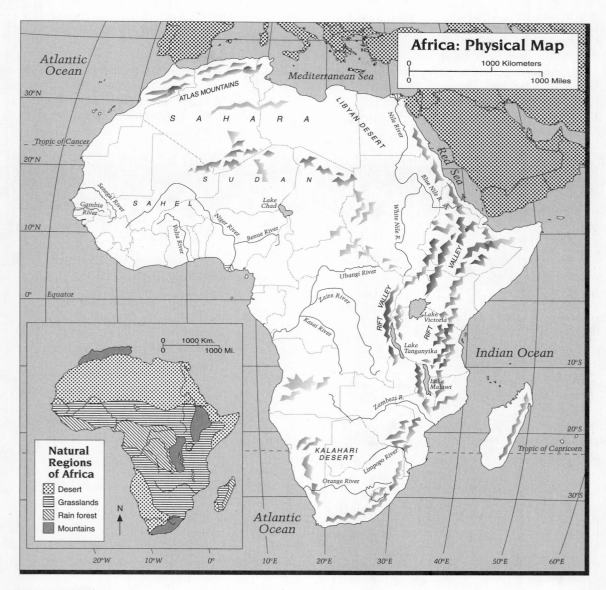

Africa: Physical Map

Atlantic Ocean
Mediterranean Sea
30°N
ATLAS MOUNTAINS
SAHARA
LIBYAN DESERT
Nile River
Tropic of Cancer
20°N
SUDAN
Red Sea
Blue Nile R.
Senegal River
SAHEL
Lake Chad
White Nile R.
Gambia River
10°N
Niger River
Benue River
Ubangi River
RIFT VALLEY
Zaire River
RIFT VALLEY
0° Equator
Kasai River
Lake Victoria
Indian Ocean
Lake Tanganyika
RIFT
10°S
Lake Malawi
Zambezi R.
20°S
KALAHARI DESERT
Tropic of Capricorn
Limpopo River
Orange River
30°S
Atlantic Ocean
20°W   10°W   0°   10°E   20°E   30°E   40°E   50°E   60°E

0   1000 Kilometers
0   1000 Miles

Natural Regions of Africa
- Desert
- Grasslands
- Rain forest
- Mountains

N

0   1000 Km.
0   1000 Mi.

Map Study

A physical map shows the natural features of a region. Notice the diversity of Africa in this physical map. Compare the physical features in the map with the photograph of Africa on the opposite page.

It took four days to finish creating the earth. On the fifth day, no work was done. This was a day to worship Olodumare, the Almighty.

This creation story has been passed down orally for centuries by the Yoruba, an ethnic group in what is now Nigeria. To the Yoruba, the place where the world began was their holy city of Ife, whose name means "that which is wide."

The Yoruba creation story is an example of the **oral tradition**. Most African societies have a well-developed oral tradition system of passing history down from one generation to the next.

Some African societies, especially in West Africa, have professional historians called **griots** who are trained in the oral tradition. In the past, griots were typically assigned to kings and were

1

entrusted with all the important facts about their people. Griots also reminded kings of traditions that had to be followed.

An African griot who practices the oral tradition today explains his work this way. "I teach kings the history of their ancestors so that the lives of the ancients might serve them as an example, for the world is old, but the future springs from the past."

Much of what we now know about Africa's distant past is a result of the griots' work. In this lesson, you will learn about Africa's past. As you will read, the history of Africa in fact goes to the very birth of humankind.

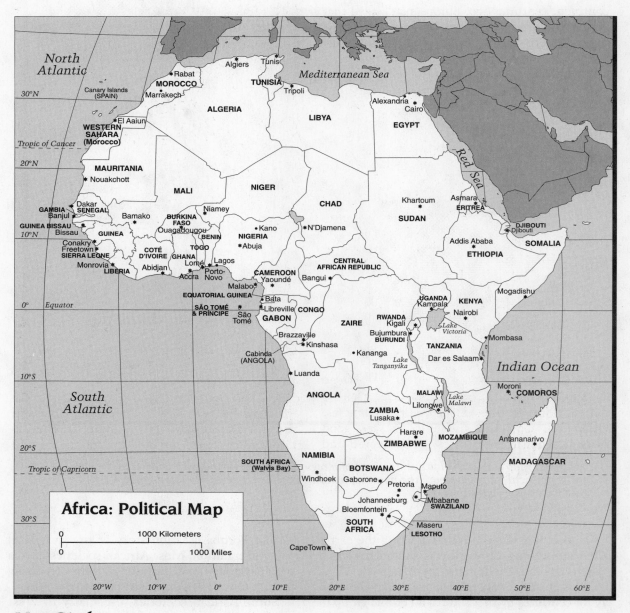

Map Study

A political map shows human boundaries such as nations and cities. Compare the political map of Africa on this page with the physical map on the previous page.

Africa is a diverse continent.

1

Western historians have not always recognized the importance of the oral tradition. Because many African societies did not have a written language when Europeans came to the continent centuries ago, Europeans decided that Africans had no history. In fact, until recently, most Western scholars believed that African history began only with the coming of Europeans.

The Europeans were using their own standards to judge African culture and therefore dismissed the Africans' rich cultural heritage and achievements. This cultural ignorance has led to many misconceptions about Africa, some of which persist to this day. For example, one popular misconception is that Africa is a land full of jungles, when in fact, only about one seventh of Africa is covered by jungles.

Africa is a continent of great diversity, both in the land and in the peoples. Perhaps one reason why Westerners have continued to see Africa in only stereotypical ways is because of an ignorance of this diversity.

Historians use many methods to study African history.

Historians are mindful of Africa's diversity as they piece together its past. They must also use many different methods. You have seen how the oral tradition is important to the study of Africa. Some stories tell about great battles. Others tell about times when crops were good or bad. When these stories are collected and analyzed by historians, they provide important knowledge and information about the African past. Other tools that African historians use, besides written records, are those of archaeologists, botanists, and linguists.

Archaeology is the study of ancient societies. Archaeologists study material remains to learn about past ways of life. **Botany** is the study of plants. Through botany, scientists learn about the development of food production and the role that it has played in the evolution and the shaping of African cultures. **Linguistics** is the study of languages. African historians use

By the 1960's, African historians wanted to preserve oral histories on tape.

linguistics to understand and interpret the movements of African peoples. By comparing languages, scientists can determine the time when related languages separated from one another.

Geography shaped Africa's history.

Perhaps the most striking feature of the African continent is its size. The landmass of the continent and its adjacent islands is 11,700,000 square miles. This area is about 3 times the size of the United States. The continent is 4,600 miles wide at its widest point. From north to south, the continent measures 5,200 miles. A single state in West Africa, Mali, is larger than the combined areas of California, Arizona, Nevada, and Utah.

Africa has great geographical diversity—deserts, snow-covered mountains, and woodland forests. Even though they are the same distance from the equator, the tropical locations of Zambia in southern Africa and Nigeria in West Africa have markedly different climates. The reason is the difference in their altitudes.

3

Clumps of vegetation, including grasses and umbrella-shaped trees, permit easy grazing on Africa's savanna. The natural balance of the savanna has been affected by the prevalence of domesticated herds. The domesticated animals eat the grasses that once were eaten only by the natural herds of grazing animals. Competition for food and overgrazing result. In addition, people often kill natural predators when they hunt near the domesticated animals, which affects nature's balance between prey and predators. What solutions would you suggest for these problems?

Tropical rain forests The tropical rain forests of the African continent are found in the western part of equatorial Africa along the Guinea coast and Zaire. The climate here is characterized by high temperatures of 68°F (20°C) and an annual rainfall in excess of 50 inches (127 mm). Trees grow well in this region and yield such valuable wood products as mahogany and ebony, as well as palm oil from the fruit of the palm tree.

A variety of crops grow in the tropical rain forest region. These crops include manioc, yams, corn, rice, sweet potatoes, plantains, bananas, coffee, and cotton. Important mineral deposits are also found in the tropical rain forest. These minerals include gold, copper, coal, diamonds, manganese, iron ore, tin, zinc, bauxite, and titanium.

Savannas The tropical forests thin off into the **savanna** belt. The savanna consists of tropical woodland and grassland. As the rainfall diminishes, the rain forest is succeeded by woodlands that cover about 25 percent of the African continent. The absence of dense woodlands allows the people in the savanna to keep herds and live a nomadic life.

From the savanna come agricultural products such as sorghum, wheat, peanuts, millet, cotton, and bananas. The economic mainstay of this region is livestock, including cattle and sheep. This area also contains mineral resources such as gold, diamonds, coal, petroleum, copper, manganese, iron ore, phosphates, zinc, copper, and tin.

Deserts The savanna woodland gives way to bush and scrub and merges with the desert. The two major desert areas of Africa are the Sahara and the Kalahari. The Sahara, whose name comes from an Arab word meaning "desert," is the world's largest wasteland. (The term *sub-Saharan* is used to describe Africa south of the Sahara.) The Sahara started to become a desert about 10,000 years ago, when the climate in the region became less wet and the rivers dried up. When green land becomes desert over a period of time, the process is known as **desertification.**

In spite of its forbidding nature, the Sahara has not been an impenetrable barrier. For centuries, trade routes across the Sahara have linked the northern and southern parts of Africa. Palm groves and oases provided convenient stopping places when crossing the desert. An **oasis** is a place where underground water comes to the surface in a spring or well.

Highlands The highlands are characterized by their elevation of more than 5,000 feet. The highlands are located in east, central, and southern Africa. The cool temperate nature of this region has attracted European settlements.

The commercial crops in the highlands consist of coffee, cotton, sisal, coconut, tea, cashew nuts, and rice. Coffee is also a highly valued crop and is widely grown. Valuable minerals in the highlands include diamonds, copper, gold, tin, soda, ash, and phosphates.

Rivers have linked African regions.

The rivers of the African continent have been a source of inspiration and imagination. The Nile, the Niger, the Zaire, and the Zambezi rivers have played important roles in the continent's history. They are among the longest and largest river systems in the world. These rivers sometimes represented cultural or political boundaries between groups of people. Sometimes they served as transportation links between regions.

The rivers also served as water highways for European exploration of the African continent in the 1800's. European explorers claimed to

The lower Volta River, shown above, is part of a 1,000-mile river system in western Africa. It is but one of Africa's great river systems that have served as a transportation routes for thousands of years. Why are rivers often considered the world's oldest ready-made roads?

have discovered these rivers, not taking into account that Africans had developed major civilizations along these rivers centuries before Europeans entered the continent. Many of these explorers gave European names to the rivers, lakes, and falls that they encountered. The Zaire, for example, was long known by its European name, the Congo. The African name for one of the world's most spectacular falls is *musi oa tunya*, which means "smoke that thunders." When the famous missionary David Livingstone came upon the falls, he named them Victoria Falls after the British queen.

Oases dot the Sahara, the world's largest desert, providing refuge for animals and travelers.

Africa has cultural diversity.

Africa's many environments have contributed to the creation of cultural diversity on the continent. A complete map of Africa would include the locations of the many hundreds of different peoples. Some scholars classify African peoples according to their physical type and skin color. Because of a mixing of peoples through centuries of intermarriage, this sort of classification is not very useful in most parts of the continent. Some nations, such as Ethiopia, Madagascar, and Egypt, have long histories of interaction between different physical types, producing populations with varying skin colors and varying genetic features. These parts of the continent have served as historical crossroads, linking Africa with other parts of the world.

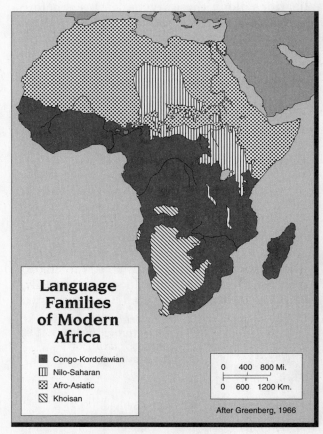

Language Families of Modern Africa

- ■ Congo-Kordofawian
- ⫿ Nilo-Saharan
- ▨ Afro-Asiatic
- ◩ Khoisan

0 400 800 Mi.

0 600 1200 Km.

After Greenberg, 1966

Map Study
Use this map and the political map on page 2 to determine which language family dominates three different African nations.

Using language classifications is one way to discuss the diverse groups in Africa. More than 800 languages are spoken on the African continent. Some of the languages are spoken by large groups of people, others by small groups. Within some language groupings are hundreds of distinct languages and many hundred more dialects.

African languages spoken on the continent are divided into four major groups: Afro-Asiatic, Congo-Kordofawian, Nilo-Saharan, and Khoisan. Afro-Asiatic group languages are common in the north, northeast, and certain parts of central Africa. The Congo-Kordofawian family of languages is the largest group and includes languages spoken in West Africa and South Africa. The Nilo-Saharan group is spoken in some areas around the Nile and Niger rivers and the western Sudan. Khoisan is characterized by sounds made with a click of the tongue. It is spoken by the Khoi and the San in southern Africa.

Many Africans are able to speak a number of local languages. There are also trade languages, such as Swahili, that are used by a large number of people. A **trade language** might be a combination of languages, or a simplification of one language. Because of colonization, (see Chapter 3) many Africans use the languages of their colonizers to communicate among themselves.

Lesson Review 1

Define: (a) oral tradition, (b) griot, (c) archaeology, (d) botany, (e) linguistics, (f) savanna, (g) desertification, (h) oasis, (i) trade language
Identify: *musi oa tunya*
Answer:
1. What functions do the griots serve?
2. In what ways is Africa geographically diverse?
3. What are the four major language groups in Africa?
4. Why are trade languages useful?

Critical Thinking
5. What factors, do you think, led Western historians to ignore the importance of the oral tradition?

Africa is the birthplace of humankind. 2

Archaeological evidence shows that human beings originated in Africa. It is the only continent with evidence of all the stages of human evolution. And recent studies suggest that all humans can be traced back to an African ancestor, although not all scientists accept the findings of these studies (text, page 22).

Africa has been called the cradle of humanity. Yet the continent was not only the cradle, but also the nursery and perhaps even the schoolyard. Distinct and important stages in the biological and cultural evolution of humans appeared on the African continent.

The first hominids, or creatures that walk upright, originated in Africa and were well established there by 4 million years ago. No one knows for sure why they began to walk upright, but scientists have come up with at least three theories to explain the development (text, page 18). Over millions of years, these creatures, called australopithecines, changed and developed. Although scientists have found no definite fossil evidence, it seems likely that the australopithecines used some primitive tools, such as sticks to dig termites out of their mounds and stones to crush nutshells.

Our knowledge of the first human species, *Homo habilis,* owes a lot to the work of Louis and Mary Leakey, who spent years at Olduvai Gorge in Tanzania and at other East African sites. *Homo habilis,* which seems to have evolved out of one of the australopithecine species, arrived on the scene about 2.5 million years ago. This hominid was the first known to fashion recognizable stone tools; thus, its arrival marks the beginning of what scientists call the Stone Age (text, page 19).

Homo habilis eventually disappeared, but before that happened a new human species arose in Africa—*Homo erectus*. This species—whose brain was significantly larger than that of *Homo habilis* and of the australopithecines—had a larger tool kit than did *Homo habilis*. At least as important, it was the first hominid to use and control fire. With fire, these hominids could live in the colder parts of Africa. And fire is probably what allowed *Homo erectus* to leave Africa and spread out across cooler climates in Eurasia.

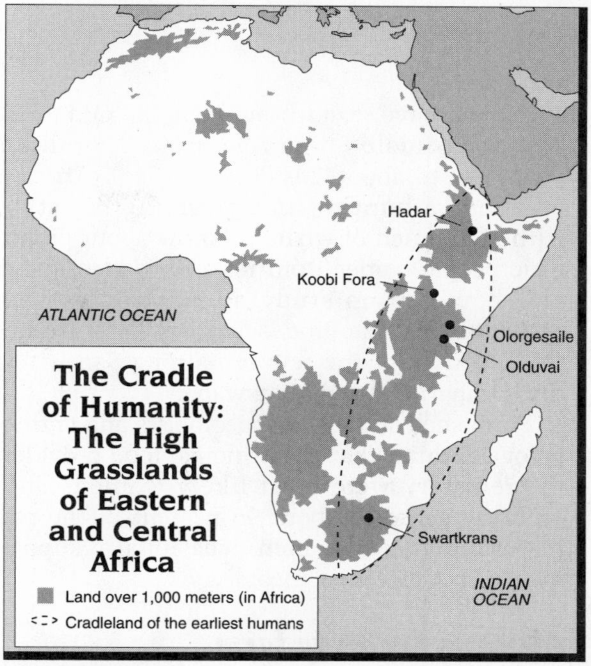

The Cradle of Humanity: The High Grasslands of Eastern and Central Africa
Land over 1,000 meters (in Africa)
Cradleland of the earliest humans
ATLANTIC OCEAN
INDIAN OCEAN
Hadar
Koobi Fora
Olorgesaile
Olduvai
Swartkrans

Map Study

Which places where early humans developed were on or near a great river or lake? What conclusions can you draw based on this information?

Some scientists believe that *Homo erectus* developed into early *Homo sapiens* (our own species) at different times and places around the world. Others believe that *Homo sapiens* first arose in Africa and spread out from there. Whatever the case may be, the early *Homo sapiens* lived in much the same way as its predecessors, *Homo habilis* and *Homo erectus*. Living in small, probably nomadic, bands, they gathered food from the wild plants around them and used stone tools to butcher animals.

Even the first anatomically modern humans, who appeared in Africa about 60,000 to 80,000 years ago, followed this same life-style. Gradually, however, their tools became more sophisticated and more numerous. These tools allowed them to do more hunting of larger animals at less risk to themselves. (Earlier hominids, while they may have caught small or young or weak animals, probably scavenged most of their meat from the kills of predatory animals or from animals that had died by accident or from disease.) People also began to create art works—paintings of animals on rocks and carvings made from stone or bone or wood. They began to develop more complex societies, living in organized groups, interacting, cooperating, and socializing.

As you have read, throughout the Old Stone Age and Middle Stone Age (from 2.5 million years ago to about 10,000 years ago), Africans practiced a hunting and gathering life-style. Although much of what we know about prehistoric people comes from fossil evidence, much also comes from studying existing hunter-gatherers. For example, scientists have studied the life-style of the few remaining San in the dry Kalahari Desert of Botswana.

From such studies, archaeologists and anthropologists think that the principal food providers in prehistory were most likely women. They probably gathered about 95 percent of the prehistoric diet, while men occasionally supplemented the diet with meat.

Africans began to farm.

The hunting and gathering way of life continued for millions of years, but in the New Stone Age, some time after about 8000 B.C., it gradually gave way to farming and herding.

Agricultural beginnings People first began farming and herding in Southwest Asia, but not long afterwards, Africans began to follow an agricultural way of life. Agriculture is the domestication or manipulation of plants or animals to make them more productive. The process occurred independently in many places around the world. Early African agricultural societies and even some pre-agricultural societies were **sedentary**. This means that people settled down and lived in one place, as a consequence of growing and harvesting crops.

Sedentary societies were more permanent, and the settlements supported a larger population. As human settlement became more permanent, their material cultures became more complex. Using new materials, such as clay, some communities produced functional items (storage jars and pots, for example), which they traded for their neighbors' farming surplus.

The Iron Age At about the same time that agriculture was winning out against the more nomadic hunting and gathering life-styles of Stone Age peoples, a revolutionary technological change

The San of the Kalahari are present-day hunters and gatherers. Based on what you have read and what you see in this photograph, describe what it might be like to be a San.

was also sweeping the continent. This was the beginning of the Iron Age. The Iron Age in Africa began between 1000 B.C. and 55 B.C. The use of iron introduced revolutionary changes and innovations in the history of African technology.

The productive use of iron tools led to significant population growth during the Iron Age. As the population grew, more land was required for food cultivation for the growing population. During this period of the Iron Age, the movements of a few families and larger-scale expansions repeatedly occurred. One of the well known and studied migrations is called the Bantu Expansion, after the string of related Bantu languages and cultures that remain intact.

The Bantu-speaking people migrated from the area of present-day Cameroon eastward around Zaire and southward through the forests of central Africa to savanna woodlands. The migrations began at least several thousand years ago and the Bantu-speakers reached Southern Africa sometime before A.D. 500.

The early Bantu-speaking farmers used stone hoes to cut and clear the forest and cultivate their new fields. The adoption of iron and iron implements helped them to produce more food and allowed them to live in villages and towns. An urban way of life brought African peoples together in towns and cities, where exchange and interaction produced even greater diversity, as they do in Africa today. As the scale and complexity of societies increased, so did the range of inequalities and the means by which elites (the privileged leaders) established and maintained advantage. Sometimes the successful use of power created great empires.

A wall painting in the tomb of Mennah, a scribe of the fields and an estate inspector for the Pharaoh Thutmose IV, graphically shows what life was like in ancient Egypt. What can you learn about Egyptian culture by studying this ancient wall painting?

Early kingdoms emerged along the Nile.

The process of agricultural growth, urbanization, and the creation of large-scale political units led to the creation of states and kingdoms in the Nile River valley. The great Egyptian pyramids of the Nile represent some of Africa's most visible monuments to this process.

Agriculture was central to the rise of the kingdoms in the Nile Valley. Between 5000 B.C. and 4000 B.C., full-time farmers established permanent settlements along the Nile. These settlements grew into regional states. By 3500 B.C., some of these kingdoms united into two states and became known as Upper and Lower Egypt. In 3100 B.C., what became known as the First Dynasty of ancient Egypt was established under Menes, King of Upper Egypt. This unification marked the beginning of the 3000-year civilization of ancient Egypt. The civilization of ancient Egypt lasted longer than any other in the history of the world.

The rulers of ancient Egypt were called **pharaohs**. Wealthy ruling classes controlled and exploited the labor of the peasantry, taxing the surplus from their crops through a highly centralized system of government. The taxes supported the pharaoh and his family in luxury and comfort, both in his lifetime and after death. The largest royal tomb was the Great Pyramid at Giza, built in about 2600 B.C. According to the Greek historian Herodotus, the Pharaoh Khufu brought his people to "utter misery," compelling them to work in gangs of a hundred thousand men over the course of twenty years to complete the pyramid's construction. So powerful did the rulers of ancient Egypt become that individual rulers were thought actually to become gods.

Some historians have even suggested that early rulers in the Nile Valley societies were religious leaders who controlled rain and floods, eventually becoming specialists in the technology and control of water systems designed to irrigate the agricultural fields.

Much of what is known about ancient Egypt comes from the archaeological excavations of the pyramids, which were elaborate tombs built for the god-kings. The Egyptian beliefs about life after death required that elaborately furnished rooms be provided for departed kings. Their treasures are famous for their beauty and workmanship.

Some information about Egypt also comes from the writings of Egyptians themselves. Extensive "documents" in stone—the picture-writing or **hieroglyphs**—on tablets and temple walls describe aspects of early Egyptian life. Destroyed in later centuries, the great library at Alexandria was a repository for the knowledge of the ancient world and was widely relied upon by Greek and other scholars.

During the period from 1570 to 1085 B.C., Egypt became a major world power. The empire expanded toward Palestine and Syria to the northeast and south into Nubia. The last Egyptian dynasty ended with Greek conquest of the Lower Nile by Alexander the Great in 323 B.C. The contact between the Mediterranean cultures and Egypt produced the foundations of western civilization.

Kush thrived on trade.

During the time known as the New Kingdom in Egypt (1570–1085 B.C.), the young Pharaoh Tutankhamen was one of many rulers to show an interest in the wealth of the southern ("upper") Nile Valley. Little did he know that within a few centuries his kingdom would be ruled by a southern state, the kingdom of Kush, beginning in 751 B.C. This ancient African kingdom underwent a period of Egyptianization and then gained control over the northern territory. Kush, with its capital at Napata and then Meroë, became a center for trade between the Nile, the Red Sea, and Africa south of the Sahara.

Meroë held a number of economic advantages, particularly in its location near rich sources of iron ore and hardwood timber. The new kingdom was based on the production and use of iron for weapons and tools, utilized in a mixed farming and hunting economy.

Meroë was also well situated for the development of trade in ivory, gold, leopard skins, ebony, wood, ostrich feathers, and manufactured goods. Elephants trained for use in warfare were exported to Egypt.

During the Period of Greek and Roman prosperity, Meroë flourished. Its script, called Meroitic, is still being deciphered by scholars.

The Kingdoms of Kush and Axum

MEDITERRANEAN SEA

EGYPT

Nile River

NUBIAN DESERT

SAHARA

KUSH

Meroë

Red Sea

ARABIA

Adulis

Axum

AXUM

Lalibela

Blue Nile R.

INDIAN OCEAN

White Nile R.

ETHIOPIA

0   500 Miles

Map Study

What natural features allowed the Kushites to become successful merchants?

Unlike Egyptian hieroglyphics, Meroitic was an alphabetic script. The religion of Kush was also distinct from that of Egypt. And Kush's political system owed much to the impact of other African societies, where male and female rulers held power jointly.

The later centuries at Meroë were marked by the decline of environment and society. The growth of the population and successful industries had a devastating impact on the local environment. The exploitation of wood fuel for iron-smelting and pottery-making led to deforestation. Forests disappeared, their elephant populations dwindled, hillsides eroded, and eventually, by about A.D. 300, Meroë and the great kingdom of Kush disappeared.

The decline of Kush gave the nearby kingdom of Axum an opportunity for expansion. Axum was situated between the area of Meroë and the Red Sea. Its large port city of Adulis was a trade center and also the recipient of peoples and cultures arriving from across the Red Sea from the Arabian region of Saba in modern Yemen. The language they introduced developed into Ge'ez, from which modern Amhara of Ethiopia is descended. After the Greek colonization of Egypt, Adulis and the kingdom of Axum developed a lucrative trade in ivory and possibly slaves. They manufactured their own coinage. Their crafts people produced luxury goods of glass and metals for export to the Roman empire and to Egypt. In the fourth century A.D., Christian merchants and scholars from Alexandria introduced Christianity to Axum, as they had to Coptic Egypt and Christian Nubia. King Ezana (320–350 A.D.) adopted the new religion, which enabled the state to secure trading connections with the Greek world of the eastern Mediterranean.

Foreign trade carried Aksumite influence back across the Red Sea to southern Arabia and northwards to Persia. The ultimate decline of Axum in the eighth century was largely due to the rise of a new and expanding religion, Islam. (You will read more about Islam in the next lesson.) The great stone monuments of its cities fell in the wake of the Islamic onslaught. The African Christian kingdom retreated to the interior of Ethiopia, where it survived for more than a thousand years because of the central highlands' isolation.

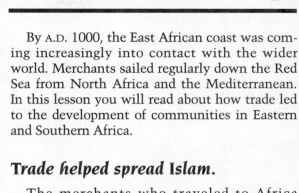

By A.D. 1000, the East African coast was coming increasingly into contact with the wider world. Merchants sailed regularly down the Red Sea from North Africa and the Mediterranean. In this lesson you will read about how trade led to the development of communities in Eastern and Southern Africa.

Trade helped spread Islam.

The merchants who traveled to Africa brought more with them than trading items. They also brought their religion, Islam.

The Islamic religion originated in Western Asia, in what today is Saudi Arabia. The origin of the Islamic calendar is the year A.D. 622, the year of the *Hijra*, the flight of the Prophet Muhammad. By the time of his death in 632, almost all Arabs were united under a single empire. Followers of the Prophet Mohammed spread the faith from West Asia south toward East Africa and northwards across Asia and North Africa in the seventh and eighth centuries. Sometimes this was accomplished by the *jihad*, a holy war against unbelievers.

From their capital at Cairo, the Arabs dominated the Nile River valley and developed a trading empire that included Syria and Arabia. In the case of East and West Africa, the trader's role was most critical to Islam's success. Those Africans who joined the new faith gained access to a large, commercial network that stretched around the globe. The occupation of North Africa was successful in gaining converts to Islam, in part because Muslims were not subject to taxes.

For many Africans, the presence of Islam made very little difference in their daily lives. For others, it was a sudden and dramatic cultural occupation, particularly transforming the lives of African women. In the new Islamic states, women found themselves under separate and strict religious rules and eliminated from most political avenues. Islam encountered many different African societies, some of which were better organized in economic and political terms,

The Church of St. George was constructed during the thirteenth century by King Lalibela. It is carved out of volcanic rock and is 40 feet deep within a hillside. The interior is decorated with fine mosaics and columns.

Lesson Review 2

Define: (a) pharaohs, (b) hieroglyphs
Identify: (a) Olduvai Gorge, (b) *Homo sapiens*, (c) the Kalahari San, (d) Bantu Expansion, (e) Kush, (f) Meroë (g) Axum
Answer:
1. Why is Africa called the cradle of humanity?
2. How did agriculture bring changes to the African hunting and gathering communities?
3. How did the use of iron help Bantu-speaking peoples?
4. What led to the creation of kingdoms in the Nile Valley?
5. What made Meroë successful?
6. What led to the decline of Axum?

Critical Thinking
7. Why is the exploitation of the environment detrimental? For example, what effect does the depletion of a wood supply have on a society?

and were able to place Islam in a relatively unimportant, yet distinct cultural position. The blending of Islam and local African beliefs was accomplished sometimes by a process called **syncretism**, in which neither one of the components was completely abandoned or completely altered, but were mixed together to create a new blend of ideas and practices. Religious change was gradual and mostly peaceful for many of the continent's converts.

Swahili culture developed in East Africa.

By A.D. 1000, the character of coastal life was strikingly cosmopolitan and international. Diplomatic and trade missions between East Africa and China were commonplace. During China's T'ang Dynasty (A.D. 618–907), a major report describes encounters between Chinese travelers and Africans. By the tenth and eleventh centuries, Arab reports and Chinese trade statistics indicate that large quantities of African goods were reaching China. In 1414, a giraffe was presented to the Chinese emperor. Arab and Persian merchants developed more permanent cultural links to the East African coast through intermarriage. The language and culture that developed from a mixture of an African base (Eastern Bantu) and Arabic influence is called Swahili. Today, Kiswahili is the most widely-spoken East African language.

The Indian Ocean world, of which Swahili culture was a part, was made up of a sea-borne trading empire. Sometime after A.D. 900, Swahili came to represent a distinctive coastal society that was Islamic and African. East African coastal ports imported large amounts of Asian fabrics and porcelain. These and other items were traded to the African interior for exotic woods, skins, spices, ivory, iron, and gold. These items were then exported to India and beyond. The organization of the trade was centered on the small islands off the coast, such as Zanzibar, Lamu, Kilwa, and Pemba. Between A.D. 1000 and 1500, these islands became city-states, integrating the land and oceanic trading empires. Their wealthy African and Arab merchants lived in luxurious palaces. Many of them minted their own coinage in silver and copper.

Mosques and palaces dotted the coastline, from the Red Sea southwards along the Indian Ocean.

Of all the new Swahili towns, Kilwa was to become the most important. Their merchants broke the Mogadishu (Somalia) control over the gold trade to the interior by A.D. 1200. They took advantage of their position near the Limpopo and Zambezi trade routes to the interior and the trade winds of the Indian Ocean to attract goods and bring foreign buyers. Local craftsmen designed remarkable, seaworthy vessels made of local stone to develop the coastal trade. The small mosque at Kilwa was carved of coral, with barrel vaults and domes. Houses had inside pit-toilets, sinks, and drainage. Doors and windows had fitted woodwork. Tiles and plaster finished the architecture to a high degree of architectural accomplishment.

Local industries included weaving, salt-making, carving in ivory and bone, and a range of local pottery styles to supplement imported wares. Foreign items remained important as luxury goods and status markers for the elite inhabitants of this African world trade center.

Great Zimbabwe became a kingdom.

Much of southern Africa and the interior regions of eastern Africa were drawn into the Indian Ocean world that revolved around Kilwa. The great empire of Zimbabwe likely had its origins in strategic control over gold mines and production associated with the trade. Beginning in the Iron Age, cattle herders living in the region of southeastern Africa along the Zimbabwe Plateau began accumulating wealth based on trade in local products, including iron, copper, tin, and gold. The society had different class levels, with the elite probably emerging from a group of religious specialists who were well positioned to take advantage of the emerging long-distance trade with the coast.

At Great Zimbabwe, one of dozens of fourteenth-century sites of impressive stone buildings, archaeologists have found Chinese porcelain and coins from the Indian Ocean trading empires. During the 1300's, this large-scale urban center housed an estimated population of 18,000. Again, trade alone did not produce this complex society. Rather, its location near

The ruins of Great Zimbabwe reflect the advanced civilization that once lived there. The first Europeans who saw these ruins believed that they must have been built by other Europeans because the building techniques used were unlike any others found in Africa. Scientific evidence gathered in the early 1900's proved that Zimbabwe was a great African civilization. However, in the 1960's some white Africans tried to deny that Africans built Great Zimbabwe. The evidence held, however, and the ancient Africans have been given due credit for this fine work of architecture.

resources and a rich agricultural region furthered the development of large-scale political and social organization. At its height, Great Zimbabwe and the state it controlled were in direct contact with the trading cities of the East African coast. The textiles, glass beads, coins, and other trade goods enhanced the prestige and authority of local rulers. When Great Zimbabwe declined the following century, the same factors that likely accounted for its wealth were likely responsible for its decay and eventual abandonment of the site. The environment collapsed from over-exploitation and the gold trade declined because of falling world prices and the depletion of many of the local deposits.

Lesson Review 3

Define: syncretism
Identify: (a) Islam, (b) Swahili, (c) Kilwa, (d) Great Zimbabwe
Answer:
1. How did the presence of Islam affect Africans?
2. What two groups formed the Swahili culture?
3. What allowed Great Zimbabwe to develop?

Critical Thinking
4. How did trade affect—both negatively and positively—the development of African kingdoms as well as the people?

Trade empires flourished in the western Sudan. 4

Far across the continent from Zimbabwe and Kilwa, West Africa peoples were also elaborating their political order to create kingdoms and states. Much of the historical knowledge of ancient West African kingdoms, such as Ghana and Mali, originated with the writings of Arab travelers and traders. This documentation is also supplemented by oral histories and by archaeological excavations.

Long-distance trade across the Sahara sands went on for many centuries before the introduction of the camel in the third or fourth century A.D. The introduction of the camel revolutionized the scope and scale of the trans-Saharan trade. New routes were opened up and trade was regularized. The trade brought products such as leather goods and gold to the markets and fairs of Europe and Asia. For many years, the trade remained in the hands of Berber nomads based in North Africa. As the transport systems were transformed, increased demand for ivory, ostrich feathers, animal skins, and gold from the south encouraged the expansion of trade networks. During the eighth and ninth centuries, Arab merchants became more involved in the trade as full-time traders. An important result of their involvement in the long-distance trade was the appearance of written records in Arabic.

Ghana was a land of gold.

The earliest mention of a West African kingdom is the description of the ancient kingdom of Ghana by the Arab geographer al-Fazari. In the 700's, he described Ghana as "the land of gold." The gold, however, came from the area south of the empire. Later writers gave more expansive accounts, though in all, the written documentation amounts to only about twenty pages. The reputation of these lands of gold lasted more than a thousand years.

During the eleventh century, the capital of Ghana was Kumbi-Saleh. It was described as a town with two quarters, one section being Muslim. Although its identification remains speculative, an actual site in Mauritania has been excavated by archaeologists and may in fact be Kumbi-Saleh. Across West Africa, from the Senegambia region westwards, many other sites reflect the accumulation of status and authority, marked by gold and other metals found in graves. Ancient Ghana was probably the pinnacle of the complex economic and political orders that emerged in the Western Sudan.

Oral histories provide information about the decline of Ghana. These histories tell about the end of the state when the kingdom's gold sources dried up, the trade abruptly ended, and its settlements withered away. In about 1051, the weakened kingdom succumbed to the invasions of the Almoravids from North Africa.

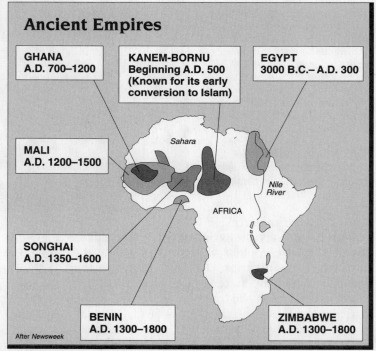

Ancient Empires

GHANA
A.D. 700–1200

KANEM-BORNU
Beginning A.D. 500
(Known for its early
conversion to Islam)

EGYPT
3000 B.C.– A.D. 300

Sahara

MALI
A.D. 1200–1500

Nile River

AFRICA

SONGHAI
A.D. 1350–1600

BENIN
A.D. 1300–1800

ZIMBABWE
A.D. 1300–1800

After *Newsweek*

Map Study

Use the Ancient Empires map to answer the following questions: How did trade affect many of the ancient cultures of Africa? What technological advancements were achieved by at least two of the cultures? How did location affect each culture?

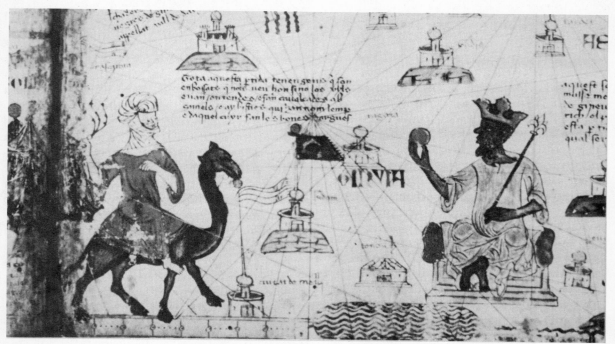

Manasa Musa, seated on a throne and holding a gold nugget, appears on the first European map of western Africa, drawn in 1375.

Mali won control of trade.

Ghana's successor was the great Mali, an empire that encompassed most of West Africa north of the forested region. At its height in the 1300's, Mali was also involved in the trans-Saharan gold trade. Gold was obtained from distant sources, including Bure and Bambuk on the upper Niger and Begho on the edge of the forest to the south, and then traded north across the desert. Eventually the trade reached Europeans. Even though Europeans' currencies were based on West African gold, they had no knowledge of its sources.

Mali began as trading confederation of smaller states. The great leader of the Keita clan of the Malinke was Sundjata. He is credited with the unification of the empire. According to the oral histories still sung by West African griots, Sundjata used magical and supernatural powers to defeat the enemy Sosso of Sumaguru. His successors built an empire linked together not only by commercial concerns, but also by a common cultural identity.

The most famous king of Mali was Mansa Musa. (You will read about him again in Chapter 5.) He was one of a number of African rulers who converted to Islam during the first few centuries after its arrival. The new faith presented opportunities to become a part of a far-flung commercial network. Mansa Musa brought Mali to the attention of the entire Muslim world by making a famous pilgrimage to Mecca, the Muslim holy city. Along the way, he gave away so much gold that he caused the price of gold currency in Cairo to drop dramatically. He is pictured on many of the European maps of the era following his reign, seated on a throne and holding an immense gold nugget. Many years would pass before Europeans had any more accurate information to update this vision of West Africa. In the meantime, the image of the gold nugget would attract their greed and attention.

In the 1400's, Mali declined after a series of weak kings. Other factors in the era of political disintegration included the deterioration of climate and the arrival of the epidemics known as the Black Death in Europe. The eras that followed were plagued by civil wars and religious conflicts. Just as the Almoravid invasion of West Africa took advantage of the uncertain economic and unstable political times in the eleventh century, competing Muslim states and a new trading partner, the Europeans, began to draw the wealth away from the center of the empire in the 1400's and 1500's.

15

Songhai conquered Mali.

In 1468, Timbuktu, a trading center in the Mali empire, was captured by a powerful Songhai army. The leader, Sonni Ali, became known as a great conquering hero, but also as an enemy of Islam. He founded the Songhai empire, which in the sixteenth century was even larger than Mali had been. The heart of the kingdom lay along the Niger River, where Sorko fishermen turned their canoe skills toward military ventures. The region of farmers and hunters was united into an interregional trading network. Its central administration remained at Gao, an early town on the Niger, but the territory was greatly expanded by Sonni Ali's use of horses. He built up a fierce army of horsemen and pushed the Songhay's control deep into the desert.

Sonni Ali's successor, Askia Muhammad, added devout adherance to the Islamic faith to the running of the empire and this resulted in a revival of trans-Saharan trade. Timbuktu became a great center of Islamic learning. Scholars from all over the Islamic world came to Timbuktu to study.

World travelers spread news about Africa.

Although many people wrote about the kingdoms and empires of the Sudan, from the time of Ghana to Songhai, few actually had visited the region themselves. Two particularly valuable eyewitness accounts do exist. Some years after the reign of Mansa Musa, the Berber (North African) traveler, Ibn Battuta visited Mali during the reign of Musa's brother in the 1300's. His account of this and other journeys has become an extraordinary historical source.

Ibn Battuta has been celebrated as one of the greatest world travelers of premodern times. He went from North Africa to West Africa, then to East Africa. He traveled to China, where he stayed with a relative of the man he had visited in Mali. He also visited Europe. His accounts reveal the cosmopolitan character of African and world societies. According to Battuta, enormous amounts of gold changed hands in the West African markets. The buildings of the Sudan were impressive for their elegant and colorfully painted patterns. The Mansa who greeted Battuta was found seated in the center of a huge palace, his attendants dressed in fine garments of silk brocade. Of the people in the kingdom, Ibn Battuta wrote: "They are seldom unjust, and have a greater abhorrence of injustice than any other people . . . There is complete security in their country. Neither the traveler nor the man who stays at home has anything to fear from robbers or men of violence."

More than a century later, a young Moroccan visited Songhai during the reign of Askiya Muhammad. The Moroccan's account, published under the name of Leo Africanus, describes the town of Timbuktu in 1510–1513.

Here are many shops of craftsmen and merchants, especially those who weave linen and cotton cloth. To this place Barbarie [Berber] merchants bring cloth from Europe. All the women of this region except maidservants go with their faces covered, and sell all necessary kinds of food. The inhabitants are exceedingly rich. Here there are many doctors, judges, priests and other learned men that are well-maintained at the king's cost. The inhabitants are people of a gentle and cheerful disposition, and spend a great part of the night in singing and dancing through all the streets of the city.

Kingdoms arose in west central Africa.

One of the early important kingdoms of west central Africa was the kingdom of Kongo. Living on the lower Zaire River, a group of successful farmers developed specialized skills in iron production and began a long-distance trade that included salt and copper. Shrines to the "spirits of the land" were located along the river. The guardians of these shrines were called *mani kabunga*. By 1400, the villages were united into a kingdom headed by the *manikongo*, or king. Like many African rulers, the king held both spiritual and political authority. An elaborate system of tribute was organized from the interregional trade the kingdom controlled between the Atlantic Ocean and the Kwango River.

By the ninth century, the West African site of Igbo Ukwu, in the forests of Nigeria, had a highly complex political system. Archaeologists have uncovered extraordinary bronze sculptures there that indicate high technical achievement. The copper used in these sculptures suggests that the people of Igbo Ukwu accumulated wealth via long distance trade. The objects themselves were likely symbols of leadership and high status.

Ancient Ife and Benin Archaeologists at Ife, in what is now Nigeria, have uncovered some of the world's most exquisite castings in copper and bronze. (You will read more about these sculptures in Chapter 5.) The sculptures are very naturalistic and may actually be portraits of kings. Dating to about the tenth century, they reveal complex systems of beliefs, economies and political organization. In fact, Ife was one of many such urban centers in West Africa.

Bronze Ife head of a king

Some Nigerian oral histories suggest that Ife technology and other aspects of its society were transmitted to the region's later kingdoms, such as Benin. A major empire, Benin had its gradual beginnings at least by the tenth century. Benin included vast territories between 1400 and the late nineteenth century. Like Ife, Benin began as an important city with claims to the surrounding territories. Benin developed an elaborate **divine kingship**, which was descended, claimed the kings, from an Ife royal. The king or *oba* of Benin represented the physical and spiritual life of the kingdom and its peoples. Like the *manikongo* of Kongo, the *oba* was both a political and spiritual head of state.

Society in the capital of Benin was organized around a central palace. Palace guilds were responsible for metalworking, trading, and other activities. Shrines in the palace were devoted to the past kings and queen mothers, portrayed in metal. Many specific historical events are represented in the Benin art, carved on ivory tusks and cast into bronze and brass plaques and sculptures. These objects record centuries of history from the royal point of view. Yet, they provide a glimpse into one of sub-Saharan Africa's most celebrated political achievements.

Benin's territory was loosely organized. Over the centuries, its size changed according to the political and economic fortunes of its rulers. By the 1400's, the city was a huge walled fortress with wide streets and fine houses. In the mid-1400's, under King Ewuare, Benin became an empire with an elaborate administrative structure of appointed chiefs. A powerful standing army expanded the territory and trade under the *oba's* control. The kingdom welcomed the trade with Europeans and exported pepper, ivory, gum, and cotton cloth to early Portuguese traders, who resold many of the goods to other coastal Africans.

After about 1500, the character of African societies began to change in fundamental ways. Africans came into close contact with Europeans who took advantage of the coastal trade. The Africans and Europeans became unequal partners, but partners nonetheless, in a new global society. Arriving by sea, the European presence would transform the very essence of African societies, their economies, and politics.

Lesson Review 4

Define: divine kingship
Identify: (a) Timbuktu, (b) Ibn Battuta, (c) Leo Africanus
Answer:
1. What was the result of the Arab merchants' involvement in the trans-Saharan trade?
2. (a) What caused Ghana to decline? (b) How do you know what happened to Ghana?
3. Who unified the Mali empire?
4. How did Mansa Musa bring Mali to the attention of the Muslim world?
5. What factors led to Mali's decline?
6. How were the *manikongo* of Kongo and the *oba* of Ife similar?

Critical Thinking
7. You have read how oral histories are valuable in studying African history. The writings of Ibn Battuta and Leo Africanus are also valuable historical sources. Why are their writings particularly useful?

Summary

1. Africa is a diverse continent. European historians who first studied Africa typically dismissed the history and diverse cultures of the continent because of two reasons. First, there were few written records in Africa. Second, the cultures of Africa were so different from European cultures that they were misunderstood. Today, however, historians are paying attention to oral tradition and other clues gained from archaeological, botanical, linguistic, and geographical studies to piece together Africa's intricate history. In the process, they are gaining an appreciation of the continent's diverse cultures.

2. Africa is the birthplace of humankind. Archaeological evidence shows that human beings probably originated in Africa. From the work done in Africa by archaeologists such as Louis and Mary Leakey, we have learned much about the evolution of humankind. We have also learned about the great early kingdoms of the Nile Valley.

3. Trading communities arose in the east and south. As trading opportunities with Arabs increased, East Africans were exposed to Islam. As the African and Islamic cultures met, syncretism often occurred. For example, the blending of Eastern Bantu and Arabic influences resulted in the Swahili language and culture. The most important Swahili town was Kilwa. In Southern Africa, the kingdom of Great Zimbabwe evolved from the struggles over gold mines and production associated with trade. When its natural resources were depleted, Great Zimbabwe declined.

4. Trade empires flourished in the western Sudan. Knowledge about the ancient West African kingdoms comes from the writings of Arabs of the time and from oral histories. The kingdom of Ghana was followed by the kingdom of Mali. Both empires had complex economic and political orders and great wealth. In the sixteenth century, the Songhai empire surpassed the achievements of the previous kingdoms. In west central Africa, the kingdom of Kongo was impressive in its political systems, extraordinary artworks, and technology. The elaborate empire of Benin developed later in the same region. After about 1500, however, most of the great kingdoms throughout Africa were gone. European influence had transformed the very essence of African societies.

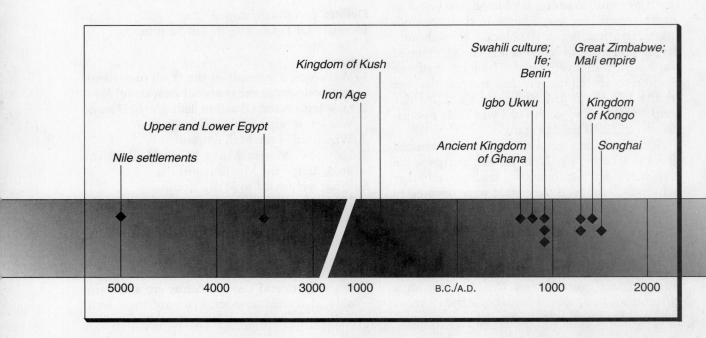

Reviewing the Facts

1. Define the following terms:
   a. oral tradition
   b. griot
   c. archaeology
   d. botany
   e. linguistics
   f. savanna
   g. desertification
   h. oasis
   i. trade language
   j. sedentary
   k. pharaoh
   l. hieroglyph
   m. divine kingship

2. Explain the importance of each of the following names or terms.
   a. the Sahara
   b. Louis and Mary Leakey
   c. Olduvai Gorge
   d. Kalahari San
   e. Iron Age
   f. Menes
   g. Axum
   h. *Hijra*
   i. Kilwa
   j. Kumbi-Saleh
   k. Sonni Ali
   l. Ibn Battuta

3. How large is Africa?

4. Describe the following geographical areas of Africa:
   a. tropical rain forests
   b. savannas
   c. highlands

5. List three ways that rivers have been important in African history.

6. What are the four major groups of African languages?

7. Why was fire important to early humans in Africa?

8. How did the Iron Age lead to urbanization in Africa?

9. What important event occurred in the Nile River valley in 3100 B.C.?

10. What contributed to the decline of Meroë?

11. How did Islam influence affect African women?

12. Why was the Swahili empire's coastal location important?

13. Why was the camel important to early civilizations in western Sudan?

14. List three factors that contributed to the decline of Mali.

15. What type of center was Timbuktu?

16. What two eyewitness accounts of the Sudan empires are particularly valuable?

17. How did the Kingdom of Kongo develop?

Basic Skills

1. **Making a chart** Create a chart for the Iron Age in Africa. Label the columns *When It Began, Types of Progress Made Possible,* and *Problems Created by Progress.*

2. **Comparing maps** Look at the political map of modern-day Africa on page 2 and the map The Cradle of Humanity on page 7. Try to find a correspondence between each labeled center on The Cradle of Humanity map and a modern-day city.

3. **Supporting the main idea** Give two supporting details you learned from this chapter to support this generalization: If historians did not use griots as sources of information, we would know very little about African history.

Critical Thinking

1. **Determining relationships** The Nile floods its banks every year, leaving behind rich soil. Ancient Africans who settled in the area spent much time keeping records of this flooding. Why was it important for them to know as much as possible about it?

2. **Applying a concept** Identify three reasons why studying African history is important.

3. **Contrasting events** Compare the developments occurring in Swahili and Mali between 1000 and 1300 A.D. How were the two empires alike? How were they different?

Perspectives on Past and Present

1. Review the answers you found for #2 of the Basic Skills section above. Choose one modern-day city that you listed and find out more about its history. Can the roots of this urban area be traced all the way back to the Cradle of Humanity?

2. How important is the Islam religion to modern-day Africa? Do research to find out (a) approximately what percentage of Africans claim this as their religion today, and (b) whether certain regions of Africa have larger Islam populations than others.

Investigating History

1. Until modern times, the origins of the Nile were unknown. Do research to find out who found its source and when.

2. The text states that relations between East Africa and China were common during the T'ang Dynasty. Do research to find out more about this Chinese dynasty. What was the culture like? What were the accomplishments of the dynasty? Who were its rulers? What from this culture might Africans have desired to gain through trade?

Chapter 2   The Atlantic Slave Trade

This painting, "Slave Deck of Albanez," an expressive watercolor by Francis Meynell (1821–1870), shows the crowded living conditions on a slave ship.

Read and Understand

1. Slavery in Africa has a long history.
2. The Triangular Trade linked three continents.
3. Africans suffered during the Middle Passage.
4. The slave trade had a lasting effect.

Key Terms

Middle Passage
asiento
Triangular Trade
abolition

Olaudah Equiano saw the whole incident from his hiding place in a tall tree. Several men came into his neighbor's yard and tried to steal the children. Young Olaudah called out and the men left without the children. Olaudah would soon find himself in the same predicament, however, when he and his sister were alone one day.

Ere long it was my fate to be thus attacked and to be carried off when none of the grown ups were nigh. One day, when all our people were out to their works as usual and only I and my dear sister were left to mind the house, two men and a woman got over our wall and in a moment seized us both, and without giving us time to cry out or make resistance they stopped our mouths and ran off with us into the nearest wood. Here they tied our hands and continued to carry us as far as they could till night.

20

Portrait of Olaudah Equiano

Slavery in Africa has a long history. 1

Slavery has existed since ancient times. Historically, slaves were people who were outsiders and chosen to perform many different kinds of work. They were distinguished from other members of society by the fact that they did not have family and community ties and did not have the freedom to choose the kind of work they wanted to do.

Slavery was known in Africa on a limited basis before the Atlantic slave trade began in the fifteenth century. Beginning in the eighth century, Arabs begin to penetrate North Africa and the Sudanese kingdoms. The Arabs participated in the trans-Saharan trade, transporting slaves, gold, and other goods. In total, an estimated 3.5 to 10 million Africans were exported through the trans-Saharan trade prior to the beginning of the Atlantic slave trade.

Within some African societies, slaves were used as soldiers and farmers. In the Songhai empire, slaves produced the majority of food crops and necessary staples.

Olaudah was 11 years old in 1756 when slave dealers kidnapped him from his home in eastern Nigeria. He reached the coast after passing through the hands of many traders and the stalls of many markets. He experienced slavery in the West Indies and Virginia, and later served as a sailor for the British Merchant Marines. During his years as a sailor, Equiano was somehow able to save enough money to purchase his freedom.

Equiano's experiences were part of the Atlantic slave trade that linked Africa, Europe, and the Americas between the fifteenth and nineteenth centuries. Equiano lived to tell his story. He was able to survive against tremendous odds; many others were not as fortunate. Unlike Equiano, millions of Africans were killed during their capture or perished on the high seas during the long voyage to the Americas—a journey that became known as the **Middle Passage.**

Those who lived through their capture and the trip from their distant African homelands frequently survived only to be maimed in the course of their slave labor. Most of these men, women, and children never had a chance to leave any record of their ordeal. They could only bear silent witness to their own tragic history, the history of slavery.

Slavery had different interpretations in Africa.

Slavery as it existed in Africa before the fifteenth century did not provide the basis of the Atlantic slave trade. In fact, the term *slavery* had different levels of meaning and did not always indicate a position involving bondage. Each society had its own understanding and interpretation of slavery. The specific significance of the word *slave* within each particular society often eluded outside visitors who could not understand the local dialect or language.

The word *slave* cannot be directly translated into African languages. There is no African equivalent of the word in the sense of a person with a total loss of freedom and whose person and labor are the property of another. In African languages, words that have historically been seen as equivalent to the notion of slavery are now known to bear little or no relationship to the use made of *slave* in the Americas.

In the language of the Asante of Ghana, for example, the term *akoa* may be translated both as *subject* and *slave*, but Europeans could not always distinguish the exact meaning of the term.

The Portuguese began the Atlantic slave trade.

In the early 1400's, Portugal's Prince Henry the Navigator supported many seagoing expeditions. He organized and paid for voyages along the west coast of Africa. The Portuguese soon recognized the commercial possibilities that the continent offered. They saw opportunities to exploit rich fishing banks and to extract quantities of gold from the African peoples.

In 1441, Antam Gonçalves, a Portuguese sailor, seized ten Africans near Cape Bojador (present-day Western Sahara). This event is often referred to as the beginning of the Atlantic slave trade. However, it was not an act of formal trade but rather an act of kidnapping. Formal trade was soon established because the Africans did not allow Europeans to kidnap Africans at will. This trade will be discussed later in this chapter.

At first, African slaves were sent to Portugal, Spain, and Italy. In fact, the first slaves sent to the Americas came from Europe, not directly from Africa. By 1551, 10 percent of the 100,000 people living in Lisbon, Portugal, were slaves. The city had more than 60 slave markets. Spain imported slaves for use in Catalonia, Aragon, Valencia, and Majorca. Italy obtained African slaves as gifts for popes and aristrocrats.

In Portugal, field slavery flourished for a time, but household slavery was more common. Portuguese slaves served as domestics and butlers. The Portuguese also used slaves on their sugar plantations located on African offshore islands. Plantations depended on a large supply of labor. Therefore, slaves were used on plantation islands such as the Cape Verdes, the Madeiras, the Canaries, and Saõ Tomé. When the plantation system was brought to the Americas, the Portuguese and other Europeans called on European traders to supply the slave labor. This led to the establishment of the direct slave trade across the Atlantic.

Europeans sought wealth across the Atlantic.

Following Christopher Columbus's voyages, the Spaniards sought to exploit the wealth in the Americas. At first, they attempted to use the Native Americans as a labor force. Heavy labor took a huge toll on the native population.

The Native American population, which numbered in the millions, declined sharply after European contact. European diseases, for which the Native Americans had no immunity, was the major cause of death. Because the Native Americans were unable to meet and sustain the labor demands of the Americas, the Europeans looked elsewhere.

Indentured servants was one source of labor in some areas of the Americas. Indentured servants agreed to work for a short period, usually about seven years, in exchange for their passage to the Americas. As a solution to the labor needs, however, indentured servitude wasn't favored for several reasons. First, Europeans wanted a permanent labor force and the term of the indenture contract was short. Second, indentured servants could run away and blend in easily with the rest of the population. And third, transporting Europeans to the Americas was expensive. When all previous attempts to find labor sources failed, the Spaniards turned to Africa.

The Spaniards initiated the asiento system.

The Spaniards had no trading posts in Africa and so they could not trade directly for slaves. They had to rely on the Portuguese, who had posts on the western African coast. Through the

An African bronze of a Portuguese soldier

22

Portuguese, the Spaniards imported their first slaves directly from Africa in 1518.

In that year, Charles I of Spain issued an **asiento** to a member of his household, Lorenzo de Gomenot. An *asiento* was a license to import slaves into the Spanish colonies. The *asiento* that De Gomenot received allowed 4,000 Africans a year to be imported to these colonies. For the rest of the sixteenth century, various individuals and groups were licensed by the Spaniards to supply such laborers for the Americas. As the demand for such laborers increased, Spanish kings charged exorbitant prices for these licenses.

Slaves delivered by these contracts were defined in terms of their labor potential. They were often young people who met specific conditions of physique and health. They were valued in terms of a unit known as a *peca de India* (an Indian piece). The definition of a *peca de India* changed over time, but in the seventeenth century, each healthy person between the ages of 15 and 25 who passed inspection was worth one *peca de India*. If they were between the ages of 8 and 15 or 25 and 35, then three of them were valued at two *peca de India*.

The *asientos* became such a great international prize that Europeans disregarded Portugal's monopoly of the trade on the African coast. These traders were known as intruders. One of the earliest and best known of the intruders was the British sea captain John Hawkins. In the 1560's, Hawkins made three voyages to Africa where he kidnapped Africans and sold them to the Spaniards in South America. Because he made such a fantastic profit from this voyage, Queen Elizabeth I of England decided to support his next venture. Elizabeth gave Hawkins a ship named *Jesus*, and Hawkins continued to steal more Africans. Elizabeth I eventually rewarded Hawkins by making him a knight. Sir John Hawkins's coat of arms depicted an African in chains.

Africans opposed the slave trade.

By the beginning of the eighteenth century, the slave trade was the major European trading activity on the African coast. Africans themselves were drawn into a formal trading system because of the great European demand for slaves. In return for securing slaves, Africans received certain goods, including firearms.

Although they were unsuccessful, many Africans tried to stop the slave trade by preventing their people from collaborating with the Europeans. One such person was Tomba, the leader of the Baga people, who tried to stop the slave trade in Guinea. He was defeated by African slave traders and their European allies. The King of Dahomey (present-day Benin), Agaja Trudo, realized that slaving in his country was destructive to his country's development. However, he participated in the slave trade so that he could acquire firearms to defend himself against his armed neighbors. Queen Nzinga Nbande, the head of the Matamba state in Angola, tried to organize a resistance against the Portuguese. When the resistance failed, she too participated in the trade to secure arms to protect her state against other Africans who were acquiring firearms.

Lesson Review 1

Define: (a) Middle Passage, (b) *akoa*, (c) *asiento*, (d) *peca de India*
Identify: (a) Olaudah Equiano, (b) Prince Henry the Navigator, (c) Tomba, (d) Agaja Trudo, (e) Queen Nzinga Nbande
Answer:
1. How is Olaudah Equiano's story different from most enslaved people's stories?
2. How were slaves used in Africa before the Atlantic slave trade?
3. What interpretations did slavery have in Africa before the Atlantic slave trade?
4. What event is referred to as the beginning of the slave trade?
5. Why did Europeans turn to Africa for a source of forced labor?
6. Why wasn't indentured servitude favored in the Americas?
7. How did the Spaniards use the *asiento*?
8. Why were the Africans who tried to oppose the slave trade unsuccessful?

Critical Thinking
9. How did the desire for low-cost labor lead to the Atlantic slave trade?

The Triangular Trade linked three continents.

2

The trade between Africa, Europe, and the Americas during the Atlantic slave trade period came to be known as the **Triangular Trade**. The Triangular Trade consisted of three main stages. Goods were shipped from Europe to Africa, where these goods were exchanged for slaves. The slaves were then taken to the Americas. These slaves were exchanged for tropical agricultural produce, cash, or promissory notes that were transported back to Europe, thus completing the triangular cycle. One exception to the triangular nature of the trade existed between Brazil and Africa; goods went straight to Africa from Brazil, and the ships returned with slaves.

All sea travel during the Atlantic slave trade period required complex arrangements.

Exporting a human cargo required an especially careful preparation. First, slave ships had to be acquired. If the voyage was not the undertaking of a company, a group of individual investors pooled their resources in order to minimize loss in case of failure. Second, a ship captain was needed to direct the voyage. Not only did the captain have to be able to run the ship, but he had to be able to deal with slave traders in Africa. Third, goods to exchange for slaves had to be secured. And finally, a crew had to be assembled for the journey.

After gathering all the necessary crew and cargo, the Europeans set out for specific stops along the African coast. Timing was critical. Arriving in the wet season made it difficult to conduct the slave trade, and the wet weather brought diseases such as malaria that often proved deadly to the Europeans. The slave markets that Europeans went to most often were located between Senegal and Angola. The Bight

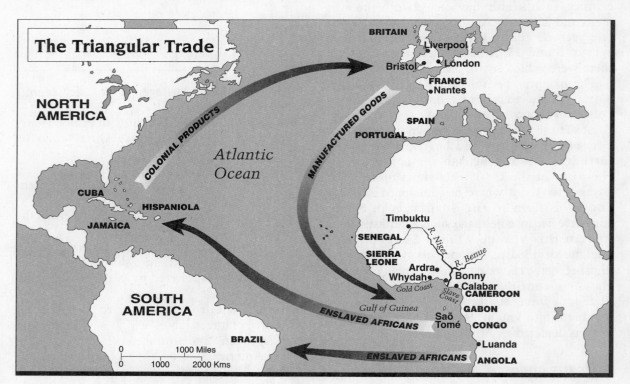

Map Study

The arrow at the bottom reflects the slaves that were exported from the west coast of Africa to Brazil. The other three arrows create a triangle for which the triangular trade is named. Use the map to determine the three regions that were involved in the triangular trade. What did each of these regions export?

24

of Benin, which covered the kingdoms of Dahomey and Oyo, exported so many slaves by the middle of the seventeenth century that the area became known as the Slave Coast.

Slaves came from many sources in Africa.

As slave labor in the Americas proved to be profitable, Europeans began to offer more goods to African slave traders. Africans soon developed a desire for the products that Europeans offered. To obtain these goods, Africans used a number of means to obtain slaves.

Wars Most of the slaves sold to Europeans were acquired through wars, which were actually nothing more than slave raids. Warfare for slaves encouraged retaliation and set off a cycle of violence.

European slave traders encouraged wars through the sale of guns and gunpowder. They were active participants in the wars and conflicts that produced slaves. For example, in 1703, Dutch traders supplied one African state with 100 soldiers and firearms to wage war against its neighbors. In return, the Dutch received the captured slaves.

Wars were started in an attempt to obtain economic benefits. One slave-ship captain wrote: "I verily believe, that the far greater part of the wars in Africa, would cease, if the Europeans would cease to tempt them with goods for slaves."

Kidnapping Like warfare, kidnapping introduced much violence into the African society. Unwary individuals, especially women and children in isolated places, were easy prey for slave kidnappers.

Debts When individuals incurred debts and were unable to repay the loans, they could be sold into slavery. Sometimes these people were sold to Europeans before their relatives could repay the debt.

Tribute In order to avoid further warfare and raiding, some states gave slaves as tributes to their oppressors. A strong state such as Ashanti maintained tributary arrangements of this sort with many of the states it had conquered.

Judicial process Individuals could be condemned to slavery for alleged crimes, including the practice of witchcraft and the violation of taboos in the society. By the seventeenth century, some societies had laws that made it quite easy for rulers to send almost anyone they wanted to into slavery. One traveler reported: "The Kings are so absolute, that upon any slight pretense of offense committed by their subjects, they order them to be sold for slaves without regard to rank or profession." Many Africans who were enslaved were not criminals and had violated no laws.

Captive Africans, escorted by armed African overseers, march to the coast where they will be sold to slave dealers.

Slaves were just one component of the trade.

Whatever the method of enslavement, the slaves were marched from the interior to the factories, forts, and castles on the coast that were staffed by Europeans. The slaves arrived on the coast dejected and exhausted.

Before Europeans could start trading for slaves, they customarily paid duties and gave gifts to the African rulers on the coast. Once trading began, African traders received textiles, guns and gunpowder, alcoholic beverages, mirrors, jewelry, and iron bars in return for the slaves. Trading products also included household goods such as pots, pans, knives, clocks, and locks.

After this exchange of gifts, the slaves were carefully examined from head to toe, without regard to gender, to see that they had no blemishes or defects. Some of the slaves were rejected if any defects were identified. One slave trader described the inspection:

They were put into a booth, or prison, built for that purpose, near the beach, all of them together; and when the Europeans are to receive them, they are brought out into a large plain, where the surgeons examine every part of every one of them . . . Such as are . . . good and sound are set on one side . . . Each of the others, which have passed as good, is marked on the breast with a red-hot iron.

The slavers had a clear preference for males aged 15 to 25 years. This group represented about two-thirds of the slaves. Only occasionally were slaves over 35 years old purchased.

Slavers also showed a preference for slaves from certain parts of Africa. The English, for example, preferred Akans who were known as *Coromantees*. The Coromantees were so named after a fort built at Cormantine on the Gold Coast. The French and Spaniards preferred Yorubas from the Bight of Benin. Once slaves became more expensive, however, slavers gave up the luxury of choice.

Lesson Review 2

Define: Triangular Trade
Answer:
1. What were the three main stages of the Triangular Trade?
2. What arrangements did the trip across the Atlantic require?
3. From what sources did African slaves come?
4. How did European slave traders encourage African wars?
5. What did the Europeans have to do before they could acquire slaves?

Critical Thinking
6. What effect do you think the removal of young males had on African society?

A captive African wears a slave yoke that would prevent him from running away into the jungle. Such yokes were also used as punishment in the West Indies to prevent enslaved people from lying down and sleeping.

Christiansborg Castle was built in the 1660's to hold captive Africans before they were shipped to the Americas. Today the castle houses Ghanaian heads of state.

Africans suffered during the Middle Passage. 3

Most slaves understandably showed extreme levels of distress and despair at being torn from their homeland. Some feared that they were being taken away to be eaten by their captors. The slavers' attempts to explain what was happening failed to calm the slaves' fears. Some slaves resisted being put on board the slave ships. Some tried to drown themselves as they were taken onto the ships.

The conditions on slave ships were foul. The decks averaged between four and five feet in height. In addition to the slave holds, some slavers built half-decks along the sides of the ships where slaves, lying in two rows, one above the other, were crowded together and fastened by leg-irons.

Because of the constant threat of disease at sea, the slave ship's captain did have to employ a doctor and maintain some measure of cleanliness. Slave cargoes were afflicted by fevers, dysentery, and smallpox. Smallpox had the most disastrous effects because there was no cure for this disease. To these health dangers

may be added the torments of seasickness and the oppressive heat in the holds.

Slaves were brought upon deck at mid-morning. Those who had died during the night were thrown into the ocean. The slaves were given water to wash themselves, and the ship's surgeon then examined them for sores and other ailments. Meals were served twice daily: breakfast around 10:00 A.M. and the other meal at 4:00 P.M.

To control the hungry captives' food consumption, the process of eating was sometimes directed by signals from a monitor, who indicated when the slaves should dip their fingers or wooden spoons into the food and when they should swallow. The monitor also was responsible for reporting those who refused to eat. Any slaves found to be attempting to starve themselves were severely whipped. According to a ship's surgeon:

Upon the negroes refusing to take sustenance, I have seen coals of fire, glowing hot, put on a shovel, and placed so near their lips as to scorch and burn them. And this has been accompanied with threat, of forcing them to swallow the coals, if they any longer persisted in refusing to eat.

27

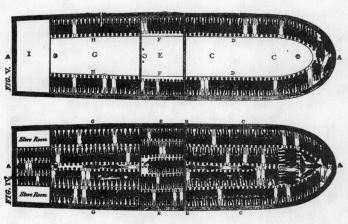

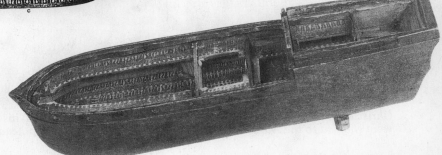

A layout of a slave ship shows cramped captives lying chained in stacked decks during the crossing from Africa to the Americas. The white spaces represent the enslaved individuals who died during transport.

Model of a slave ship used to show people in Britain the abominable conditions on board

At other times, the speculum orum, a mouth opener, was used to force feed the slaves.

The ship's provisions were carefully accounted for in log books. These records were vital, since the vessel's capacity did not allow for emergency provisions. Thus, when bad weather prolonged the Middle Passage, food and water allowances were reduced. In September of 1781, the slave ship *Zong* sailed from West Africa with a cargo of 470 slaves. The ship was bound for Jamaica. As it neared its destination 12 weeks later, it ran short of water and food. There was also an outbreak of disease on the ship. When the *Zong's* captain saw impending disaster, he proposed jettisoning those slaves who in his opinion were too sick to recover. He reasoned that the insurance underwriters, rather than the ship's owners, would bear the loss. Furthermore, he argued, this action would save slaves from lingering deaths. One hundred and thirty-six slaves were dragged to the deck and flung overboard. Later, the underwriters refused to carry the loss.

Slavers took precautions against revolts.

Given the oppressive conditions and the yearning for freedom, slaves inevitably revolted against their ordeal. Although all would have welcomed the opportunity to escape, slaves from certain areas earned a reputation for rebellion. The Coromantees of the Gold Coast were particularly known for their pride and mutinous behavior. Often, slaves sought to kill the European traders and set the vessel ashore. Rebellious slaves were severely punished.

Slavers went to great lengths to prevent rebellions and mutinies. They visited the holds daily and searched every corner between the decks for pieces of iron, wood, or knives gathered by the slaves. Great care was taken not to leave lying about any object that could be used as a weapon.

Rebellions, contagious diseases, and lack of adequate food compounded the discomfort and difficulty of the passage, which took many African lives. Mortality often depended upon the length of the journey to the Americas and the incubating period of diseases. An estimated 3 to 5 percent of the slaves died before embarkation and another 18 percent died during the Middle Passage. This high mortality rate was reduced to about 6 percent toward the end of the eighteenth century through efforts to better living conditions on the ships.

The crew members were subject to similar conditions of disease, faulty provisions, and the length of the voyage. Thus, the mortality rate among crew members was also high.

Slaves were taken to European colonies in the Americas.

The slaves were taken to the Spanish, British, French, Dutch, and Danish colonies. The number of slaves that landed in the Americas has intrigued scholars, and many books have been devoted to the subject. Recent scholarship in the United States suggests that about 12 million people were exported from Africa during the period of the Atlantic slave trade. Scholars in Africa, however, believe the number may begin at about 15 million and go as high as 100 million. Brazil imported the most slaves (38 percent) from Africa. The British Caribbean imported 17 percent; the French Caribbean, 17 percent; Spanish America, 17 percent; North America, 6 percent; and Dutch and Danish Caribbean, 6 percent.

Whatever the final destination of the slaves, the purpose of their importation was always economic. They were used on sugar, coffee, tobacco, and cotton plantations. They were also used for other

agricultural pursuits and for mining enterprises. The demands of the sugar plantations were especially high. During harvesting seasons, the slaves labored for 16 to 20 hours a day, leading to a high mortality rate. Many of the slaves on the sugar plantations survived for only eight to ten years. For that reason, some sugar planters periodically replaced whole populations of slaves. Gold mining, especially in Brazil, also exacted a heavy toll. Prospecting in icy streams seriously affected the Africans, who quickly deteriorated physically.

Abolitionists worked toward ending the slave trade.

The demand and need that brought Africans to the Americas reached its peak during the 1700's and early 1800's. By then forces were at work to end the trade, a movement known as **abolition**.

There were two stages to the abolition movement. The first stage took place from the 1770's to 1808 when Great Britain ended the trade in the British empire. Sweden abolished the trade in 1813; Holland and France in 1814; and Spain in 1820. The second phase took place from 1808 to the 1850's when Britain made efforts to abolish slavery itself in the British empire. Britain did abolish slavery in 1833. The United States abolished slavery in 1863, and Brazil followed in 1888.

Slave chains

29

Africans were active in the antislavery movement. Ottobah Cugoano (christened as John Stewart) and Olaudah Equiano (later renamed Gustavus Vassa) were leaders in the British antislavery movement. Their autobiographical works were published in conjunction with their work for the movement. Cugoano published *Thoughts and Sentiments on the Evils of Slavery* in 1787, and Equiano published his personal narrative, *Equiano's Travels*, in 1789. The two men wrote of their experiences as slaves, bringing to the general public's attention the destructive impact of the slave trade.

Slave revolts Slaves in the Americas also participated in their own liberation. Slaves had revolted in the Americas as early as the early 1700's, but the rebellions that had the most impact on the slave trade began late in the same century. In 1791, former slaves joined forces and revolted against the French. In 1794, Toussaint L'Ouverture, a former slave, became the leader of the revolutionaries and drove out the French from Haiti. His actions inspired Gabriel Prosser who led a revolt in Virginia in 1800 and Denmark Vesey who led a rebellion in South Carolina in 1822.

Portrait of Pierre-Dominique Toussaint L'Ouverture

Runaway slave rebels, called maroons, fought to help other enslaved people escape or revolt.

Lesson Review 3

Define: abolition
Identify: (a) the *Zong,* (b) Ottobah Cugoano
Answer:
1. What were the conditions on the slave ships?
2. What happened on the *Zong?*
3. How did the slavers attempt to prevent revolts?
4. (a) Where were the enslaved Africans taken? (b) About how many slaves landed in the Americas?
5. What kinds of labor did the slaves do?
6. Why were the books written by Ottobah Cugoano and Olaudah Equiano important to the antislavery movement?

Critical Thinking
7. Why do you think African scholars and United States scholars differ on the number of slaves that landed in the Americas? Why do you think knowing the actual number has intrigued many people?

The slave trade had a lasting effect.

4

As you read, the Portuguese first seized Africans in 1441. No one at the time could have imagined the magnitude of the impact this act would ultimately have. One African in the Congo, named Dom Affonso by the Portuguese, quickly realized that contact with Europeans would prove to be detrimental to Africans. Dom Affonso converted to Christianity after meeting with the Portuguese. He believed that the Portuguese were mostly interested in spreading Christianity and conducting trade. Affonso, with Portuguese backing, became king of the Congo. By 1526, he was well aware of the injustices done to Africans. He wrote letters to the king of Portugal, trying to persuade him to stop the trade.

Your Highness should know how our Kingdom is being lost in so many ways. . . . We cannot reckon how great the damage is, since the merchants are taking every day our natives . . . so great, Sir, is the corruption . . . that our country is being completely depopulated, and Your Highness should not agree with this nor accept it as in your service. And to avoid it we need from [your] Kingdoms no more than some priests and a few people to teach in schools, and no other goods except wine and flour for the holy sacrament. That is why we beg of Your Highness to help and assist us in this matter, commanding your [traders] that they should not send here either merchants or wares, because it is our will that in these Kingdoms there should not be any trade of slaves nor outlet for them.

Dom Affonso was not successful in his attempt to reason with the Portuguese. His kingdom was eventually completely destroyed by the slave trade.

The slave trade sacrificed millions of Africans for the transformation of Europe and the Americas. The forced migration of Africans caused immense cultural and economic changes in Africa, Europe, and the Americas. Societies in the United States and Africa continue to deal with the repercussions of the slave trade. This lesson will explore some of these repercussions.

The slave trade greatly affected Africa.

The impact of the slave trade was greater in Africa than in any other region. As the demand for slaves grew, African societies became increasingly violent. African leaders used their growing supply of guns to find new captives and to fend off neighboring enemies, many of whom were also involved in the slave trade. As a result, the slave trade created an atmosphere of violence and instability that reverberates into present-day Africa. As you will read in Chapter 3, this weakened Africa was no match for the European powers who came to Africa to claim territory.

Depopulation An estimated 20 million Africans died or were transported from their homelands during the centuries of slave trading. The loss must be counted in more than numbers, however. The majority of captives were between the ages of 15 and 25 years. They were also the healthiest and strongest members of African communities. This loss robbed Africa of a creative, productive, and inventive part of its population. It also took away the segment of society most likely to have children, depleting the population even further.

The slave trade also caused depopulation because of the wars and raiding associated with it. Through enslavement, large numbers of people were forced to migrate from their homelands. The slave trade also divided Africans among themselves because it led different groups to fight and enslave one another.

Economic problems The uncertainty that wars, raiding, and violence created in African society hurt the development of African businesses and trade. It was hard for African businesses to plan for the future when the future was so uncertain. Also, slaves who came to the Americas brought with them talents and skills that were then lost to the African community.

The slave trade presented another economic problem for Africans. Europeans extracted valuable labor resources through the slave trade. In return, Africans received guns, alcohol, and luxury goods. None of these items helped Africa to develop economically in the way slaves helped to build farms and businesses in the Americas. Even when goods such as cotton and iron were exchanged for slaves, they often hurt local industries producing the same goods.

Racism Enslavement increased the perception of Africans as an inferior race. In business reports, Africans were often lumped together with gold and ivory as things and commodities. Africans were reduced to the level of lesser human beings in many non-African minds. One reason for this was the Europeans' need to justify the enslavement of Africans. As money from the slave trade poured into European coffers, elaborate justifications were created to ease any moral qualms some traders had about slavery. A common justification was the belief that Europeans were transporting Africans to a "better place." Over time the image of exhausted Africans being unloaded from slave ships became the overriding image most whites had of Africans.

Sierra Leone and Liberia The slave trade is responsible for the founding of two present-day African countries: Sierra Leone and Liberia. In 1787, the British established Sierra Leone as a settlement for ex-slaves who had attempted to settle in Britain. Olaudah Equiano was among the first group to arrive. His group named their settlement Freetown; today it is the capital of Sierra Leone.

In the 1820's, Liberia was founded as a colony for freed slaves from the southern United States. Liberians issued a Declaration of Independence in 1847 and adopted the motto, "The love of liberty brought us here."

The slave trade affected Europe.

Europe was engaged in the slave trade for more than three centuries. Africa's misfortune benefitted Europe economically in several ways. Plantations in the Americas and West Indies reaped huge profits for their European owners. The precious metals mined by slaves created wealth for European mine operators and owners. Major ports such as Liverpool in England and Nantes in France grew because of the slave trade. The shipping industries that supplied the slaves for the voyages also grew. Money accumulated from the slave trade was invested in European industries and fueled an economic boom in Europe. In fact, many scholars believe that profit and capital accumulated from the slave trade contributed to the Industrial Revolution.

Some scholars have argued that the slave trade was a risky venture and many European businesses lost money pursuing it. Considering how many Europeans continued to invest in the trade, however, it seems logical that the profits outweighed the risks.

The Americas benefitted from the slave trade.

Africans who came to the Americas as slaves did so with much more than their chains. They brought with them something of far greater and more lasting value—their culture. (See Chapter 5.) These Africans brought their ideas, language, religion, views of government, music, foods, folklore, art, working technology, and creativity in all areas of life. They made an inestimable and enduring cultural contribution to the Americas well beyond the prosperity their enforced labor generated.

Africans impacted the history and development of the Americas in countless ways. They provided plantation owners with the skill and endurance to farm tropical regions. Africans' ability to withstand extreme heat and tropical disease made them the foundation of the agricultural industry that was exploding in the Americas. Slaves also developed prosperity in the North American colonies as slave carpenters, masons, and mechanics. In 1835 and 1836, a slave in the state of Maryland received a patent for two corn harvesters that he had developed. Slaves also applied skills learned in Africa to mining and the search for minerals and gems, especially in South America.

Examples of African-inspired culture that has nothing to do with economics can be found in the Americas. For example, Africans brought much of their culture to their religion as it developed in their enslavement. Religion often became a powerful force in their lives. Africans interpreted Christianity in their own ways, often combining traditional African beliefs.

Elmina Castle in Ghana

Perhaps the most profound evidence of the African influence on religion is found in spirituals. Sometimes these songs were used as a way to communicate. Often they were used to express the slaves' oppression as enslaved people, as the following example shows.

*O, stand the storm, it won't be long
We'll anchor bye and bye, O brethren!
Stand the storm, it won't be long,
We'll anchor bye and bye*

African Americans look back on their past.

The first enslaved Africans who were brought to what is now the United States arrived in the Jamestown settlement in 1619. Centuries later, a controversial debate is now growing in the United States over what impact the slave trade has on African Americans today. Some people feel that the United States government should compensate the descendants of enslaved Africans. This compensation would come in the form of some kind of monetary settlement, called a reparation.

Proponents of this debate feel that African Americans today deserve reparations because their ancestors were deprived of their culture and their fundamental human rights. Opponents feel that African Americans today are too far removed from the slave trade to be affected by it. Furthermore, they feel that the govern-ment could not afford to compensate such a large group of people.

The debate has reached the United States government, where a bill has been recently introduced. This bill would create a committee to further examine the effects of the slave trade on African Americans.

Some African Americans return to Africa to find their cultural roots. Often it is a poignant experience. One much visited spot in Africa is the old slave castle at Elmina in Ghana. After a tour of the grounds and slave dungeons of the castle, some African Americas are overcome by such deep emotions that they cry out in anguish. Ironically, no plaque or memorial is on the grounds to commemorate the multitudes of Africans who perished in the slave trade during the capture, march to the west, the Middle Passage, and on the plantations and mines in the Americas.

Lesson Review 4

Identify: Elmina Castle
Answer:
1. The majority of captives transported from their homelands during the slave trade were between the ages of 15 and 25 years. How did this affect Africa after the slave trade ended?
2. What economic problems did slavery cause in Africa?
3. How did Europe benefit by the slave trade?
4. What cultural contributions did the enslaved Africans bring with them to the Americas? What technological advances were made by enslaved Africans in North America?
5. Why do many African Americans return to Africa as visitors?

Critical Thinking
6. Why are the effects of the slave trade still felt in Africa and the United States?

Chapter 2 Review

Summary

1. Slavery in Africa has a long history. Arabs had begun a trans-Saharan slave trade in Africa during the fifteenth century. Within some African societies, slavery existed. However, this slavery did not provide the basis of the Atlantic slave trade. The Atlantic slave trade is usually viewed as beginning in 1441, and enslaved Africans were originally sent to Europe and African off-shore plantation islands. When other sources of labor proved unsatisfactory in the Americas, however, most African slaves were shipped across the Atlantic to fulfill the need. The Spanish *asiento* system made the Atlantic slave trade fabulously profitable, guaranteeing its continuance. Africans often tried to oppose the slave trade, but were unable to do so successfully without sacrificing their freedom entirely.

2. The Triangular Trade linked three continents. In the Triangular Trade, goods were shipped from Europe to Africa and exchanged for slaves. The slaves were then taken to the Americas. In the final stage, the slaves were exchanged for produce, cash, or promissory notes that were then transported back to Europe. For the supply of slaves the Europeans wanted, African slave traders relied on wars, kidnapping, and tributary arrangements. Africans who were in legal or financial trouble also often ended up as slaves. Once captured, the slaves were marched from the interior of Africa to the coast.

3. Africans suffered during the Middle Passage. Conditions aboard slave ships were foul and crowded. The mortality rate was often as high as 18 percent. Disease was a constant threat, and hunger was common. Slavers went to great lengths to prevent the rebellions that often resulted from the miserable conditions aboard the ships. Slave ships took the slaves to European colonies, where they were used for agricultural and mining enterprises. The labor was hard, and many slaves died at a young age. The abolition movement began in the 1770's, with slave trade being abolished in various countries through 1820 and slavery itself ending in the United States in 1863.

4. The slave trade had a lasting effect. Immense changes in Africa, Europe, and the Americas occurred because of the slave trade, and repercussions of it continue to be felt. In Africa, increased violence, depopulation, and economic problems were among the costs of the slave trade that are still being felt. Racism toward Africans and African Americans is another huge cost of the slave trade. In Europe, on the other hand, the slave trade resulted mostly in benefits. The profits were huge and helped to fund the healthy growth of Europe during the time of the slave trade. Similarly, the Americas developed largely because of the labor of enslaved Africans. Today, many Africans and African Americans are personally dealing with the legacy of slavery.

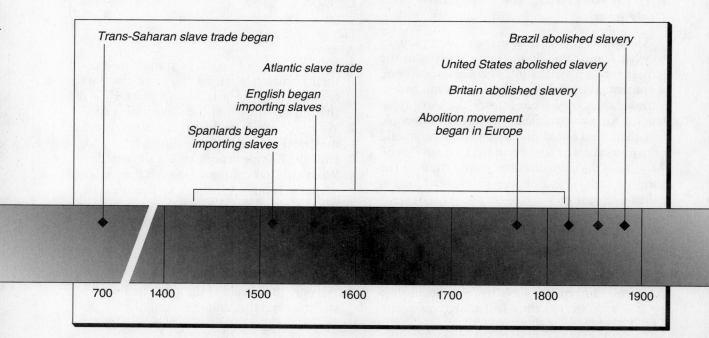

Trans-Saharan slave trade began

Atlantic slave trade

English began importing slaves

Spaniards began importing slaves

Brazil abolished slavery

United States abolished slavery

Britain abolished slavery

Abolition movement began in Europe

700 1400 1500 1600 1700 1800 1900

Reviewing the Facts

1. Define the following terms:
   a. Middle Passage   d. Triangular Trade
   b. *asiento*   e. abolition
   c. *peca de India*
2. Explain the importance of each of the following names or terms:
   a. Olaudah Equiano   d. Bight of Benin
   b. Toussaint L'Ouverture e. Tomba
   c. Prince Henry   f. Elmina Castle
      the Navigator
3. How do we know that slavery in Africa before European influence was nothing like the Atlantic slave trade?
4. Where were the first enslaved Africans sent?
5. How did the Spaniards gain a monopoly on the slave trade?
6. What did European slavers gain from African wars?
7. Describe the actual slave trading process that occurred on the African coast.
8. What happened to the bodies of slaves who died during the Middle Passage?
9. Why was keeping careful track of a slave ship's provisions so important?
10. Why was the mortality rate high among slaves who labored in the Americas?
11. What were the two stages of abolition?
12. Why did racism toward African Americans result from the slave trade?
13. How did Europeans benefit from the slave trade?

Basic Skills

1. **Using visuals** (a) Why are the pictures in this chapter particularly important? (b) To which picture did you react most strongly? Why?
2. **Making an outline** Make an outline of Lesson 3. Look for the four main ideas in the lesson. Then look for supporting details to include under each main idea in the outline.
3. **Making a chart** Make a chart titled *Hardships Endured by Enslaved Africans*. Label the columns "On the March to the Coast," "During the Middle Passage," and "In the Americas." In each column list the hardships discussed in this chapter.

Critical Thinking

1. **Drawing conclusions** Violence is a problem for many African countries today. (See Chapter 6 for more information on this topic.) How could the slave trade be viewed as leaving a legacy of violence that still continues?
2. **Evaluating sources** Reference was made in this chapter to autobiographies by Olaudah Equiano and Ottobah Cugoano. (a) Why might these sources be viewed as crucial reading for anyone who wants to know the truth about the slave trade? (b) What should people keep in mind when reading accounts of the slave trade written by European slavers?
3. **Identifying bias and point of view** In this chapter a slave-ship captain (page 25), a slave trader (page 26), and a slave-ship surgeon (page 27) are quoted. What point of view do these men seem to share?
4. **Problem solving** Finding qualified captains for the slave ships was difficult. Make a list of qualifications that a captain needed to have. Order the list from most important to least important. Then create an advertisement that could have been used to attract qualified captains.

Perspectives on Past and Present

The significance of the magnificent kingdoms of ancient Africa has often been overlooked in history texts, which dwell instead on the time since European influence on the continent. As a result, many African Americans have not known the details of their proud heritage. Alex Haley's book *Roots* did much to change this, however. In researching this book, Haley traced his own family history to Africa and discovered many wonderful things about his relatives. After reading *Roots*, many other African Americans have been inspired to research their own family histories. Read a portion of *Roots* or a review of the book, or watch a segment of the movie (often available in video stores or local libraries). Then write a statement about how discovering one's heritage can help build pride and self-esteem in a person who has experienced discrimination.

Investigating History

1. Do research to find out approximately how many weeks an enslaved African was in transit from the moment of capture to the time the slave ship landed in the Americas. How long was the march from the interior to the coastline? How much time was spent in the holding place on the coast? How long was the voyage? Create a time line to show your findings.
2. You read in this chapter about the tragedy aboard the slave ship *Zong*. See if you can find other accounts of tragedies involving slave ships.

Chapter 3 · The Partition and Colonization of Africa

How does this European engraving of the battle between Henry Stanley and Chief Mojimba differ from Mojimba's account of what happened? How are the two versions alike?

Key Terms

imperialism
colonialism
legitimate trade
assimilation
direct rule
indirect rule

Read and Understand

1. Explorers and missionaries changed Africa.
2. Colonialism affected all facets of African life.

Chief Mojimba was astonished by the news of a man with white skin traveling down the Lualaba River. No one in the village had seen such a man before. The chief speculated on who the man was and where he might have come from. Perhaps he was a long lost brother who was believed drowned in the river. Mojimba believed that life came from the water. Maybe in the river this brother had found life and now he was coming home.

The chief ordered that a great feast should be prepared as a greeting for this man. Everyone was to wear clothing usually reserved for ceremonies. Soon they gathered in their great canoes on the river and began the journey to meet this brother. As they moved through the water, they sang songs of joy.

Mojimba couldn't believe what happened next. As his canoes approached the man's party, loud bangs pierced the air. Several of Mojimba's men fell into the river, dead.

Cecil Rhodes, a wealthy diamond-mine owner, used his fortune and political power to further his dream of making much of Africa, and indeed the world, part of the British empire. His vision included building a railway from the Cape to Cairo. How does this Punch cartoon reflect the dreams of Cecil Rhodes?

Stanley wrote about his travels in Africa in his book called *Through the Dark Continent*. The title fittingly describes how most Europeans in the late 1800's thought of Africa—as a dark continent full of savages. This belief was used as a rationale to bring "progress" to Africa. At this time, Europeans were committed to **imperialism**, a policy of conquering and then ruling other lands as colonies. The process of acquiring and maintaining colonies is called **colonialism**.

Colonialism can be traced to the time of European expansion beginning with the fifteenth century. The motivating influences of the period were what was known as the three G's: gold, glory, and God. European enthusiasm for acquiring colonies diminished during the 1700's, but it returned during the last decade of the 1800's. The nineteenth-century imperialism became known as the three C's: commerce, Christianity, and civilization.

This chapter looks at reasons such as these behind colonialism. It will also look at the Africans' response to the coming of Europeans into their lands.

What Mojimba could not have known at the time was that his village had come to meet a man who would soon become famous for his experiences in Africa. This man, Henry M. Stanley, had come to Africa to explore the river he knew as the Congo. In a horrible misunderstanding, Stanley believed Mojimba's actions were a sign of war. He wrote:

We had sufficient time to take a view of the mighty force bearing down on us and to count the number of the war vessels. There were 54 of them! A monster canoe led the way, with two rows of upstanding paddles, 40 men on a side, their bodies bending and swaying in unison as with a swelling barbarous chorus they drove her down toward us.

Explorers and missionaries changed Africa. 1

During the early days of the slave trade, Europeans had been content to stay on the coast and wait to purchase enslaved Africans. Although some European countries had established a permanent presence on the coast, few Europeans actually lived in Africa or knew anything about the interior. This changed by the late eighteenth century, when Europeans developed a great desire to explore the continent. The early explorers and their sponsors knew that the information gained on such trips would be useful over the long term for trading and colonization.

The partition of Africa was often carried out by various agents and European chartered companies doing business in Africa. These chartered companies became involved in the process because some European nations were at first reluctant to spend the funds that were necessary for effective occupation. In fact, European nations often used the work of chartered companies in various African lands as the basis for their claim to that area.

The European powers soon recognized that each nation would have to work quickly to establish a claim to African territory. In a matter of two decades Africa was divided, or partitioned, among the various European powers. This process is known as the Scramble for Africa because of the speed with which the partition was carried out.

Many factors contributed to the partition of Africa.

Before the slave trade was abolished in the nineteenth century, Africa's largest export was enslaved Africans. After abolition, Europeans began to ask for trade items such as gold, ivory, cloves, peanuts, cotton, and rubber. This period of change from a slave-trade economy to an economy based on natural products was known as the era of **legitimate trade**.

Wealth One of the most successful African exports during this time was palm oil, which was used to manufacture soap and to lubricate machinery. Europeans were in the midst of a great growth in industrialization and they needed huge quantities of palm oil to keep their machines running.

The success of the palm oil export proved that Africa was a good source for raw materials to keep European factories and industries busy. However, as the legitimate trade expanded in Africa, Europeans saw more opportunities to increase their own wealth. They looked to Africa as a place to invest and make money.

Competition Part of the reason European powers wanted African territories had to do with competition. Some countries, having lost European territories as a result of wars, looked to Africa as a way to increase their holdings.

In this Punch *cartoon, the snake represents the Belgian King Leopold and the man represents the people of the Congo. According to the cartoon, what effect did Leopold have on the Congo?*

France's interest in Africa, for example, was influenced by its loss of Alsace-Lorraine in a war in 1871.

The first European to seize territory in Africa was King Leopold II of Belgium. In 1879, he hired Henry Stanley to investigate the Congo River. Stanley eventually claimed, in Leopold's name, an area more than 80 times larger than the small country of Belgium.

Meanwhile, Otto von Bismarck, Chancellor of Germany, gained his own African territories. While Leopold II was motivated by wealth, Bismarck was motivated by politics. At the time, Germany and France were enemies. Bismarck hoped that his actions would bring Britain into Africa, creating competition with France and improving Germany's standing back in Europe. Bismarck's plan worked and soon Britain and France were actively pursuing territories in Africa.

Bringing the "light" Explorers were joined by missionaries who wanted to carry the Christian gospel to the Africans. Missionaries, for the most part, felt that Africa was a "dark" continent and they wanted to bring it "light."

Many Europeans agreed with the missionaries. In fact, they felt it was their duty to bring their "superior" European civilization to the "backward" Africans. This view was known as the "White Man's Burden." The name comes from a poem written by Rudyard Kipling, a well-known writer of the time:

> Take up the White Man's Burden—
> Send forth the best ye breed—
> Go bind your sons to exile
> To serve your captives' need . . .

The most famous European missionary to Africa was Dr. David Livingstone. During his extensive travels through Central Africa, he found evidence of continuing slave trade after abolition. He felt that by spreading Christianity and introducing other forms of trade, the slave trade could be stopped.

In general, Africans responded to early missionaries with friendliness. However, they were surprised by some of their customs. When Livingstone wrote about the Bakalahari people, he said:

> It is, however, difficult to give an idea to a European of the little effect the [Christian] instruction produces . . . When we kneel and address an unseen Being, the act often appears to them so ridiculous that they burst into laughter.

European settlement Besides claiming territories and establishing colonies in Africa, some European countries encouraged their citizens to move to Africa. Germany promoted white settlements in East Africa (Tanganyika) and southwest Africa. The British promoted white settlement in Kenya and present-day Zimbabwe. French colonists settled in North Africa; in fact, the French came to view Algeria as an extension of France. The Portuguese encouraged white settlement in their colonies of Angola and Mozambique. In South Africa, white settlement that had begun in 1652 exploded with the discovery of diamonds in 1867 and the discovery of gold in 1885.

The Scramble for Africa had rules.

The European powers involved in the Scramble for Africa soon realized that rules had to be established. For that reason, Bismarck called for a conference to be held in Berlin beginning in 1884. Here, the Europeans would decide how the official colonization of Africa was to take place. As King Leopold put it, the conference was a chance for the European powers to divide "the magnificent African cake." Even though the decisions that came out of this conference would greatly affect Africa, no Africans were invited to attend.

On February 26, 1885, three months after the conference began, thirteen countries were prepared to sign the Berlin Act and to abide by its regulations, which included the following.

1. King Leopold was to allow free trade for all European nations in the Congo, an area he had already claimed.
2. European countries were free to colonize coastal territories that they already occupied and to extend their rule some distance inland.
3. Each nation was required to notify all other signing countries when they occupied a new country.
4. Treaties with African kings were to be accepted as valid titles to territories.
5. European powers were to state their intent toward the African people. This included promises for the protection of Africans "in their moral and material being, the suppression of slavery and the slave trade [and] the education of the natives."

Partition required three stages.

The Berlin Conference did not actually partition Africa. Rather, it set up rules and regulations for a process that was already underway. That process was carried out in three stages. By the end of the process, many African countries were firmly under European control.

The first stage of the process involved treaty-making between European nations and African rulers. During this stage, an agent representing a European nation approached an African ruler and asked him to recognize that particular nation as his people's protector. The Treaty of Protection prevented the African ruler from entering into any relationship with another European nation. The African ruler simply had to make an X mark on the document agreeing to the so-called treaty.

Many African rulers did not fully understand the implications of signing a treaty. Some agents were deceitful and did not interpret the contents accurately to the Africans, so rulers signed the documents thinking that they were only signing treaties of friendship. Many times African rulers were forced to sign by military force.

The second stage of the process involved treaty-making between European nations. One purpose of the treaties was to define the exact boundaries of the colonial possessions. This stage was necessary because the boundaries made by European agents were sometimes vague. The boundaries were drawn without African input. Frequently, nations and ethnic groups were split and placed under different colonial rulers.

The third stage of the process was the actual occupation of the African countries. Often called the pacification stage, it was a brutal process during which European nations used troops to put down the rebellions of Africans who did not welcome the occupation of their land. Since there were virtually no wars in Europe between 1870 and 1914, many European military officers seeking advancement often

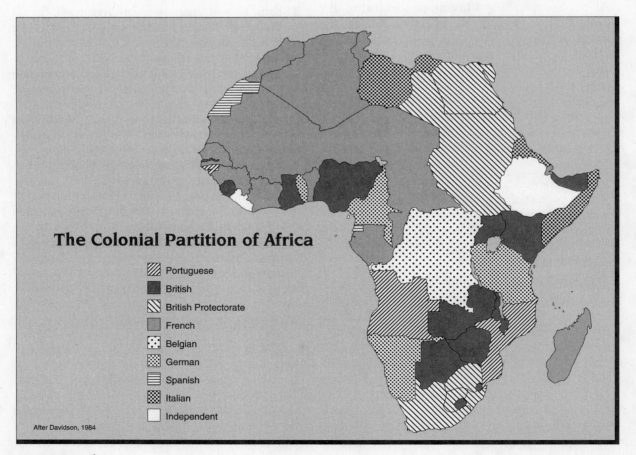

The Colonial Partition of Africa

- //// Portuguese
- ■ British
- \\\ British Protectorate
- French
- Belgian
- German
- Spanish
- Italian
- Independent

After Davidson, 1984

Map Study
Much of Africa was partitioned and colonized by a few European countries. Use the map to determine which European country controlled the largest area of Africa. Which two countries of Africa were independent from outside controls?

ended up in Africa during this phase of colonization. Some of them stayed in Africa to become the governors of various territories.

Europeans believed that pacification was necessary because until African rebellions against colonial rule had been put down, Europeans could not establish effective governments. Furthermore, Europeans could not construct the roads, railways, and telegraph lines that were needed to govern and to extract resources from the colony.

The Europeans neglected their promises.

When the European rulers signed the General Act of the Berlin Conference, they promised to protect the Africans, to suppress the slave trade, and to educate the African people. As you will read in the next lesson, the Europeans did not keep these promises. The truth was that colonialism, as confessed by a French colonist, was "not an act to civilize, [but] an act of force, motivated by European self-interest."

Lesson Review 1

Define: (a) imperialism, (b) colonialism, (c) legitimate trade
Identify: (a) Chief Mojimba, (b) Henry M. Stanley, (c) King Leopold II, (d) Otto von Bismarck, (e) the Berlin Conference
Answer:
1. What were the motivating forces behind imperialism in the nineteenth century?
2. What was the most successful African export during the era of legitimate trade? Why was it successful?
3. How did competition among European powers factor into the partition of Africa?
4. What were the three stages of the process?

Critical Thinking
5. Rudyard Kipling, like many other Europeans, believed that part of the White Man's Burden was to bring Western benefits to societies he believed to be primitive. What examples would you have given Kipling to persuade him that Africans did not need or appreciate these benefits?

Colonialism affected all facets of African life. 2

Africans did not make it easy for the Europeans to continue on their colonizing path. In 1890, Chief Machemba of the Yao told the German commander, Hermann Von Wissman the following.

> I have listened to your words but can find no reason why I should obey you—I would rather die first . . . I do not fall at your feet, for you are God's creature just as I am . . . I am Sultan here in my land. You are Sultan there in yours. Yet listen, I do not say to you that you should obey me, for I know that you are a free man. . . . As for me, I will not come to you, and if you are strong enough, then come and fetch me.

Africans resisted colonialism.

Europeans had one significant advantage over the Africans they encountered as they formed their colonies: superior weapons. European armies usually had no difficulty defeating African soldiers. Such defeats, however, did not always result in complete conquest. And as Europeans tried to conquer inland territories, they found energetic resistance among larger, well-organized militant states.

Samori Touré To protect his Mandinka empire in West Africa, Samori Touré engaged in a full-scale, seven-year war with the French. He established a military workshop that employed 300 to 400 men. They manufactured gunpowder and repaired quick-firing rifles.

By 1898, he was forced into surrender. As he handed his Muslim prayer leaflets to the French, he said, "Allah [God] made you stronger. He abandoned me. I no longer have the need to pray. This prayer book is for you."

Queen Mother Yaa Asatewa In British West Africa, the leading resisters included Queen Mother Yaa Asatewa of the Asante. In 1896, a British officer demanded that an Asante golden stool be brought for him to sit upon. This stool was a ceremonial stool believed to hold the soul of the Asante nation. No one ever sat upon it,

The Europeans used the Maxim machine gun along with other advanced weapons in their conquest of Africa.

not even the rulers of the Asante. This insult was more than the Asante could bear. Led by Queen Mother Yaa Asatewa, the Asante held the officer and his wife in a fort for several weeks until they eventually escaped. The Asante fought against the British for four more years until they were finally overpowered.

King Menelik II In Ethiopia, King Menelik II and his army effectively held off the Italians who wanted his country. In a famous battle, called the Battle of Adowa, Italy suffered great losses. The defeat came as a shock to the Europeans; however, the colonizing powers did not stop trying to gain colonies elsewhere.

Europeans had different methods of rule.

To make colonial rule effective, Europeans had to put down resistance and devise policies and ways of governing suitable for their colonies. The policies that Europeans adopted for Africa were influenced by a racist attitude that assumed the inferiority of the African peoples and their cultures.

Assimilation The way Europeans viewed their colonies influenced the type of administration that evolved. While the French and the Portuguese viewed their colonies as part of their countries, the British and Germans regarded their colonies as independent entities that were to be separately treated.

French policy in Africa was characterized by the policy of **assimilation**. Its colonized people were expected to assimilate, or become absorbed into, French culture. Through western education, Africans in the French colonies could become French and enjoy the rights and privileges accorded all French citizens. These Africans were known as *evolués*. The Portuguese had a similar system whereby Africans who met certain educational and cultural standards were accorded Portuguese citizenship. These Africans were known as *assimilados*.

Direct rule vs. indirect rule European colonizers employed two main administrative methods in Africa—**direct rule** and **indirect rule**. The French, Belgians, Germans, and Portuguese generally employed direct rule, while the British employed indirect rule. French direct rule involved a centralized administrative system. In French West Africa, for example, the administration was headed by a governor general who received his orders and direction from Paris. A similar situation operated in the Portuguese colonies, where all the laws and regulations came from Portugal. The French and the Portuguese colonies used appointed officials to carry out the policy of direct rule.

Under British indirect rule, African rulers were allowed to form village and district governing councils known as "native authorities." Each district was assigned a British district officer whose duties included maintaining the peace, mediating disputes, and acting as judge to uphold British law. Any changes the African councils wanted to enforce had to be approved by the British central government. The British adopted a paternal attitude toward their subjects.

The colonial economies grew.

By 1914, the colonial powers were firmly established in Africa, and colonial economies were beginning to take shape. The colonies were expected to provide raw materials for the industries of the controlling countries and to import finished manufactured goods from the controlling countries.

While the governments of the controlling countries wished the colonies to serve their economic purpose, those governments generally did not direct the everyday economic activities. Those activities were handled by commercial companies, mining firms, and banks. Many of the foreign commercial institutions, often acting together with the colonial authorities, obtained concessions from the colonial governments that benefitted them economically. It was these commercial firms that bought and collected agricultural goods, employed African labor, and established prices of imports and exports.

Agriculture The major emphasis of the colonial agricultural economy was the production of cash crops for export. Since production for domestic use did not earn foreign currency, it did not receive encouragement from colonial authorities. Production for export was concentrated in the hands of small producers, with individual colonies specialized in different crops. The Gold Coast (present-day Ghana) exported cocoa; Western Nigeria, cocoa and palm kernels; Gambia, groundnuts; Uganda, Nigeria, and Tanganyika, cotton; and Uganda and Tanganyika, coffee. In return, the colonies were expected to import goods from Europe.

The long-term effect of this emphasis on exports was that many African nations failed to produce enough food to feed themselves. The system made Africans dependent on Europe. Since many African economies were based on one crop, the entire economy of a country was affected when the crop failed because of lack of rain or the price of the crop fell on the world market. In areas of European settlement such as

During the colonial period, Africans were forced to work on European agricultural estates. In this photograph taken in the early 1900's, African workers tend the cotton fields in a plantation in the Belgian Congo.

Kenya, African were forbidden to grow certain crops. In such areas, Africans were also forced to support the agricultural activities of European settlers by working on their crops.

Mining In addition to agriculture, minerals played an important role in colonial economic development in Africa. Many areas were rich in minerals: gold and diamonds in the Gold Coast and South Africa; copper in Zambia; and coal in Nigeria. However, because much money had to be spent to make mining profitable, the control of mining was confined to European firms that had a great deal of capital. While the capital came from abroad, the labor was supplied by Africans who were paid very poorly for their work. Many miners lost their lives through accidents in the mines.

The price of African labor African labor made agricultural and mining activities possible. Much of this labor was not a spontaneous response to the growing economy, however; it was coerced.

In some French, Portuguese, and Belgian colonies, Africans were forced to perform certain forms of labor for projects of local or colonial interest. The laborers received little or no compensation. In the Portuguese colonies, for example, convicts were used as laborers. The Portuguese regarded the giving of labor to the state as a moral and social obligation for their African subjects.

43

Economic development brought services to European settlers.

As economies grew, colonial banks were established and standard currencies were introduced in place of barter. The use of European currency led to a huge reduction in the value of African traditional currency—even though it was still used for paying the labor force. This meant that Africans who worked received even lower wages than it appeared. Yet they were taxed at European currency rates. While the existence of colonial banks facilitated economic activities, the banks provided no credit terms for Africans, even though some deposited their money in these banks.

Railroads, roads, telegraph lines, harbors, and post offices were established by colonial administrators to assist in the task of economic development. These things were needed and used to facilitate European trade rather than for the convenience of Africans.

Social services such as hospitals and clinics followed economic development, but these services were not donated by the colonial governments. Africans had to bear the cost. Consequently, African colonies that performed well economically received better services. In addition, Europeans in the colonies often received the bulk of social services—far out of proportion to their numbers. Many of these services went to the urban areas; thus, Africans who lived in the countryside generally did not benefit from them.

Colonialism caused social changes.

A major transformation that took place under colonial rule was rapid social change. Before colonial rule, most Africans lived in rural areas. Under colonial rule, new opportunities for employment and the attractions of urban life lured many to the cities. A new range of occupations was open to Africans who migrated from the rural areas. Work in offices and industries created a pattern of relationships different from those that had operated in the traditional societies.

Urbanization Although urban centers had existed in precolonial Africa, new cities grew rapidly under colonial rule. Some of the cities were the seats of government; others were major ports or industrial centers. As the urban centers grew, they became a mecca for people in the countryside who were looking for better prospects in life.

Education Education also became important in colonial Africa. The standard and level of education varied from country to country. Portugal and Belgium provided the least educational opportunities for Africans in their colonies. The British, in general, provided a good education for their colonists. In colonies where the education level was high, a vocal, Western-educated elite emerged. As you will read in Chapter 4, the educated elite began to rival the African traditional elite and to play a leading role in various nationalist groups.

Religion Missionary activities in Africa affected the traditional societies and brought important changes to the lives of many Africans. Especially during the 1800's and the early part of the 1900's, missionary activity spread Christianity to many parts of the continent. Missionaries did not only bring religion, however. They also brought education and helped accelerate the process of westernization.

Christianity affected African traditional society in many ways. For example, Africans were asked to commit themselves to one wife. In some traditional African societies, having more than one wife was not considered wrong. After adopting Christian ways, some traditional African Christians came to regard their own societies and cultures as inferior and pagan.

In response to the attitude of missionaries and church leaders toward African culture, some Africans began to look for ways to adapt Christianity to the needs of the African people. Africans also realized that the Christian churches were firmly controlled by Europeans: they were the administrators, preachers, and teachers. Africans who supported the churches were upset that those who advocated fairness for all in the church would practice supremacy. As a result, Africans started to form their own independent churches and break away from the European-controlled denominations. Thus the rise of the African independent churches, known as Ethiopianist churches, was a reaction against European domination and an acknowledgement of the value of African culture and institutions.

Colonial and missionary schools were started in many parts of Africa. What positive and negative effects might these schools have had on the African people?

Some of the African independent churches were anti-European and participated in early nationalist movements to regain African independence. For example, the African John Chilembwe who returned to Nyasaland (Malawi) led an independent church movement in that area. Chilembwe felt that European rule in Africa was a mockery and it was only through force that Africans could extricate themselves from colonial rule. Chilembwe and his followers therefore supported a local effort to overthrow the government of Nyasaland in 1915, but the revolt failed and Chilembwe was killed.

In Central Africa, the Jehovah's Witness movement had a powerful influence and led to the founding of African independent churches. In Nyasaland and Rhodesia, the followers became part of what was known as the Watchtower movement. In the Congo, the movement—which was begun by a prophet known as Simon Kimbangu in 1921—was known as the Kitawal movement. Although Kimbangu's preaching was primarily Biblical, he was arrested for disrupting order and sentenced to death. Later, his sentence was changed to life imprisonment. Kimbangu died in jail some thirty years later.

Lesson Review 2

Define: (a) assimilation, (b) direct rule, (c) indirect rule
Identify: (a) Samori Touré, (b) Queen Mother Yaa Asatewa, (c) King Menelik II, (d) John Chilembwe, (e) Simon Kimbangu
Answer:

1. As Europeans formed their colonies, what advantage did they have over the Africans?
2. How did direct rule and indirect rule differ?
3. Why didn't the controlling countries encourage the production of crops for domestic use? What long term effect did this have on many African nations?
4. In what ways were European settlers affected by economic development in the colonies? How were the Africans affected by this?
5. What three major social changes did colonialism cause?

Critical Thinking

6. Africans had no weapons to match the European guns. Therefore, Africans failed in their early attempts to resist colonial rule. How did Africans begin to work toward their own liberation once this rule was in place?

Chapter 3 Review

Summary

1. Explorers and missionaries changed Africa.

Colonialism in Africa began with European expansionism of the fifteenth century. As more and more countries became interested in gaining control over parts of Africa, the partition of the continent became very important. Countries scrambled for control for various reasons, including the desire for wealth and power, and religious fervor. By 1885, the Berlin Act established rules for how African colonization was to occur. Thirteen countries signed this act. Three stages were part of the partition process. First, the colonizing European nation and the African country's ruler had to agree to a Treaty of Protection. Second, the European nation had to make treaties with other European nations regarding the boundaries of the new colony. Third, occupation occurred. Often this stage was characterized by brutal suppression of any African rebellions.

2. Colonialism affected all facets of African life.

Although Europeans had superior weapons to use in defeating Africans who rebelled, complete conquest was not always possible. Several African countries resisted colonialism with valiant and organized efforts that often gained them additional years of independence. No matter what the individual policies regarding colonial rule were, the European belief that Africans and their cultures were inferior was evident. Also apparent was the fact that the colonies were expected to serve an economic purpose. Only cash crops could be farmed, and Africans were forced to labor in the fields and mines for very low wages. The development of service industries in Africa occurred during colonialism to benefit the Europeans, not the Africans. No regard was given to traditional African societies, and urbanization, education, and religion forced many rapid social changes.

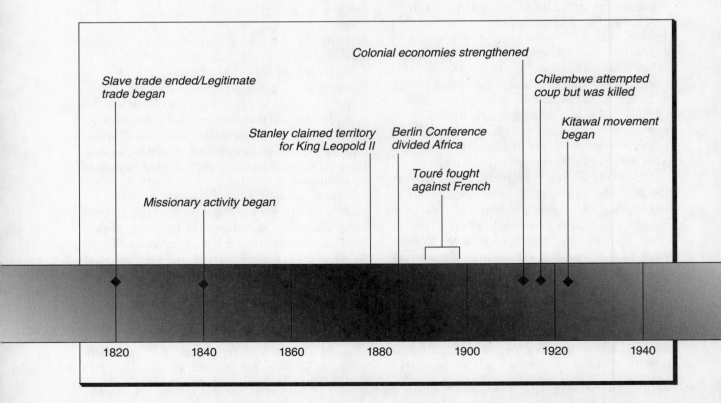

46

Reviewing the Facts

1. Define the following terms:
   a. imperialism
   b. colonialism
   c. legitimate trade
   d. assimilation
   e. direct rule
   f. indirect rule
2. Explain the importance of each of the following names or terms.
   a. Chief Mojimba
   b. Scramble for Africa
   c. King Leopold II
   d. Otto von Bismarck
   e. Dr. David Livingstone
   f. Berlin Act
   g. John Chilembwe
   h. Battle of Adowa
   i. Ethiopianist churches
   j. Queen Mother Yaa Asatewa
3. Why did Europeans desire to explore the African continent in the late eighteenth century?
4. Why was palm oil important to Europeans?
5. How did the motivations that King Leopold II and Otto von Bismarck had for acquiring African territories differ?
6. What was the "White Man's Burden"?
7. List five regulations of the Berlin Act.
8. What wrongs were often done Africans during the Treaty of Protection stage?
9. Why was the third stage of the partition process known as the pacification stage?
10. What was impressive about Samori Touré's efforts to resist the French?
11. Why were Africans called *assimilados* given Portuguese citizenship?
12. What were long term effects of centering African agriculture on cash crops?
13. What was unfair about the financial systems set up by Europeans in Africa?
14. What did John Chilembwe believe about overcoming colonial rule?
15. What happened to Simon Kimbangu?

Basic Skills

1. **Reading strategically** Skim Lesson 1. Be sure to note the heads, subheads, and key words (in boldface type). Examine the map and the art, and their captions. Write three questions that you think you can find answers to in this lesson. Then read to find the answers.

2. **Summarizing** Summarize what you believe to be the single most important factor behind the colonization of Africa. Include at least three facts that support your view.
3. **Organizing information** (a) To organize the information in Lesson 1, create a three-part chart. Label the sections *gold, glory,* and *God.* In each section, write statements that support the heading as a motivating force behind colonialism. (b) Organize the information in Lesson 2 in the same way, labeling the chart sections *commerce, Christianity,* and *civilization.*

Critical Thinking

1. **Analyzing** What basic problem between Europeans and Africans does the incident on the Lualaba River, described at the beginning of the chapter, illustrate? What would have had to happen from the very beginning between Africans and Europeans for such misunderstandings not to have occured?
2. **Identifying cause and effect** What effect did the adversarial relationship between Germany and France have on the Scramble for Africa?
3. **Determining relationships** What was the relationship between King Leopold's seizure of territory in Africa and the need for the Berlin Conference?
4. **Comparing** Compare France's direct rule to Britain's indirect rule in Africa.

Perspectives on Past and Present

The boundaries drawn by Europeans during the Scramble for Africa were decided upon without African input. Often, nations and ethnic groups were divided. Research to find one example of when this occurred. Trace the negative impact of this European decision to the present day.

Investigating History

European colonialism occurred in areas other than Africa. For example, India was subject to colonialism under Great Britain. Find out more about the history of colonialism in India. How was what happened there similar to what happened in Africa? What are some differences?

Chapter 4

African Nationalism

Jomo Kenyatta, shown here waving his symbolic fly whisk, inspired many Kenyans during their struggle for independence.

Key Terms

nationalism
pan-Africanism
protectorate
apartheid

Read and Understand

1. Many events inspired African nationalism.
2. Africans began to form nationalist goals.
3. World War II deepened African resolve.
4. Many roads led to independence.

It was just a few minutes before midnight. The old man looked out across the stadium at the thousands who had gathered for this celebration of freedom. He stood in the glare of floodlights, one hand leaning on a black stick, a symbol of power.

The man's name was Jomo Kenyatta, which means "burning spear" in the language of his people, the Kikuyu. But tonight "his people" were more than the Kikuyu. They came from many regions and many clans, from many villages spread across the East African grasslands and up into mountains. On this night, December 12, 1963, he stood before them as leader of the new country of Kenya.

The British had ruled Kenya for more than sixty years. The British flag still flew from the flagpole. Just before midnight, the floodlights went out and the British flag was lowered in the dark. As the lights went on again, the black, red, and green flag of Kenya was raised, as cries of "Uhuru!" "Freedom!" filled the night. Fireworks flashed across the African sky.

Jomo Kenyatta had come a long way to this day of Uhuru. As a little boy, he had traveled the green land helping his grandfather, who was a medicine man. Kenyatta carried his grandfather's bag, which held herbs and bark and other things to heal and help his people. Kenyatta had it in his mind to help his people, too, in ways quite different from his grandfather's. He went to England as a young man and studied at English schools. As he talked to English leaders and learned about their ideas, he thought of ways these ideas could help his people. Soon he was saying that the British should not rule Kenya, that the old African way of living was good and that change should come when the Africans wanted change, not when forced on them by the Europeans. In fairness, the British settlers in Kenya should give back to the Africans the good land they had taken. Kenyatta met with others from all over the world who felt that African culture should be preserved and respected, and that Africans should rule their own destiny.

Back home in Kenya, Kenyatta was soon sent to jail, accused of leading a secret organization that the British called the Mau Mau. Perhaps being in jail saved his life, for during the next bloody years, many people were killed, both by the Mau Mau and by the British. The struggle split African Kenyans into factions, many unwilling to work together. Then, just two years before the night of Uhuru, Jomo Kenyatta had been released from jail. He had been able to bring the factions back together to work for independence.

There are threads in Jomo Kenyatta's story that run through much of the history of Africa as it developed a sense of **nationalism**, which is a feeling of loyalty for one's own land and people. Many African leaders as students in Europe encountered ideas about freedom that they then turned against those same European powers in their own struggle for independence.

They took part in the colonial struggle at home, some suffering imprisonment and even death.

In this chapter, we will explore the course of events that led millions of Africans to bind themselves together in more than 50 independent nations.

Many events inspired African nationalism. 1

Nation is not an easy word to define. When does a group of people become a nation? The concept of a nation-state is fairly new, just a few hundred years old. Within a nation, people have decided to join together to govern themselves. They call themselves a nation and other peoples recognize them as a nation.

Europeans were unaware of powerful African kingdoms, such as that of the Asante. A commanding Asante king is shown here sitting under a ceremonial umbrella that symbolized his office.

49

As you read in Chapter 1, many distinct groups are spread across the vast continent of Africa. In the past, the members of each group lived in a particular landscape that sustained them and defined their way of life. Until the twentieth century, most people living on the African continent did not think of themselves primarily as African, or even as Yoruba, Bakongo, or Swahili. They thought of themselves as members of their own family or clan. As a rule, only a large religious movement, such as Islam, could blur the boundaries of these local loyalties.

So how could the concept of nationalism take hold in Africa? Each nation in the world was formed to expand the power of the groups within it. In Africa, nations were formed for this same reason, but they were formed under particular circumstances and with a particular enemy in mind—colonialism. This anticolonial nationalism swept through both the Asian and African colonies of Britain and France after World War II, under leaders who spread the idea that all people, not just Europeans, have the right to their own independent nation-states. This lesson will describe some early events that set these ideas in motion.

Colonial abuses inflamed anticolonial feeling.

Chapter 3 tells how European colonists assumed the power to dictate how Africans should live. It was a rare European who could look past prejudice to see the richness of rural African life. Colonialism was not just an economic and political policy, it was also a racist attitude that allowed many kinds of abuses. In the years that followed colonization, both the policy and the attitude had to be challenged.

The policy in each colony toward European settlers and the use of the land was an important factor in setting the course of that colony's nationalist history. Where white settlement was encouraged, the newcomers were given land that had been taken from Africans. The Africans who had been displaced often had to work for these new owners at low wages.

Some colonies had many settlers, while some had a smaller but still significant number, and others had almost none at all. In the countries with few settlers, Africans found it easier to regain their freedom.

Without exception, Africans resisted the takeover of their land, but the consequences were often bitter. For example, by the time Muslim patriots in Algeria had finally lost their long war of resistance, they had also lost not only their right to govern themselves, but much of their best land. By 1939, European settlers made up about one tenth of the population, but owned one third of the land that was rich enough to grow crops.

Another important example of settler land use was in Kenya, where the British government wanted to make their Kenya-Uganda railroad profitable by encouraging Europeans to settle in the fertile interior highlands. This was where the Kikuyu lived. The Kikuyu were forced onto smaller plots, into the city, or into taking jobs with the new European owners. The Kikuyu had to pay a "hut tax," and when they were unable to raise the money, their land was taken away. Henry Thuku, who formed the Young Kikuyu Association in 1921, said of the colonial government, "It is their task to steal the property of the Kikuyu people." It is not surprising that the Kikuyu took the lead in developing anticolonial nationalism in Kenya.

Although the Africans were courageous defenders of their lands, in most cases they had neither the weapons nor the unity to fight successfully. The first step toward nationalism was taken when African leaders in each colony realized that they needed to join together if they were going to be strong enough to prevail.

Pan-Africanism arose as a cultural and political movement.

The racist attitude on which colonialism was built was evident in the African and Asian colonies, but it was also evident in the United States. In the early part of the twentieth century, African American intellectuals began to challenge this attitude and to focus on African heritage in a positive way. They reminded the world that two of the greatest libraries of the ancient world had been in Egypt and Timbuktu and that the medieval empires of West Africa had been centers of wealth and learning.

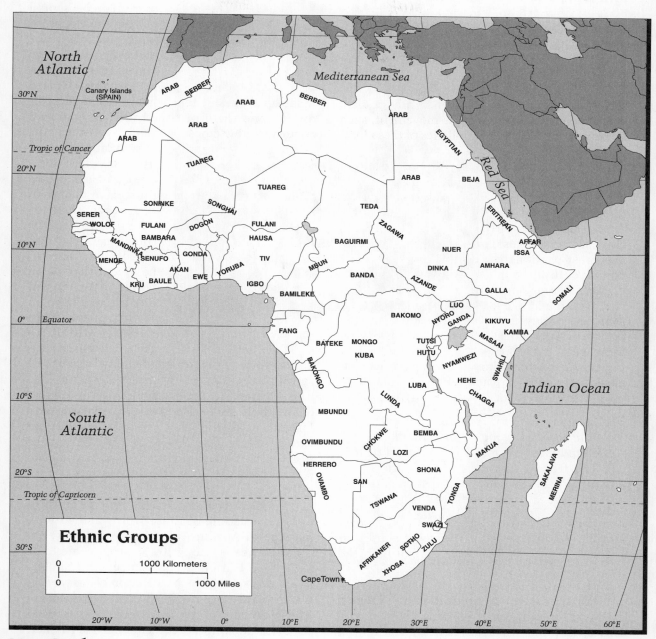

Ethnic Groups

| 0 | 1000 Kilometers |
| 0 | 1000 Miles |

Map Study

Notice that no political lines are drawn between the various ethnic groups in this map.
How might this map be different if the ethnic groups had organized themselves politically?

They also looked at the world of their own time and saw people of African descent, including those living in quiet traditional ways, whose lives were full of beauty and culture. They developed the concept of **pan-Africanism**, which celebrated the kinship of all those of African descent and aimed to improve their lives.

Marcus Garvey One of the earliest and most passionate voices calling for a united "Africa for the Africans" was Marcus Garvey. He lived in New York but was born in

Marcus Garvey in 1921

Jamaica and spent time in London, where his encounters with Africans influenced his interest in Africa. He said

> *If liberty is good for certain sets of humanity it is good for all. Black men, Colored men, Negroes have as much right to be free as any other race that God Almighty ever created, and we desire freedom that is unfettered, freedom that is unlimited, freedom that will give us a chance and opportunity to rise to the fullest of our ambition and that we cannot get in countries where other men rule and dominate.*

Although Garvey's organization, the Universal Negro Improvement Association, soon collapsed, its pride in African heritage and its call for African Americans to return to Africa struck a chord that rang loudly throughout Africa.

W.E.B. Du Bois Another African American who influenced pan-Africanism was W.E.B. Du Bois. A professor at Atlanta University, he was probably the first American author to describe the great medieval kingdoms of West Africa. His

themes were that those of African descent, wherever they might be, should feel an emotional tie with one another; that they have a deep attachment to Africa as their ancestral home; that an educated few, an educated "elite," must lead the way to improving the lives of all black people; that black people must take charge of their own lives by developing such things as businesses, schools, and newspapers; and that black people "have a contribution to make in civilization and humanity, which no other race can make."

Pan-African Congresses Du Bois organized a series of conferences on pan-Africanism. The first was held in London in 1900, followed by others held in Paris, Brussels, London, and Lisbon, and then in New York City in 1927. At these conferences, people of African descent from all over the world, but mainly from North America and the West Indies, came together for the first time.

The Harlem Renaissance and négritude Du Bois was one of those who watched with pleasure as African Americans found their full artistic voice in the 1920's in what came to be called the Harlem Renaissance. The Renaissance was sparked by a collection of essays that was printed in 1925. In the collection, called *The New Negro: An Interpretation*, African Americans explored the connection to their ancestral African past.

At this same time, a literary black consciousness movement known by its French name, *négritude*, flourished among West Indians of African descent and French-speaking African students in Paris. These poets and writers founded the magazine, *Présence Africaine*,

What symbols about African American culture did Senegal artist Papa Ibra Tall include in his oil painting entitled "Harlem"?

which published new works exploring the African experience.

Négritude was a reaction against France's colonial policy of forcing Africans to assimilate into the French culture (see Chapter 3). French-speaking Africans wanted to embrace the uniqueness of their own African culture. Léopold Sédar Senghor, a leader of the movement, said

> *The British speak of "Anglo-Saxon civilization" because they are men, and the French speak of "French civilization" or "Greco-Latin civilization." We Negroes speak of* Négritude, *for we too are men—men who, forty thousand years ago, were the first to emerge as* Homo sapiens, *the first men to express themselves in art, the first to create the earliest agrarian civilizations in the valleys of the Nile. . . .*

As black artistic expression came out of the shadows, pride in African descent and in the legacy of African culture reinforced the feeling that Africans should be governed by no one but themselves. Although only a few Africans heard about these international movements, those few included the people who were developing their own ideas about the rights of African peoples, the need for African unity, and the ways to go about reaching their goals.

International events influenced nationalism.

By World War I (1914–1918), colonialism seemed to be a stronger force than nationalism. With the exception of North Africa, both colonial rulers and the African people believed that the colonial systems were there to stay.

World War I The war that began in 1914, though essentially a war among European powers, was in truth a world war, with a direct effect on Africa. For instance, Egypt was put under a Christian **protectorate** by the British during this war, which means that Britain controlled the Egyptian government. This action was greatly resented by the vast majority of Egyptians, who were Muslim, and their resentment played a part in the Egyptians' search for true independence.

Many Africans fought on the side of the empires that ruled them. The Gold Coast raised 3,000 soldiers to fight for the British empire, and the logical conclusion was drawn in a Gold Coast newspaper in 1921: If these Africans "were good enough to fight and die in the Empire's cause, they were good enough . . . to have a share in their government's country."

League of Nations Some nationalistic ideas came from the League of Nations, forerunner of today's United Nations, which had been formed as an answer to the many horrors of World War I. The League talked about eventual independence for colonial peoples and ideas such as the right of all peoples to self-determination. Although only Europeans were included in the discussions, some educated Africans read about them and became even more convinced that such rights must belong to the peoples of Africa.

The global depression In the early 1930's, the deep economic depression that hit the world's industrialized nations also shook the colonies. The demand for raw materials from Africa dwindled, so that many African workers lost their already small wages. At the same time, European powers had less money to spend in their colonies. The cities became crowded with rural Africans who had been forced off their lands. These same cities became places where new ideas could be heard and discussed. They became fertile places for nationalist ideas.

Lesson Review 1

Define: (a) nationalism, (b) pan-Africanism (c) protectorate
Identify: (a) Jomo Kenyatta, (b) Marcus Garvey, (c) W.E.B. Du Bois, (d) Harlem Renaissance, (e) *négritude*, (f) Léopold Sédar Senghor
Answer:
1. How did white settlement affect Africans' ability to regain their freedom?
2. What were the goals of the people who influenced pan-Africanism?
3. How did World War I affect nationalism?

Critical Thinking
4. What point do you think Léopold Senghor was making in his statement about *négritude*?

Africans began to form nationalist goals. 2

Colonialism was especially powerful between the two World Wars (1918–1939). During this time, African leaders mainly wanted to correct abuses, not demand independence. There were clear signs, however, that something was stirring. The older nationalist organizations were being shaken up by the ideas of educated young men who had grown impatient with their elders' inaction. People in many parts of the continent were growing more aware of one another and of ideas that could lead to a better Africa.

Education played a leading role.

As early as 1900, three regions of the continent had significant numbers of western-educated Africans: North Africa, especially Egypt; West Africa, especially around Dakar in Senegal, along the Gold Coast in Sierra Leone, and in southern Nigeria; and in what by 1910 would become the Union of South Africa.

Except in North Africa, where nationalist leaders were Muslims, most of these educated people had gone to Christian mission schools. Some of the people were devout believers who recognized that the message of the Church ran counter to the racist colonial practices they saw all around them.

Because colonial governments all over the continent supported the spread of missions along with their schools and clinics, the numbers of Africans exposed to these Christian ideals were bound to grow. In this way, through western education, Africans from different parts of a colony or even from different areas of the continent could talk to one another, even though they had to speak in the language of their oppressors. Ironically, the English and French languages became keys to African unity.

In Muslim communities, education was perhaps even more important. In Algeria, for instance, no political nationalist movements were allowed before World War II, so the only force that could work to keep national feeling alive were those religious movements that supported Islamic education. In this way, traditional values and national pride were preserved.

The western-style suit makes it easy to pick out the person who was western educated. Notice that he is seated close to and as high as the chief of his ethnic group, the Asante. What does this imply about the status of the educated man?

55

Egypt gained an early, flawed independence.

In North Africa, the history of nationalism in the Muslim, Arabic-speaking countries is closely tied to the destiny of their neighbors in the Middle East. In 1914, Egypt was supposedly a self-governing province of the weakening Ottoman empire, though British agents had really run it for years. Ships laden with goods paid well to steam through the Suez Canal, a vital route between Europe and Asia. Britain was resolved to keep control of the profits. Egyptians resented the fact that all these profits went to European shareholders rather than to relieve the poverty of the Egyptian people. They also resented the British preference for Egyptians with a Turkish background.

Two nationalist movements were in place by World War I. The more conservative, ruling-class Egyptians with Turkish backgrounds were pitted against middle-class native Egyptians. The native Egyptians were led by Saad Zaghlul, who had the support of most Egyptian people.

When the Ottoman empire collapsed after World War I, Britain set the course of Egypt's future. Britain made Egypt a self-governing constitutional monarchy in 1922 and made an Egyptian with a Turkish background, Sultan Fuad, the king of Egypt. He usually ignored the constitution and ruled by decree because the majority in the Egyptian parliament belonged to Saad Zaghlul's Wafd party, the first true nationalist party in Egypt. In 1936, Britain loosened its hold on the Egyptian government, but Sultan Fuad was still in power as World War II began.

West African politics varied.

The French and British left little intact after their conquests in West Africa. They set up new boundaries for their colonies and gave them new names. They imposed new governments, new laws, new economic systems, and new educational and religious institutions. Conquered communities, from the once-powerful Asante to the smallest Igbo town, were swallowed up into these new colonies.

There were three areas in which nationalist thinking had been known from the earliest colonial times. They were the coastal communities of Senegal, called the Four Communes; the coastal towns of the Gold Coast, with their long history of commercial ties to Europe; and southern Nigeria, especially Yoruba and Igbo territory, where Christian missions were active.

People born in one of the Four Communes of the Senegalese coast were citizens of France itself and were treated much better than their Muslim neighbors in the interior, who suffered under heavy taxes and could even be trapped into forced labor. Because of the harsh tyranny of life in the interior, it was left to those living in the relative freedom of Senegal—or those living in the French capital of Paris itself—to take part in political activity. In 1914, for the first time a black African, Blaise Daigne, was elected Senegalese deputy to the French National Assembly. At first, he worked for the benefit of Africans, but later represented the views of the French government rather than those of French West Africans. His career set a pattern for nationalist activity among French-speaking Africans, who usually identified strongly with France.

East Africa was ripe for nationalism.

European colonialists had an especially strong hold on East Africa. By the outbreak of World War in I in 1914, the British had set up a white settler colony in Kenya and had established protectorates over the rulers of Buganda and Zanzibar. The Germans were in Tanganyika, and the Italians were in the southern part of Somaliland and in Eritrea, just north of Ethiopia.

Ethiopia As you read in Chapter 3, Menelik II, King of Ethiopia, had avoided being conquered by delivering a stunning defeat to the Italian army at the battle of Adowa in 1896. News of the Ethiopian success spread throughout the world, giving hope to the oppressed, since it proved that Europeans could be defeated. After World War I, Ethiopia was a recognized member of the international community. But the Europeans did not take Ethiopia very seriously as a nation and did little to help when Fascist Italy attacked in 1935. Ethiopian Emperor Haile Selassie fled into exile and the country came under Italian control from 1936 to 1941, a blow to the cause of African nationalism.

Kenya Modern nationalism in East Africa got its start in Kenya, especially among the Kikuyu people, much of whose land had been taken from them and given to European settlers in the early 1900's. To add to African discontent, thousands of Kenyan men were used as bearers for British troops fighting against the Germans in neighboring Tanganyika, the scene of many battles.

In the early 1920's, a white settler community made its first move to try to gain control of the colonial government. They failed. The British government said their policy would be based on what was best for the "native interests," but the dominant voices in setting the laws for the colony were still European.

The Africans of Kenya had watched with interest as the settlers pressured the British government. They formed lobbying organizations like those used by the settler community. The most important was the Young Kikuyu Association, founded by a young telephone operator, Harry Thuku. This group worked for the abolition of a new pass system—a way of controlling people's movements by making them carry cards saying who they were and where they could and could not go. They also worked for the return of Kikuyu lands and for lowering the taxes Africans had to pay. After two years of mass gatherings and petitions, colonial troops fired on one of the rallies and Thuku was arrested; the movement died down.

South Africa laid the foundation for a troubled future.

The European settlers controlled South Africa in a way that neither the settler community of Algeria nor the settlers of the "white highlands" in Kenya could ever do. Almost 90 percent of the land, most of the resources, and all of the political rights and military power were in the hands of the Europeans who had settled there over the past 300 years. The vast majority of the population, however, was descended from Bantu-speaking African peoples who had farmed and kept cattle in those lands for more than a thousand years.

Independent churches As you read in Chapter 3, one of the earliest forms of independence gained by Africans was freedom to establish their own Christian congregations, separate from those of the missionaries. South Africa, for instance, had many independent Christian churches before World War II.

Africans who took up careers in the churches were often disappointed that the missionaries insisted on keeping leadership roles for themselves. The Africans began setting up independent African Christian churches, which became centers for the discussion of new ideas and hopes.

The African National Congress Before the Union of South Africa was formed in 1910, nationalist pressure groups had already sprung up in each of the colonies that eventually made up South Africa. Once the Union actually came into being, educated Africans realized that they would have to have a nationwide organization to advocate their goal, which even then was a society based not on race but on individual merit. In 1912, representatives of various regional associations met in Bloemfontein, under the leadership of Pixly ka Isaka Seme, and established the African National Congress (ANC), which was known until 1923 as the South African Native National Congress.

For many years, members of the ANC clung to the belief that their point of view would be bound to win acceptance if they could just explain it clearly enough in petitions, newspaper articles, and meetings with people in power. They underestimated the political deafness of self-interest. On the eve of World War II, South African nationalist hopes were in place, but so was the resolve of the white settler government.

Lesson Review 2

Identify: (a) Saad Zaghlul, (b) Sultan Fuad, (c) Blaise Daigne, (d) African National Congress
Answer:
1. What role did education play in nationalism?
2. Why was Egypt's early independence flawed?
3. What was the Young Kikuyu Association and what did it do?

Critical Thinking
4. Why was the white settler government in South Africa deaf to the ANC point of view?

World War II deepened African resolve. 3

During the years 1939 to 1945, most of the powerful countries of the world were at war with one another. Radio and film took their place along with the printed word as wartime weapons. Stirring speeches crackled over radio sets around the world and film footage showed flags whipped by a breeze as soldiers marched off to fight for freedom. That was the theme of these sounds and images—the fight for freedom and human rights. Africa was listening.

Africans suffered hardships for freedom.

From the very beginning of the war, the French and British asked the people of their African colonies to help them defeat the Axis Powers (Germany, Italy, and Japan) in the name of freedom. In 1941, this appeal was written in a document called the Atlantic Charter. Among other things, the charter promised that after the war those who signed would "respect the right of all peoples to choose the form of government

Soldiers from British West Africa are shown enroute to their post during World War II. Africans defended their continent against invaders, as well as fighting abroad defending Allied territory.

under which they will live." Africans looked at this charter as a promise of freedom from colonial rule.

Two hundred thousand Africans from French and British colonies served as soldiers in campaigns from North Africa to Burma. Their war experience helped change their own feelings about European superiority. White settlers and officials led privileged lives in the colonies. In East Africa, for instance, a European was never seen carrying a package, however small. The colonial customs were meant to impress on the Africans how different Europeans were. But in the mud of the trenches, African soldiers came eye to eye with European soldiers and saw that they were not so different after all.

World power shifted after the war.

The war devastated Europe. The European powers were so weakened that they were replaced by two new superpowers, the United States and the Soviet Union. These two soon began a struggle for global dominance called the Cold War. These countries did have one thing in common: neither supported British or French colonialism. Both wanted to attract the support of African nationalist leaders who might side with them in their own emerging struggle with each other.

After the war, Britain did grant independence to some of its Asian colonies. However, the British did not plan to grant immediate independence to those in Africa. Both the British and the French at first thought they could satisfy African demands by making minor reforms that would give a limited number of Africans a voice in their governments, but even these changes were to take place only in colonies that had few white settlers. In countries with heavy populations of settlers, the European-descended minority was demanding more power, not less, so that they could control the African majority.

Before long, however, Britain and France were forced to recognize the power of African discontent. Pressures that had been building during the war exploded into mass protests. A new generation of nationalist leaders worked to organize not only the well-educated few but also the masses in both the cities and the countryside.

In 1938, Italy set out to obtain territory in Africa. Among the Italian goals was French Tunisia. In response, France sent troops from other regions in its African colonies to defend Tunisia. Here, members of the Eighteenth Senegalese Regiment of the French Colonial Infantry parade at the Oasis of Gabes before leaving for their post in the desert.

Labor unions and ethnic associations both grew more militant and nationalist in tone. Nationalist newspapers, pamphlets, and books attracted larger and larger audiences.

By 1950, the force of the new movement could no longer be denied, and Britain and France were rethinking their strategies, at least for those colonies in which there were no large settler populations pushing their own demands. For example, in the North African colonies of Tunisia and Morocco, the French first met nationalist demands with soldiers and guns, but soon sought to compromise with more moderate elements of the nationalist leadership. Both of these territories gained their independence in 1956.

Future leaders gathered at the fifth Pan-African Congress.

A new phase in the story of pan-Africanism began with the Fifth Pan-African Congress, held in 1945 in Manchester, England. Among the participants were Jomo Kenyatta of Kenya and Kwame Nkrumah of Ghana, two future leaders of their countries.

The participants were inspired by the promises of the Atlantic Charter and by their sense of unity. Kwame Nkrumah of the Gold Coast and some of the other leaders returned home determined to work for freedom. You will read about Nkrumah's efforts in the next lesson.

Lesson Review 3

Identify: (a) Atlantic Charter,
(b) Fifth Pan-African Congress
Answer:
1. What role did Africans play in World War II?
2. Why did the fact that the United States and the Soviet Union became superpowers change colonialism?
3. How were Britain and France forced to recognize the African demand for independence?

Critical Thinking
4. Why do you think both the United States and the Soviet Union wanted the support of Africa's nationalist leaders?

Many roads led to independence.

4

The slow, often painful process of gathering together into nationhood was drawing to its climax in the years after World War II. The educated elite had led the Africans of each colony to break down the barriers that separated them, and now they could hope to speak with one voice.

A war-weary Europe, land-hungry settlers, and an Africa on the rise made an explosive mixture. In this lesson, you will see that sometimes colonies became nations peacefully and sometimes only after much blood had been shed.

Ghana became the model of a peaceful transition.

Young, American-educated Kwame Nkrumah came home to the Gold Coast in 1947 determined to win independence for his people without delay. His radical ideas soon pitted him against the older Gold Coast leaders, so he founded a new party—the Convention People's party (CPP). The party led the people of the Gold Coast in strikes, boycotts, and passive resistance campaigns. Nkrumah was arrested and jailed. The protests were so successful, however, that the British realized they had to prepare for independence. With no settlers to stand in the way, Britain hoped to make the transition peacefully, keeping hold of some valuable economic ties with the region.

The turning point came in 1951 when the first national election for an all-African parliament was held and the candidates of Nkrumah's party won. Nkrumah was released from jail to head the government. From this time forward, the newly elected African officials and the British colonial officials worked together in harmony toward independence. On March 6, 1957, the old colonial Gold Coast became the new independent country of Ghana.

From the time of those 1951 elections, Ghana became a model for African nationalists. Kwame Nkrumah became an advocate for independence throughout Africa. In a speech to the first All-African Peoples Conference, held in Accra in 1958, he stressed the need for all of the peoples of the continent to stand together. This pan-African viewpoint spread across Africa, and today it is represented by the Organization of African Unity (page 62).

A banner at the 1958 All-African Peoples Conference in Accra, Ghana, reads: "Hands off Africa! Africa must be free!"

French West Africans negotiated independence.

France had regained its own independence after the war, when it was freed from German occupation. The new French government knew what it was like to be under another country's heel, and it was sensitive to the issue of freedom. A constitution, adopted in 1946, called for the election of African deputies both to the French National Assembly and to a new Assembly of the French Union, made up of France and all its colonies.

For the first few years, these deputies were able to improve the conditions for French West Africans. Forced labor was abolished and French Africans were given more of the rights given to French citizens. But there was still a rising demand among the Africans that they be able to manage their own affairs.

In the early 1950's, the situation began to change rapidly. The neighboring British colonies were moving toward independence, and Algeria had begun its armed struggle in North Africa. The French hold on its African colonies was loosening. In 1958, the war hero Charles de Gaulle became president of France. He felt that the most important thing for France was to keep its colonies economically dependent even if that meant giving up some political control. He proposed a new French community of self-governing countries under French leadership. But French Guinea, led by Sékou Touré, rejected the idea and the other colonies soon followed. The De Gaulle government bowed to the inevitable, and eight separate countries took their place on the roster of free nations.

East Africa moved toward independence.

Other parts of Africa watched as West African countries won their independence. At the end of the war, Ethiopia was free again after five years under Fascist Italy. Somaliland had been liberated from Italy's hold, too, by British-led African forces, only to come under joint British-French control. Tanganyika was still under British control, but now became a United

Kwame Nkrumah (inset) is shown above, speaking in the parliament of independent Ghana. He inspired African nationalists throughout the continent.

Nations Trust Territory. Uganda, under the British system of indirect rule, was still dominated by the Ganda people. Kenya too was under indirect British rule.

The more than 50,000 white settlers in Kenya not only owned the best lands, but also had the strongest voice in the colonial council. While the British government looked on, the African people and the settlers now clashed over who would control the country. The Kikuyu people, whose best lands had been wrenched away from them, led the resistance to settler control. Jomo Kenyatta used an old party, the Kenya African Union (KAU), to rally the ordinary African people of the colony who were suffering the poverty brought on by the loss of their land, low wages, and the hardships of war.

As more and more people flocked to the KAU, the white settlers became very uneasy. As a result, the colonial government declared a state of emergency in 1952. Several thousand Kikuyu fled into the forests of the central highlands and formed the Land and Freedom party (which the British called the Mau Mau).

61

For the next four years, bitter warfare raged in Kenya. Thousands of Africans were killed, both by fellow-Africans and by the British. Many more, including Jomo Kenyatta, were rounded up by the British army and sent to prison camps. The conflict never spread throughout the country, and the Kikuyu resistance was put down, but the British realized that they could not support the settlers' demands in the long run. In 1955, they ended the state of emergency and once more allowed African political parties. This meant that Kenya would now move toward African majority rule. Jomo Kenyatta and other leaders were released from jail. In 1963, under Kenyatta, Kenya was declared independent.

The OAU *became the voice of Africa.*

In 1963, the newly independent African nations formed the Organization of African Unity (OAU). It has its headquarters in Addis Ababa, the capital of Ethiopia.

From the beginning, the OAU was devoted not just to the idea of African unity, but to the proposition that none of its members would be really free until all were. Thus, when the end of the season of negotiated independence came, the OAU took up the cause of those who now faced long and bloody wars of liberation to gain their freedom. The peaceful transitions of power in the mid-1960's came to an end, and armed liberation struggles began. But one struggle had begun ten years earlier, in North Africa.

Algeria finally gained independence.

Guerrillas of the Front for National Liberation (FLN) had launched a war against the French in Algeria, and hundreds of thousands of French troops fought against them from 1954 to 1962. Algerian freedom fighters not only did battle on several fronts under able leaders, such as Ahmed Ben Bella, they also were careful to tend to their cause in other ways. They set up services to take care of the people in liberated zones. They got the support of foreign allies, and they kept the support of the Algerians who were in the areas the French army had taken over.

The masses of the Algerians grew more loyal to the FLN as the war grew more ferocious. By

1962, despite their military strength, the French knew they had lost politically. They were forced to grant Algeria independence under FLN leadership. The new FLN government not only turned itself to the task of rebuilding the war-torn country, but also became a haven for refugees from other liberation movements, especially those fighting against the Portuguese.

The Portuguese colonies struggled.

In West Africa, only the Portuguese colony of Guinea-Bissau had no hope of achieving independence peacefully. Portugal, a small country, feared that the loss of the markets and the natural resources of its colonies would mean economic ruin. Portugal was under a dictatorship itself at the time, so all those who sought independence or even reform were suppressed. The same harsh policies were in place in Angola and Mozambique, the Portuguese colonies in southern Africa. Nationalist movements were forced to go underground or into exile, and they secretly took up arms.

Not until 1974 did freedom fighters, many from Angola and Mozambique, topple the Portuguese dictatorship. In 1975, all three colonies were made independent. The new anti-colonial governments of Angola and Mozambique became allies with the other Africans in southern Africa, where the trend was not toward liberation, but toward ever harsher and more racist control by settlers of European-descent.

Angolan demonstrators air their opinion. What message are they trying to convey, and why?

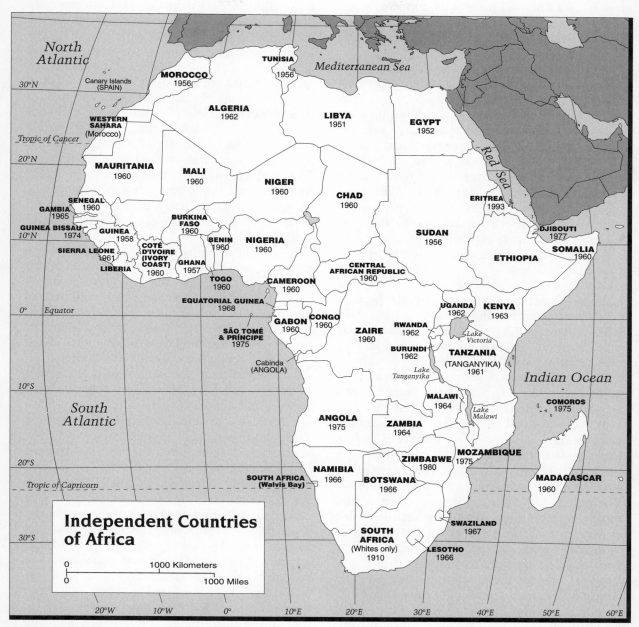

North Atlantic

30°N

Canary Islands (SPAIN)

Tropic of Cancer

20°N

10°N

0° Equator

10°S

South Atlantic

20°S

Tropic of Capricorn

30°S

TUNISIA 1956

MOROCCO 1956

Mediterranean Sea

ALGERIA 1962

LIBYA 1951

EGYPT 1952

WESTERN SAHARA (Morocco)

MAURITANIA 1960

MALI 1960

NIGER 1960

CHAD 1960

Red Sea

ERITREA 1993

SENEGAL 1960

GAMBIA 1965

GUINEA BISSAU 1974

GUINEA 1958

BURKINA FASO 1960

SUDAN 1956

DJIBOUTI 1977

SIERRA LEONE 1961

COTÉ D'IVOIRE (IVORY COAST)

BENIN 1960

NIGERIA 1960

ETHIOPIA

SOMALIA 1960

LIBERIA

GHANA 1957

TOGO 1960

CAMEROON 1960

CENTRAL AFRICAN REPUBLIC 1960

EQUATORIAL GUINEA 1968

GABON 1960

CONGO 1960

ZAIRE 1960

UGANDA 1962

KENYA 1963

RWANDA 1962

SÃO TOMÉ & PRÍNCIPE 1975

Lake Victoria

BURUNDI 1962

TANZANIA (TANGANYIKA) 1961

Cabinda (ANGOLA)

Lake Tanganyika

Indian Ocean

MALAWI 1964

COMOROS 1975

ANGOLA 1975

ZAMBIA 1964

Lake Malawi

ZIMBABWE 1980

MOZAMBIQUE 1975

MADAGASCAR 1960

SOUTH AFRICA (Walvis Bay)

NAMIBIA 1966

BOTSWANA 1966

SWAZILAND 1967

Independent Countries of Africa

0   1000 Kilometers
0   1000 Miles

SOUTH AFRICA (Whites only) 1910

LESOTHO 1966

20°W   10°W   0°   10°E   20°E   30°E   40°E   50°E   60°E

Map Study

The map shows the year in which each African nation was formed. According to the map, which nations have been independent for more than 40 years?

South Africa played out the tragedy.

South Africa held the key to white rule in the region. Not only did it serve as a model of settler domination, it also supported other racist regimes with its industrial strength and even with its army.

Apartheid After World War II, white South Africans instituted **apartheid**, a system separating the country into racial groups under white control. Each ethnic group was to have its own homeland, which would eventually become self-governing. The true nature of this system is shown by the fact that the Africans had no choice in the matter. They were given a territory and their South African citizenship was taken away from them. By stripping Africans of citizenship in South Africa in this way, the white minority was magically transformed into a majority over the remaining non-whites—the Coloureds and Asians.

Many new laws governed all aspects of the black South Africans' lives, including who they could marry, where they could go to school, where they could live, and what kind of work they could do. Africans could not own land or rent an apartment in the white 87 percent of South Africa without permission. These laws made living very difficult for the majority who were listed as African, Coloured, or Asian.

It was a criminal offense even to criticize the government. Those who did were jailed as Communists or were put under a form of house arrest called banning, without even being given a trial. Newspapers and books were censored. The police and army were strengthened, and torture was common. White civilians were not only given guns, they were trained to use them.

In this explosive situation, African leaders continued to struggle for national unity and freedom, though their methods changed. The ANC had been using peaceful means since 1912. During World War II, a youth wing was founded by younger men who wanted more action, among them Nelson Mandela and Oliver Tambo. After the war, as the poisonous effects of apartheid spread, the ANC and other movements gradually added armed struggle and international pressure to their arsenal of weapons.

The Freedom Charter South African nationalists realized that they had to develop mass support and that they also had to agree on common goals in order to defeat the divide-and-rule tactics of apartheid. A large-scale passive resistance effort in 1952 increased ANC membership dramatically, though it failed to change any of the harsh laws. A few years later, a multiracial, multiethnic conference, set up by the ANC, met and adopted the Freedom Charter. This document stated that there could be only one unified South Africa under democratic, majority rule.

Sharpeville Now new and more militant organizations, such as the Pan-Africanist Congress (PAC), rose to challenge the moderate ANC. The turning point came in a town called Sharpeville. In 1960, hundreds of peaceful marchers gathered to protest harsh laws such as those that required non-whites to carry special papers at all times. Police opened fire, killing 69 and wounding 186.

News photographs showed the scene of the massacre, and the world was shocked. In South Africa, protests against the killing immediately broke out, and the government banned all African nationalists, forcing them underground. Members of the ANC, under Nelson Mandela, now formed an underground military wing called *Umkhonto we Sizwe*, "Spear of the Nation."

The government's answer was to bear down even harder. In 1964, Mandela was charged with treason and sent to prison for life.

SASO *and growing antiapartheid support* With nationalist organizations banned and their leaders jailed, it appeared that the government had won. But anger at apartheid injustice was not so easily silenced. In 1969, the South African Student Organization (SASO) was launched by black university students under the leadership of Steven Biko. SASO was designed to fight the divide-and-rule tactics in higher education, where Africans were assigned to schools on the basis of ethnic origin. Biko was arrested and later murdered in prison, but SASO became part of a wider black consciousness movement unifying all those South Africans classified by the government as non-white.

In 1976, police fired on a demonstration of schoolchildren in Soweto, killing or injuring hundreds. Resistance to apartheid again grew fierce. As the government cracked down in one area, a new grass-roots movement would spring up in a nearby church or in a community group.

World opinion turned against the violent actions of the South African government, resulting in protests, boycotts, and sanctions. Here, protestors at an antiapartheid rally in New York City show their support for black South Africans and their outrage against apartheid. Notice the diversity among the individuals and among the signs.

The antiapartheid movement now included people from all races, including those South African whites who were appalled by their government's policy. Interracial organizations, such as the South African Council of Churches, appealed to the rest of the world for support. First the OAU, then the United Nations, and finally many of the UN member nations joined in condemning apartheid. The South African government found itself more and more isolated, subject to sanctions and boycotts in everything from sports events to the purchase of oil and weapons.

Meanwhile, the political scene in the southern part of Africa was changing dramatically. In spite of South Africa's best efforts to keep white rule in its neighboring countries, independence came to them, one by one.

The end of apartheid By the early 1990's, the South African government, under the more moderate presidency of F.W. de Klerk, began moving toward majority rule. Nationalist organizations were unbanned and their leaders freed, among them Nelson Mandela, who was greeted as a hero in the capitals of the world. In 1994, South Africa held all-race elections. Mandela became South Africa's new president. You will read more in Chapter 6 about the challenges that South Africans face following Mandela's election.

Lesson Review 4

Define: apartheid
Identify: (a) Kwame Nkrumah, (b) Convention People's party, (c) Organization of African Unity, (d) Charles de Gaulle, (e) Sékou Touré, (f) Land and Freedom Party, (g) Front for National Liberation, (h) Ahmed Ben Bella, (i) Freedom Charter, (j) Sharpeville, (k) South African Student Organization, (l) Steven Biko, (m) Soweto
Answer:
1. Describe Kwame Nkrumah's efforts to win independence for the Gold Coast.
2. What message did Nkrumah deliver to all Africans?
3. How did French West African colonies gain their independence?
4. (a) Who led the resistance to settler control in Kenya? (b) How did the British respond to the white settlers' demands?
5. To what idea was the Organization of African Unity devoted?
6. Describe the liberation movements in Algeria, Guinea-Bissau, Angola, and Mozambique.
7. In what ways did black South Africans resist apartheid?

Critical Thinking
8. Some former colonies gained their independence peacefully, while in others much blood was shed. What factors created this difference?

65

Chapter 4 Review

Summary

1. Many events inspired African nationalism. Until the twentieth century, most people living in Africa related only to the bigger group that was their family or clan—not to a nation. Nationalism emerged in Africa as the people fought against the abuses of colonialism. Each colony had different policies regarding settler land use, which influenced the course of that colony's nationalism. Pan-Africanism also arose in the early twentieth century, as a response to the racist attitudes resulting from colonialism. African nationalism was spurred on by African participation in World War I, by certain League of Nations comments, and by the global depression of the 1930's.

2. Africans began to form nationalist goals. Western-style education, Christianity, and Muslim foundations all gave unity and voice to nationalistic feelings among Africans. Different areas of the continent experienced different results from their early pursuits of nationalism, however. In Egypt, problems arose between native Egyptians and Egyptians with a Turkish background. In West Africa, those under French control were more successful in nationalistic pursuits than others were. In East Africa, nationalism was an especially strong force, with Kenya setting the standard.

3. World War II deepened African resolve. As a result of the Atlantic Charter, many Africans felt the promise of freedom and so fought in World War II to help defeat the Axis Powers. After the war, Africans were caught up in the Cold War struggle between the United States and the Soviet Union, as both sides hoped to gain the support of African nationalist leaders. By 1950, Britain and France could no longer ignore the force of nationalism in Africa and began making compromises that led to the independence of the colonies. The promise of the Atlantic Charter and the Fifth Pan-African Congress inspired future African leaders to seek freedom.

4. Many roads led to independence. Colonies gained their independence in different ways. In Ghana, the transition was a peaceful one, with African officials and British colonial officials working together harmoniously. French West Africa gained independence through negotiation. In East Africa, however, the price of independence was often violent warfare. The Organization of African Unity was formed in 1963 to help all African nations gain their freedom. Nevertheless, certain areas such as Guinea-Bissau and South Africa had a long struggle ahead of them. In South Africa, the apartheid system—which lasted until the 1990's—was particularly disturbing.

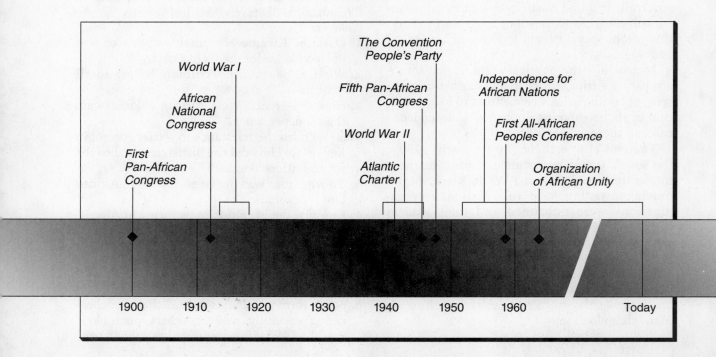

First Pan-African Congress

African National Congress

World War I

World War II

Atlantic Charter

Fifth Pan-African Congress

The Convention People's Party

First All-African Peoples Conference

Independence for African Nations

Organization of African Unity

1900   1910   1920   1930   1940   1950   1960   Today

Reviewing the Facts

1. Define the following terms:
   a. nationalism
   c. apartheid
   b. pan-Africanism
   d. protectorate
2. Explain the importance of each of the following names or terms.
   a. Jomo Kenyatta
   f. Saad Zaghlul
   b. Henry Thuku
   g. Blaise Daigne
   c. Marcus Garvey
   h. W.E.B. Du Bois
   d. Harlem Renaissance
   i. Kwame Nkrumah
   e. South African Student Organization
   j. Fifth Pan-African Congress
3. How did settler land-use policies affect the course of nationalism in Euopean colonies in Africa?
4. What themes did W.E.B. Du Bois express in his writings?
5. What contributions to pan-Africanism did the *négritude* movement make?
6. How did the League of Nations contribute to nationalism?
7. Name two ways that western education helped the African nationalism movement.
8. What set apart the Four Communes of West Africa from other African colonies?
9. Why was the Young Kikuyu Association formed?
10. Name two ways the formation of independent churches in Africa impacted nationalism.
11. What promise of freedom was included in the Atlantic Charter?
12. Describe the warfare in Kenya leading to that country's independence.
13. How did Algerian freedom fighters help their cause in non-warring ways?
14. What harsh restrictions were part of South African apartheid?
15. What happened at Sharpeville?

Basic Skills

1. **Making a time line** Choose one of these countries: Kenya, Ethiopia, or Ghana. Make a time line that shows the struggles in that country leading to independence. Include important dates and brief descriptions of what happened on those dates.
2. **Making an outline** Outline the content of Lesson 1. Your outline should show the main ideas along with key supporting details.
3. **Taking tests** Suppose you saw a True/False question that said "All European colonial rulers were prejudiced against Africans." What is there about the way this question is asked that can help you determine the answer?

Critical Thinking

1. **Drawing conclusions** You read in this chapter about different ways independence has been obtained in Africa. (a) How effective and costly has violent warfare been in moving the cause forward? (b) What would you say De Klerk of South Africa learned from the history of other African countries? Explain.
2. **Contrasting events** How were the feelings associated with the Harlem Renaissance in the United States different from those of African movements such as the Young Kikuyu Association?
3. **Making generalizations** List some facts from this chapter that support this statement: "The power of the media was very important in furthering nationalism in Africa."

Perspectives on Past and Present

Often Africans did not have the weapons necessary to fight their colonial rulers with any hope of success. Do some research to find out if, as a result of this perceived inadequacy, newly independent African nations placed emphasis on acquiring arms. Your librarian can help you find journal articles that reveal how much money the new African governments have typically spent on arms.

Investigating History

1. Read some of the writings of W.E.B. Du Bois. Look for statements that support the themes described on pages 52–54 of this chapter.
2. Learn more about the League of Nations. (a) What nations were part of the League? (b) How was the League the forerunner of the United Nations?

Chapter 5

Africa's Cultural Contributions

Kpeli *mask in use in Africa (left);* kpeli *mask as displayed in a museum (right)*

Key Terms

orisha
hadj
polyrhythm
patina

Read and Understand

1. African culture has a distinguished history.
2. Africans have influenced cultures of other lands.

If a person wandered through a museum and saw the African mask (above right), he or she might appreciate the beauty of its form, its design, and the skill of its craftsmanship. But this person might miss the meaning of the mask's design and the larger context of its use.

African masks were and are used as part of a performance. The performance can have any of a number of purposes. Some performances are religious while others are educational. Still others are organized to enrich the lives of the audience. Performances often include music, dance, and song.

The *kpeli* mask pictured here is often associated with female qualities. A small face mask of this type is often paired in performance with a fearsome "combat" male mask, a combination of dangerous animal forms that emphasizes the difference between male and female roles.

The *kpeli* is not meant to show a realistic woman's face. Instead, the facial features express specific Senufo values. In a convention common to many African carving traditions, the partially closed eyes express deep spiritual awareness. The tightly closed mouth reflects the importance the Senufo place on control of the mouth. The Senufo believe this is essential to self-control. They teach that carefully watching what goes into the mouth and the words that come out of it are important goals.

The parallel cuts on the face of the mask reflect the same markings that every Senufo has. Similar lines radiate from every woman's navel. These marks suggest the twins of the Senufo creation myth, linking each person to Katyeleeo, the Ancient Mother.

The outer markings of the mask are also significant. The style of the headdress stands for the men's association that ordered the mask to be made. The objects on the side of the mask represent the wings and legs of the hornbill, a bird that represents Senufo ideas of intelligence, beauty, and cooperation between male and female.

Viewing the mask in isolation in a gallery or museum is a bit like looking at African culture with a blindfold. Traditional African culture is music, dance, sculpture, song, and religion all tied together. The mask can be appreciated on its own, but it can only be understood as part of a larger whole.

This chapter will describe African cultural contributions from ancient times to the present. It will also highlight how African culture has influenced the arts and culture of lands outside of Africa.

African culture has a distinguished history. 1

From the southern to the northern part of the continent, Africans left traces of their richly creative talents. This section will describe the culture and art of the kingdoms and city-states that arose in Africa. It will also discuss the challenges facing archaeologists in their efforts to learn more about ancient African cultures.

African art began thousands of years ago.

The earliest examples of African art date back many thousands of years. In the southwestern part of the continent, there are naturalistic—or realistic, like the way things look in nature— drawings of African animals that were placed on rock surfaces 23,000 years ago.

Archaeologists were able to date these rock drawings accurately when they found fragments of the drawings while digging in the area around the drawings. Along with the rock fragments, archaeologists found charcoal. Because charcoal is burned wood, it was once part of a living tree. This means that it can be dated through radiocarbon tests.

In northern Africa, the Sahara has been called the world's greatest picture gallery. For 12,000 years or more, the inhabitants of this vast region have placed engravings and paintings on the surfaces of its rocks. As you may recall from Chapter 1, the Sahara was not always a desert. Between 11,000 B.C. and 3500 B.C., it had abundant rainfall. From the Nile River westward, the continent was green and fertile. For countless generations, people who lived there engraved on rock very large, lifelike images of many African animals. Sometimes the engravings included simple outlines of people as well.

One of the best-known sites of this Saharan rock art is the high, rocky Tassili plateau in southern Algeria. By about 7000 B.C., in what is known as the Archaic, or Roundhead, Period, the inhabitants of the Tassili were making paintings as well as engravings. These painted scenes suggest religious ceremonies, including masked performances.

As the climate slowly changed, so did Saharan rock art. In the Pastoral, or Cattle Herdsman, Period, which began between 5000 B.C. and 4000 B.C., pictures of ordinary human activities were added to the engravings. These paintings show detailed, realistic hunting and fishing scenes, village life, organized warfare, and people herding cattle, sheep, and goats.

By 1500 B.C. most of the Saharan population appears to have moved out of this vast region into areas where more water was available. The dry riverbeds, however, provided routes for travelers with pack animals. The long Saharan

Stone Age rock engraving of a bull at Tassili in the Sahara

trade routes were eventually taken over by camels. These sturdy animals are also portrayed on the desert rocks.

Ancient African kingdoms developed unique cultures.

Africans created brilliant civilizations in the Nile River valley and on the shores and islands of the Mediterranean Sea. While the cultures that developed there were strongly affected by contacts with Middle Eastern peoples, African cultures possessed unique and distinct characteristics. For example, African cultures emphasized the role played in life and death by the divine king. The office of the Queen Mother was also shown as important. Finally, African cultures made extensive use of masks during splendid religious festivals.

These three characteristics form a group of culture traits that has been long established in many African states. In the Kuba and Ashanti kingdoms, for example, the Queen Mother represented the royal lineage and assisted in choosing the new ruler. The same was true of the New Kingdom of Egypt. In the Kingdom of Benin, while royal descent was through the male line, the Queen Mother still had the important role of protecting the king, her son.

African art contains numerous images of kings, Queen Mothers, and religious activities. In addition, many masks have been found that were used by priests during religious activities. Although artists were capable of realistic art, it was customary in many African cultures to use the "official" style. In the Old Kingdom of Egypt, for example, this meant that men were portrayed with dark skin and women with light skin.

Queen Mother brass head, Kingdom of Benin, early sixteenth century

The cultures of Egypt and Kush influenced each other.

From about 2000 B.C. onward, there was continual diplomatic, cultural, commercial, and military contact between the rulers of Egypt and the leaders of Kush, a prosperous African state.(See Chapter 1.) From time to time, portions of northern Kush became part of Egypt, and the ancestors of several pharaohs and queens of the Middle and New Kingdoms of Egypt were linked to several prominent Kushite families.

About 750 B.C., the Kushite leaders Kashka and his successor, Piankhi, conquered Egypt and founded the Twenty-fifth Dynasty. The dynasty lasted approximately 100 years before it was forced to retreat to its original homeland by invading Assyrians.

From their capital at Napata, the Kushite rulers continued their prominence in the ancient world after their withdrawal from Egypt. Napata was a great religious center with important stone temples on a holy hill called Jebel Barkal. The largest of these temples was dedicated to Amon. Kushite kings and queens were buried in royal pyramids near Napata. Kushite pyramids are similar in plan to those of Egypt, but they are smaller and more sharply pointed. Precious objects, such as jewelry of gold with inset stones, and delicate images of gods and goddesses were placed in these tombs to accompany the dead. The ceiling of the tomb of King Tanwetamani, covered with golden stars, is particularly beautiful and well-preserved.

About 550 B.C., the capital of Kush was moved to Meroë, which offered many advantages. This area is watered by the annual flooding of the Nile and Atbara rivers, allowing agriculture to flourish. The city was also located near an east–west trade route that carried goods along the Atbara River. In addition, Meroë was a center for the smelting of iron. This new and important technology brought the Kushites prominence, military strength, and wealth.

After Alexander the Great conquered Egypt in 332 B.C., a Greek dynasty of pharaohs brought colonial governors and settlers from other Mediterranean civilizations to the Nile River valley. Because of their crossroads location, the Kushites prospered. They encouraged the arts of ceramics, sculpture, and stone architecture. Although the ruins of Meroë have been only partially excavated, archaeologists have found palaces, temples, engraved writings, glassware, tableware, bowls and lamps of bronze or silver, and fine jewelry. At least one Kushite king, Ergamenes (248–220 B.C.), was educated by Greek scholars. He joined the Greek pharaoh, Ptolemy IV, in building two temples on the border between Egypt and Kush.

Kushite pyramids of Meroë

In time, the Romans replaced the Greeks in Egypt. When the last Ptolemy, Cleopatra, committed suicide, the Emperor Caesar Augustus became the ruler of Egypt. A Roman writer tells us that this brought about a clash between Augustus and a kandake, or queen, of Kush. Kandake Amanirenas may have resented the sudden Roman presence so close to her kingdom. In 24 B.C., Kushite soldiers crossed the border into southern Egypt and brought down a bronze statue of Caesar Augustus in the center of a small town. They cut off its head and carried the head back to Napata.

The following year, Augustus sent an expedition into Kush to punish Amanirenas and to retrieve the head. The Romans reached Napata and sacked the city, which had been abandoned by the Kushites. The Romans were unable to find the bronze head, and they were unwilling to march deeper into hostile African territory. The Roman commander withdrew his troops, and Augustus negotiated a peace treaty with Kush. He never recovered the most important part of his statue.

During excavations in Kush in 1912, the missing bronze head of Caesar Augustus was finally found. It was hidden under the threshold of a door in a royal palace at Meroë.

The Kushites maintained their nation and culture for 1,000 years after they withdrew from Egypt. Kush was at its height between 250 B.C. and A.D. 100. It was during this time that the Kushites built their greatest stone monuments.

Although the Kushites used Egyptian hieroglyphics for centuries, they also invented their own phonetic writing system. This system was superior in many ways to the Egyptian system. The Kushites reduced the multitude of hieroglyphics used in Egypt to an alphabet of 23 signs. The Kushites also added vowel sounds, which were missing in hieroglyphic writing. Moreover, they included a sign marking the division between one word and the next. Unfortunately, although scholars have been working for more than 100 years to decipher this script, they have not yet been successful. The historical records of the Kushites remain a mystery.

Hieroglyphic   Cursive   Phonetic

Nok clay head circa 500 B.C.

The Nok culture produced magnificent sculpture.

Archaeological investigations in West Africa have yielded remarkable discoveries. Since 1943, hundreds of sculptural fragments of men, women, and animals have been found on the Jos Plateau in central Nigeria. These excavations indicate that about 500 B.C., Nok artists were making nearly life-sized figures out of terracotta, or baked clay. These large images apparently were made for religious purposes.

Most Nok works have been discovered by accident during the course of modern tin mining. Usually, only the head has survived the mining operations. A few of these heads are life-sized, while one is fourteen inches high. Since Nok artists used a convention in which the head is about one-fifth the height of the body, most of the larger figures were probably a little taller than four feet. This ratio of the head to the body has been called "African Proportion" because it is common in some, but not all, African art.

Clay sculptures of this size are unusual in art history. They would be extremely difficult to bake in an open fire. Instead, they were probably fired in large clay furnaces. The Nok used similar furnaces to smelt iron.

There is much variety in the Nok heads and in the elaborate hairstyles, headbands, hoods, hats, caps, beards, and mustaches portrayed by the artists. The eyes are represented as triangles or as segments of a circle, and the pupils of the eyes almost always have holes. The clothing of both men and women is neat and decorative. Like the Greeks, Egyptians, and Kushites of their time, Nok men wore short kilts. These kilts and the ankle-length skirts of Nok women are portrayed with carefully hemmed edges, and the figures are depicted with bracelets and anklets made of multiple strands of beads. They also wear layers of beaded necklaces in various lengths. It is believed that the Nok placed their sculptured figures on raised platforms or altars inside small shrine houses.

Little is known of the Nok except that they were an iron- and tin-working people. The Nok were among the first to smelt iron in Africa. Although most of the population lived in the cool highlands north of the Niger and Benue rivers, their culture may have spread over a wider area during the seven centuries that they were active in this region. Scholars do not yet know what happened to the Nok or which of the many modern peoples in Nigeria are their direct descendants.

Ancient Africans were skilled metalworkers.

The chance discovery of elaborate brass and copper objects in Igbo Ukwu, a small community in southeastern Nigeria, proves that during the ninth century, the Africans who lived there were extremely skilled in metalwork. In a 1959 excavation, archaeologists in Nigeria found fancy vases and ceremonial containers. They also found decorated staffs, ornaments, and pendants all cast in bronze. The makers had used the lost-wax method of bronze-casting in a style not found elsewhere.

While every bronze object from this site is unusual and skillfully cast, the pendants found at Igbo Ukwu are extraordinary. For example, there are four tiny elephant heads. Each is covered with bronze crickets and is trimmed with what looks like networks of beads. Two other

pendants show small human heads with parallel lines upon their faces and elaborate headdresses. Another type is of a bird with outstretched wings resting upon two enormous eggs decorated with flies. Beaded chains hang below the eggs. From the chains hang crescent-shaped bells.

The descendants of those who created the Igbo Ukwu treasure now make art that is quite different. However, until recently there continued to be an elite class of men and women who marked their foreheads with distinguishing lines, similar to the markings on some of the pendants.

Igbo Ukwu bronze pendant depicting human head with parallel lines on face, ninth century

The Yoruba produced sculptures that rival the world's finest masterpieces.

In addition to the Jos Plateau and Igbo Ukwu, there are other areas near the Niger River where works of ancient African art have been discovered. The ancient walled city of Ile Ife in Nigeria is particularly rich in archaeological sites. Ile Ife was a special to the Yoruba, who believed it was where the human world was created.

Archaeologists have found sculptures and other objects near the present palace of the Oni, or hereditary king of Ife. Objects have also been found in religious centers throughout the city and near sacred groves, shrines, and free-standing altars. Two ancient sculptures have been carefully stored for centuries in the Oni's palace. Others have been preserved by religious leaders for use during long-established rituals.

The Yoruba sculptures were made between about 1100 and 1300. They are naturalistic, but the artists also used classical ideas of beauty in showing the human figure. In making their sculptures, the Yoruba molded the figures and portrait heads in terracotta, a type of clay, and then fired them. The sculptures ranged in size from a few inches high to life-sized.

One excavation revealed a number of the terracotta sculptures in a shrine, with crowned figures accompanied by several uncrowned attendants. The sculptures in the shrine are thought to have honored the **orisha**, the officially recognized gods and goddesses of Yorubaland.

In addition to terracotta, the Yoruba used brass and copper to create their art. One remarkable group of brass figures shows a king and queen in royal dress. Another extraordinary work is "The Seated Figure from Tada," which is three-fourths life-sized and cast in pure copper. These figures were expertly cast by the lost-wax method.

"The Seated Figure from Tada," bronze, Yoruba, circa 1400

The original function of the brass objects is not clear. One possibility is that the heads and figures were created to celebrate early kings and queens. They probably were used in important ceremonies.

The Yoruba people still produce naturalistic art in present-day Nigeria, along with art that is stylized and conventional. Many master sculptors work in wood. One of the most well-known sculptors is Olowe of Ise.

The architecture of the north African coast has enriched the world.

Unlike Africa south of the Sahara, the north African coast was prone to continual invasions over the centuries. The Berbers are probably the best modern representatives of the original population.

In spite of centuries of foreign influence, the Berbers preserved aspects of their original culture. Long before the Arabs introduced Islam to this region, the Berbers built extensive forts and palaces of stone and sun-dried bricks. Their fortified apartment buildings, often placed on hilltops, were each inhabited by five or six families. These dwellings were attached to huge storage silos for grain and other food supplies. After the Arab conquest, influential early mosques were also constructed. These served as models for mosque styles throughout the Islamic world.

Trade stimulated the spread and development of arts and culture.

As you read in Chapter 1, rivers in Africa formed great highways carrying goods and people in and out of the African interior. The prosperous salt and gold trade stimulated trade in many other goods. African states on the southern Guinea coast exported beads of glass and semi-precious stones, ivory tusks, spices, and textiles. Africans in western Sudan did intricate work in dyed leather, which was prized in Europe. African leatherwork became known as Moroccan leather, because merchants in the coastal cities of Morocco imported it from the African interior.

The three great empires that you read about in Chapter 1 developed on the upper Niger as a result of this thriving trade. The first of these was Ghana which lasted from roughly A.D. 500 to 1240. Ghana's superior weapons technology enabled its rulers to maintain stability, wealth, and a flourishing culture for seven centuries. The growing power of the Muslims who settled in Ghana brought the empire to an end.

The second of the trading empires to reach great prominence was Mali. The capital of Mali was on the Niger River at Niani, and the official religion was Islam. As Islam became established in the region of the Niger bend, countless West African men and women used routes through Mali to make the *hadj*, or pilgrimage, to the Arabian city of Mecca.

The most celebrated *hadj* in Africa was made by Mansa Kankan Musa, the emperor of Mali who came to the throne in 1307. Mansa Musa was one of the richest rulers in the world. He dazzled all of Islam in 1324. In this year he travelled through Cairo with 100 camels, each loaded down with gold. He is said to have given away so much gold on this journey that he devalued the currency of Egypt.

Mansa Musa encouraged the intellectuals of Mali and arranged for el Saheli, the most famous architect of the day, to build the Sankore Mosque in Timbuktu. Sankore University, a center of learning and culture, grew out of this famous mosque and its circle of scholars.

The Arab traveler Ibn Battuta described the luxurious court of Mali in the 1350's: "The interpreter Dugha stands at the door of the audience chamber wearing splendid robes . . . he is girt with a sword whose sheath is of gold, on his feet are light boots and spurs. The soldiers, the district governors, the pages . . . , and the others are seated outside of the place of audience in the broad street which has trees along it. Each commander has his followers before him with their spears, bows, drums, and bugles made of elephants' tusks. The men at arms come with wonderful weaponry: quivers of silver and gold, swords covered with gold, their sheaths of the same, spears of silver and gold and wands of crystal. Four of the emirs stand behind [the king] . . . with ornaments of silver in their hands. . . ." Describing the women he said, "[O]n them are fine clothes and on their heads they have bands of silver and gold, with silver and gold apples as pendants."

Disputes among rulers weakened Mali during the fifteenth century, and various states began to declare their independence. In 1464, a strong leader named Sunni Ali of Songhai became dominant. He was followed in 1492 by Askia Muhammad. Under Askia, Songhai became one of the greatest civilizations in West African history. The contributions of jurists, scholars, philosophers, and other authors have been preserved in Songhai literature, which includes two histories of the empire written in Arabic, *Tarikh al-Fattash* and *Tarikh al-Sudan*. The decline of the trans-Sahara trade and a Moroccan invasion led to Songhai's fall in 1591.

Sankore Mosque in Timbuktu, circa 1300's

Archaeologists' work is crucial to the study of ancient African culture.

Much of Africa's ancient art has yet to be unearthed. For every ton of earth that has been excavated and studied in Egypt, less than a teaspoon has been excavated south of the Sahara.

While many ancient terracotta sculptures have been found in the ruins of Jenne Jeno, one of the principal cities of the Songhai empire, only a few have been found during controlled excavation. The rest have been stolen and smuggled out of Africa for sale to people who are willing to pay high prices for antiquities.

Archaeologists must work slowly and thoroughly in order to learn as much as possible about cultures of the past. Profiteers work quickly but destroy each archaeological site in order to steal its treasures. Once a site has been looted, the information that it could have provided through scientific excavation is lost forever. Only through controlled excavation can our knowledge and appreciation of ancient African history and culture grow.

Lesson Review 1

Define: (a) *orisha*, (b) *hadj*
Identify: (a) Tassili, (b) Napata, (c) Jos Plateau, (d) Igbo Ukwu, (e) Ile Ife, (f) Mansa Musa, (g) Askia Muhammad
Answer:
1. How is seeing an art object in use different from seeing it in a museum?
2. Why has the Sahara been called the world's greatest picture gallery?
3. What three characteristics are unique to Nile River African cultures?
4. Why was Meroë a good site for a capital city?
5. What is unusual about Nok sculptures?
6. How do we know that early African cultures had skilled metalworkers?
7. In what ways were Yoruba sculptures made?
8. How did trade affect the arts and culture? Give two or more examples.

Critical Thinking
9. What can African nations do to protect the ancient art that has yet to be excavated by archaeologists?

Africans have influenced cultures of other lands. 2

Cultural exchanges can occur in a number of ways. Members of one culture may visit a different culture and return home with artworks or other objects that are unique to the other culture. This kind of exchange occurs every time tourists visit a foreign country and return home with items that were made in the country they visited. In another kind of exchange, members of one culture may leave their homeland, willingly or unwillingly, and begin a new life in a different culture. In this situation, as time passes, elements of the newcomers' culture alter the dominant culture. This section will explain how African culture came to influence the arts and culture of Europe and the Americas.

African and European societies had similarities.

When Europeans first arrived on the southern coasts of Africa in the 1470's, they found a society very similar to their own. In both Africa and Europe, there were prosperous city-states with fortifications and palaces. Both Africa and Europe also included small rural hamlets where simple huts with thatched roofs sheltered people. As in Europe, African crafts guilds supplied the upper classes with furniture, weapons, cloth, leatherwork, metal implements, insignia, jewelry, sculpture, and finery worn in ceremonies. Professional musicians entertained the people in both parts of the world.

Europeans who visited Africa not only recognized these similarities, but they also admired the differences. A Dutch visitor to the capital of Benin described the city in the early 1600's in this way: "The town seems to be very great, when you enter into it you go into a great broad street which seems to be seven or eight times broader than the main street in Amsterdam . . . The houses in this town stand in good order, close next to each other, like houses in Holland. They are not higher than one storey, but are large with walls of red clay earth, so sleek and smooth that they shine like a mirror." Note how he tried to compare the city to his homeland.

Although the inhabitants of African coastal kingdoms did not read or write, neither did many of the Europeans who visited Africa. Moreover, in some cases, African non-literacy was apparently deliberate. The Benin people, for example, rejected the idea of literacy, preferring to train their memories and to develop skills in their children through intensely personal tutoring.

African art and culture were admired by Renaissance Europeans.

Some African kingdoms sent ambassadors to Europe early in the sixteenth century. Between 1491 and 1543, the Christian ruler of the Kongo Kingdom, which controlled the mouth of the Zaire River, sent a series of ambassadors to Rome. The king, or Manicongo, presented the Medici popes with gifts of embroidered textiles made from fine raffia fiber, a cloth much like linen in texture. Europeans considered these textiles to be "rare treasures."

The Manicongo also sent the popes some exceptionally fine ivory hunting horns carved with precise geometric patterns. Such intricate designs were already characteristic of the Kongo when the Portuguese first saw and described them in 1490. Seven of these magnificent African instruments are in museum collections today.

By 1500, professional artists' guilds in Africa were exporting carved ivories to Europe. Today more than 100 sophisticated ivory carvings from Sierra Leone can be found in museums. These art works were created by Bullom artists and include delicate ivory spoons with ornate handles, intricate containers for spices and salt, and elaborate hunting horns.

Benin bronze plaque showing a seated oba with two kneeling attendants. The two smaller figures near his head represent Portuguese soldiers. Nigeria, late seventeenth century

In the Kingdom of Benin, the hereditary *Igbesanmwan* carver's guild also exported spoons and spice containers. Benin artists often showed the Portuguese sea captains, missionaries, and traders who visited their kingdom. For the next 400 years, the descendants of these artists continued to use Portuguese figures on their ivory carvings.

The slave trade carried African influence to the Americas.

The slave trade enriched Europeans and Americans not only through the profits of African forced labor in the Americas, but also by the introduction of African culture into Euro-American life. Africans who were enslaved carried their religions, music, dance, literature, food, customs, and ideals across the Atlantic. In Brazil, Haiti, Jamaica, and Cuba, these cultural components found fertile soil. Religious concepts from the Fon, Yoruba, and Kongo people were fused with Catholicism. This fusion found expression in new religions such as Condomble in Brazil, Santoria in Cuba, and Voudon in Haiti. In the drumming of Jamaica or the rural Bahamas, African roots remain clearly visible.

In North America, however, attempts were made to wipe out African culture. Slave owners deliberately mixed the population groups and stifled cultural expression. This was done to prevent a sense of ethnic identity from fostering rebellion among the laborers. In spite of this effort, sparks of African culture survived that lent warmth and vigor to American life. The beloved stories of Brer Rabbit translate African animal fables. Brer Rabbit's roots are in the East African stories of Kalulu the Rabbit. In these tales, Kalulu's wit constantly gets him into trouble and then delivers him from doom. In music as well, the polyrhythmic responses of African American church congregations echo the call and response of certain African music. A **polyrhythm** is the combination of contrasting rhythms in a musical composition.

Like most American women of the nineteenth century, African American women spent long hours making quilts to keep their families warm. While many African American quilts share the patterns of traditional Euro-American

Three Portuguese men support a ship in this ivory saltcellar carved by Benin artists in the 1500's.

quilting, some use patterns that seem to have been made up as the quilts were worked. These quilts are works of art clearly based upon African designs, even though their creators had never been to Africa.

Africans influenced the music, dance, and art of Europe and the Americas.

African music is known for its liveliness, its polyrhythms, its "play it as it comes to you" nature, and its emotional depth. These qualities were at the root of new musical forms, such as jazz, blues, be-bop, soul, boogie-woogie, mambo, reggae, and salsa that developed outside of Africa. According to jazz scholar Samuel Charters, "[T]he structure of jazz drumming—the steady rhythm on the metal cymbal, strong rhythm in a heavy floor drum, shifting central rhythms on smaller drums, and accents on wooden or metal strikers—is an elaboration of the structure of the drum orchestra typical of the southern Guinea Coast of Africa."

Besides the multitextured rhythms of jazz, there are other elements of American music that have been inspired by Africa. A certain African way of using the voice so that it is heavy and seems to echo can sometimes be heard in the blues. Some of the techniques that are used in the blues, in addition to subtle rhythmic shifts and the use of call and response in group vocals, also have African roots.

Certain instruments also have African origins. Several types of drums and shakers are identical to those used by the drum orchestras of Africa's coastal forests. The Senegalese *bania* is a plucked string instrument that resembles the banjo. The modern xylophone originated as the Bantu *marimba* in central Africa.

Americans of African descent also contributed to a revolution in dance. In African dance, the relationship between the dancer and the musicians is fluid and intimate. The cultures of the Americas added elements from English, French, Spanish, and Portuguese traditions to this vital African interaction with musicians and dancers.

As for art, European and American painters and sculptors were revitalized by African sculpture. Artists such as Picasso, Matisse, and Derain realized the brilliance of African visual

The "Men's Weave" kente cloth (top) is from Ghana, Africa. The quilt, entitled "String," was made by the American quilter Rosie Lee Tompkins. Compare and contrast the African kente cloth with the American quilt. In what ways might the quilter have been influenced by African designs such as one found in this kente cloth?

explorations and used elements of African art in their work. However, some Europeans and Americans, in their ignorance of Africa and their belief in the superiority of their own culture, labeled African art as "primitive." Thus, they kept alive the European myth that Africans had no history, that they had not advanced past the Stone Age, and that the sense of mystery and power one gets from African sculpture stemmed from superstition rather than genius.

"Mti" (foreground) and "Secrets and Revelations" by Betye Saar, detail from Resurrection: Site Installations, 1977–1987

As the end of the colonial era approached in the mid-1900's, the richness of African visual arts, religion, philosophy, music, and theater became apparent. The beauty of African sculpture can be widely appreciated across cultures, even without knowledge of its context. The messages conveyed in this sculpture, however, are lost unless the cultural background is understood.

African art inspires American artists today.

In Africa, when a mask or figure has been carved by a sculptor and delivered to the person who arranged to have it made, it is not considered finished. Additional colors and textures may be added to the surface by a performer or by the purchaser. A religious specialist may also anoint the sculpture with sacrificial materials that will change its appearance. These additions, often repeated over many years, add a special **patina**, or surface texture, that enhances the work and is highly prized.

Betye Saar, an African American visual artist, has responded to this idea that a work of art can undergo continual alterations. Saar works with constructed altarpieces that are actually changed by the museum visitors who experience them.

Artists such as David Hammons have been influenced by African arts of accumulation, in which an object or structure gains power from the addition of materials. Hammons' lively structure, "Delta Spirit," takes on a multicultural familiarity through his use of discarded lumber, bottle caps, signs, timepieces, feathers, and other found objects.

One of the few American artists able to capture the sense of authority that classical African art communicates is Renee Stout. Stout has cast her own body in plaster, thereby turning herself into a figure of empowerment. Like a Kongo *Nkisi* sculpture, Stout's figure has a medicinal container in its abdomen. The container in a *Nkisi* is filled with substances and objects considered to be spiritually effective. The *Nkisi* itself is used to seal agreements and to resolve disputes.

In Stout's dramatic work, the empowering objects in the medicinal container include a stamp from Niger, dried flowers, and a photograph of a young African American girl. The slitted openings of the cowrie shells that represent the eyes of the figure suggest the spiritual concentration found on many female African face masks. The way the figure stands, the assembled materials hung on the torso, and the pelt of monkey hair that forms the headdress convey a brilliantly African sensibility.

New forms of art continue to come from Africa.

While European, Euro-American, and African American artists have been learning from Africa, African artists have also been learning from their past and from the outside world. There is strength and enormous variety in contemporary African art. Some artists are devising new forms for ancient ceremonies and masquerade festivals, often incorporating Euro-American influences. Others are using the techniques of folk art, advertising, photography, or tourist art to make serious social statements.

Airplane-shaped coffin by Kane Kwei

Since World War II, the natural-istic shrine sculptures of ancient Nigerian cultures have been showing up in modern forms on the southern Guinea Coast. These are life-sized tomb sculptures made of cement. They are placed in cement or cinder-block structures that are open-sided and roofed, like traditional shrines. Sunday Jack Akpan is an urban Ibibio artist who works in this art form. His painted figures are commissioned not only for shrines but also for Nigerian restaurants, homes, and businesses.

The late Kane Kwei of Accra, Ghana, produced his first fantasy coffin in the mid-1970's at the request of a dying relative. For the coffin, he fashioned a realistic boat out of painted wood and won immediate popularity for his work. Until his death in 1992, he maintained a large workshop that supplied representational coffins for local clients and European collectors. His designs have included coffins that looked like an airplane, a leopard, a cocoa pod, a hen, an elephant, and a luxury car.

In Mozambique, the tragedy of endless war over the past 30 years has given birth to a different kind of art. Voicing his horror with such paintings as "Where Are My Mother, My Brothers, My Sisters, and All the Others?" Malangatana Valente Ngwenya has become a spokesperson for his people.

Zairian urban painting has been affected by influences from tourist art, advertising, cartoon-ing, fine art, and political upheaval. Captions are written on the paintings to assist in communicating messages clearly. While the art is heavily oriented toward social issues, lighthearted works are also typical.

Cheri Samba is a well-known, popular painter in Kinshasha who also exhibits in Paris and New York. His work is sophisticated and amusing, usually with a moralizing theme. The verbal messages on his paintings include comments on tardiness, civic administration, mosquito abatement, sexual permissiveness, or AIDS.

In "Ta Tele," Congolese artist Trigo Piula makes fun of the control electronic communication has over the minds of the members of an audience. In his amusing characterization of a television as a modern *Nkisi* fetish, he addresses a concept of power that is quite different from the personal empowerment of Renee Stout's "Fetish #2." The charm of the painting masks a warning that this twentieth-century *Nkisi* is dangerous, spellbinding, and impossible to evade.

African musicians have also gained international recognition. Miriam Makeba, Sunny Ade, and Juluka are familiar to audiences everywhere, and the lovely liturgical composition *Missa Luba* has become classic religious music. Chinua Achebe and Wole Soyinka are highly acclaimed, contemporary writers who make use of the traditional modes and motifs of African storytelling. Soyinka has won the Nobel Prize for Literature. Truly, in all areas of the arts, original African cultural contributions continue to enrich the world today.

Lesson Review 2

Define: (a) polyrhythm, (b) patina
Identify: (a) Manicongo, (b) Brer Rabbit,
(c) Betye Saar, (d) Renee Stout, (e) Trigo Piula,
(f) Wole Soyinka
Answer:
1. How were European and African societies of the late 1400's similar?
2. What arts of Africa were admired by Europeans during the Renaissance?
3. Why were attempts made to wipe out African culture in North America?
4. How are African influences apparent in American music?
5. What kinds of art are African artists producing today?

Critical Thinking
6. Look at the examples and descriptions of contemporary African art in this chapter. Which one do you think is the most powerful? Why?

Chapter 5 Review

Summary

1. African culture has a distinguished history. The earliest known African art, the rock drawings of the southwestern part of the continent, are more than 20,000 years old. By 7000 B.C., drawings, engravings, and paintings were frequently done in the Tassili region. Although these scenes focused on religion and ceremony, by 4000 B.C. ordinary human activities were also featured. Cultures of the ancient Nile River African kingdoms featured three characteristics—the divine king's role in life and death, the Queen Mother, and the use of masks—that are often present in art from these kingdoms. The culture of the Kush Kingdom also reveals Egyptian influences. Some ancient western African masterpieces include the nearly life-sized Nok sculptures, which must have been fired in large clay furnaces, the intricate bronze objects from Igbo Ukwu, and the Yoruba sculptures produced in terracotta, brass, and copper. The impressive architecture of the Berbers is also considered masterful. In the interior of ancient Africa, the Niger River provided a trade corridor that allowed arts and culture to thrive through the 1500's. Archaeologists have uncovered many treasures from ancient Africa, but much work must still be done. The work is slow and careful and is often disrupted by profiteers.

2. Africans have influenced cultures of other lands. Many similarities existed between African and European societies of the late 1400's. These similarities were found in the structure of city-states, the hierarchy of classes, the look of rural and populous areas, the beliefs of people, and the level of literacy among citizens. Europeans appreciated the beauty of African textiles, artworks, and functional art pieces such as hunting horns, spoons, and spice containers. These items were valued as gifts and imported from Africa by the Europeans. The slave trade brought African influences to the Americas, even though slave owners often tried to suppress the cultural expression of enslaved people. American stories, music, textiles, and dance have been enriched by African traditions. Worldwide, the visual arts reflect African sensibilities. In Africa today, the exchange of culture with the outside world has resulted in renewed vitality and variety in the arts. African artists, musicians, and writers enrich the world with their unique contributions.

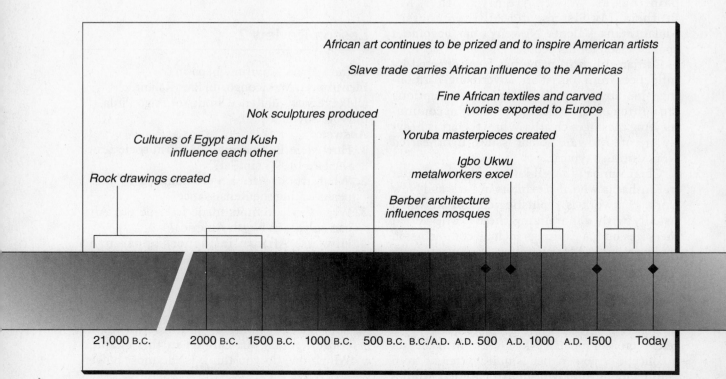

African art continues to be prized and to inspire American artists

Slave trade carries African influence to the Americas

Fine African textiles and carved ivories exported to Europe

Nok sculptures produced

Yoruba masterpieces created

Cultures of Egypt and Kush influence each other

Igbo Ukwu metalworkers excel

Rock drawings created

Berber architecture influences mosques

21,000 B.C.　　2000 B.C.　1500 B.C.　1000 B.C.　500 B.C. B.C./A.D. A.D. 500　A.D. 1000　A.D. 1500　Today

Reviewing the Facts

1. Define the following terms:
   a. *orisha*
   b. *hadj*
   c. polyrhythm
   d. *patina*
2. Explain the importance of each of the following names or terms:
   a. Tassili
   b. Jos Plateau
   c. Ile Ife
   d. Mansa Musa
   e. Manicongo
   f. Brer Rabbit
   g. Renee Stout
   h. Wole Soyinka
3. What are three prevalent characteristics of ancient African cultures?
4. Name three different materials used by ancient African sculptors, and give specific examples of each.
5. What impact did Askia Muhammad have on West African history?
6. Why is controlled excavation so important?
7. List three similarities found between European and African societies of the 1470's.
8. Describe African influences on American music.
9. Name two contemporary African artists. Describe each artist's work.

Basic Skills

1. **Using reference materials** Suppose you wanted to find out more about one of the contemporary artists, musicians, or writers mentioned in this chapter. What library resources would you use?
2. **Organizing information** Use note cards to organize the information presented in Lesson 1 about each African group's artistic contributions. Label each card with the group's name. Then fill in these details: time period, location, type of art, materials used, distinguishing features. Using cards gives you flexibility in organizing your thoughts; you can arrange the cards in time sequence, sort them by common features, and so on.
3. **Supporting the main idea** Give two details from the chapter to support this main idea: People cannot appreciate the magnificence of ancient African art unless they accurately place it in world history.
4. **Building vocabulary** What two parts make up the word *polyrhythm*? How is the meaning of this word made from the meanings of the parts?
5. **Taking tests** How might you organize your answer to the following essay question: How did trade affect African arts and culture?

Critical Thinking

1. **Analyzing** Why were Africa's major rivers so important to the continent's cultural development?
2. **Making generalizations** Why might sadness be an underlying theme in African-influenced musical forms such as blues and jazz?
3. **Applying a concept** How are the three characteristics of African cultures revealed in the *kpeli* mask pictured and described at the beginning of the chapter?
4. **Identifying cause and effect** (a) What are two consequences of profiteers taking treasures from archaeological sites? (b) How did Africans influence European art?

Perspectives on Past and Present

1. Although ancient civilizations were often very separate, parallel developments are common among the major cultures. Research to find out what was happening in the Americas during the rule of Mansa Musa. Look for similarities among art forms, styles of government, and available materials.
2. At the end of the chapter, some suggestions of modern influences on contemporary African art are given. Think of other contemporary issues and technological advances that might affect African art in the twenty-first century.

Investigating History

1. Find out how important the interpretation of various cultures' systems of writing have been to an understanding of those cultures. For example, how significant was the cracking of the code of Egyptian hieroglyphics? Then speculate on what new information might be learned about the Kushites in the event their script is deciphered.
2. This chapter has presented evidence that art, music, and literature can be revealing about what is happening in a culture. Several modern examples were presented, but none from turbulent South Africa. Find visual or written arts by a contemporary South African and see what the works reveal about life in South Africa.
3. African influence on American culture is not limited to the past. Research the Kwanzaa festival that is celebrated by many families in the United States. Include in your research the ways in which African culture has been incorporated into this American holiday.

Chapter **6** Issues in Africa Today

Uhuru Park in Nairobi, Kenya

Key Terms

refugee
Second Liberation
neo-colonialism
export-led development
structural adjustment
deforestation
Naam
sanctions

Read and Understand

1. African democracy struggles to take hold.
2. Leaders favor cash crops over food crops.
3. Africans organize to help themselves.
4. A new South Africa is born.

Uhuru Park is an oasis of open space in downtown Nairobi, the capital of Kenya. During the week, office workers find shade and a restful place to eat lunch here. But on the weekends, poor people flock to Uhuru Park to escape from the noisy and crowded slums where they live.

But maybe not for long. The government has just announced plans to build a 60-story skyscraper right in the middle of Uhuru Park. It will become the tallest building in Africa, and it will also feature an enormous statue of Kenya's president.

At first no one objects. It is not wise to criticize government decisions or express an opinion that goes against official policy. There is too much to lose, such as privileges or positions, perhaps even one's freedom.

Then someone dares to ask, "We can provide parks for rhinos and elephants; why can't we provide open spaces for the people?" The woman asking the question is Wangari Maathai, organizer of the Green Belt Movement, an internationally recognized project to plant trees in Kenya. She wants to know why the government wants to borrow $200 million to build a building when the government is already billions of dollars in debt and people are starving.

President Moi responds by calling her a "mad woman" and a "threat to the order and security of the country." But Wangari Maathai doesn't go away. She and her supporters file a lawsuit against the building plan and ask for permission to hold a public rally. The government denies her permission and a judge throws her lawsuit out of court. She is publicly shamed, and the Green Belt organization is forced to leave its downtown offices.

It doesn't matter to the ruling party that Wangari Maathai has been honored by the United Nations for organizing the Green Belt Movement or that she has won many international awards for her efforts to save the environment. She is considered a traitor.

Just when it seems that Wangari Maathai and her supporters have failed, the skyscraper plan is dropped. The fence around the building site comes down. It appears that the foreign investors have realized how unpopular their project will be, and they have changed their minds. They have withdrawn their funding. The fight to save Uhuru Park has been won! In a country where the government does not tolerate dissent, it is an amazing victory.

Like individuals in many parts of the world, Wangari Maathai recognizes the importance of our relationship to nature. By taking action to protect the environment, she has become part of an international effort to save the ecology of our planet. At the local level, Wangari Maathai is part of another movement. It is a movement of the people to take back their freedom and their traditions. Like Maathai's trees, it is taking seed and springing up all over the continent.

African democracy struggles to take hold. 1

Today, most of the world sees Africa as a continent in constant crisis—civil war, poverty, starvation, drought, overpopulation, AIDS. Dry, barren, windswept lands and starving children leap out from the TV screen. Newspaper headlines tell of brutal regimes, wars, and famines. These powerful and vivid images are part of Africa's story.

There is another side, however, that is rarely told. Not many hear about the African citizens, often at great risk, who challenge their governments to offer free elections or to honor basic human rights. Not many read about editors and reporters who risk going to jail each time they expose corruption at the highest levels. Few people hear about small farmers in Africa who achieve success despite a lack of tools, transportation to market, and government help.

What has happened to the African nations that won their independence some 30 years ago? In the 1960's, the world was confident that once freed from colonial rule, Africa would prosper. The continent was rich in mineral resources and raw materials. At the time of independence, world market prices were high for African exports such as cocoa, coffee, cotton, tea, copper, and palm oil. Ghana's Kwame Nkrumah and other African leaders called for rapid industrialization and sweeping changes. National plans called for many ambitious building projects, from new hospitals and schools to high-rise offices, hotels, and manufacturing plants.

Yet, the African dream of a better way of life that would follow independence has not been realized. Instead, African nations have endured two decades of ruined economies, civil wars, repression, and widespread disease and hunger.

Africa has suffered from political instability and economic decline.

Confronting all of the newly independent African nations were the problems of economic development, of creating stable government institutions, of encouraging national unity, and of establishing programs for health, education, and transportation. African leaders tackled these problems with different degrees of success. Yet, by the 1970's, almost all democratic regimes had failed, and civil war, violence, and political unrest had become increasingly frequent. In some countries, military takeovers brought tyrannical dictators to power, and along with them came death, destruction, and a ruptured economy. Uganda's Idi Amin, for example, is blamed for the deaths of hundreds of thousands of citizens during his eight-year reign.

Idi Amin

Economic crisis During the 1970's, more bad news hit Africa when prices for African exports took a sudden and unexpected drop. A drop in market prices is devasting to the African economy, since African nations depend on exports of minerals or agricultural products. Not only did African nations lose money on what they exported, but they had to pay much higher prices for the things they needed to buy from other countries.

The farmers had troubles, too. Good weather patterns had shifted and droughts repeatedly visited the African landscape. Despite billions of dollars in foreign aid, African economies were steadily declining by the end of the decade. The United Nations reported that Africa was deteriorating rapidly from political instability, repeated droughts, and a threatened environment.

Poverty and refugees By 1991, the standard of living of the average African was about the same as it was in the 1960's, when the colonial

period ended. Millions of Africans had died as a direct result of civil wars, or as a result of the hardships and famine brought on by the violence. In Ethiopia, for example, more than 1 million died in wars between ethnic groups.

The **refugees**—people left homeless because of famine, drought, and political instability— who swell the outer edges of African cities may be as many as 10 million. These refugees are barely surviving. Poverty is so pervasive that an estimated 12,000 children die each day for lack of food or medicine. In sub-Saharan Africa, for example, only 37 percent of the people have clean drinking water.

The statistics are grim, and it is clear that things may get worse before they get better. How did all of this happen? Although no one seems to agree on exactly what caused Africa's decline, many do agree that colonialism left Africa with more problems than solutions.

Colonialism did not prepare Africa for democracy.

African ethnic groups put their differences aside and fought together to win their indepedence. However, once the colonial governments were turned over, a new struggle for power began to take place.

Ethnic differences There have been many wars in Africa since independence, and almost all of these wars have been between different ethnic groups, not between nations. The root of the problem goes back to the Berlin Conference of 1885, when the European powers divided up the continent of Africa. The map they drew satisfied European interests, but not the interests of Africa's more than 800 different ethnic groups.

Groups with different customs were forced to live within the same boundaries, often with tragic results. In Rwanda in 1994, for example, tensions between Hutus and Tutsis exploded into genocide after the Hutu president was killed. Hundreds of thousands of Tutsis were massacred, and countless others fled the country. Later that year, after Tutsi forces gained control of the country, it was the Hutus who fled in terror. Rwanda's inability to build a stable government shows the difficulty African nations face in dealing with artificial boundaries.

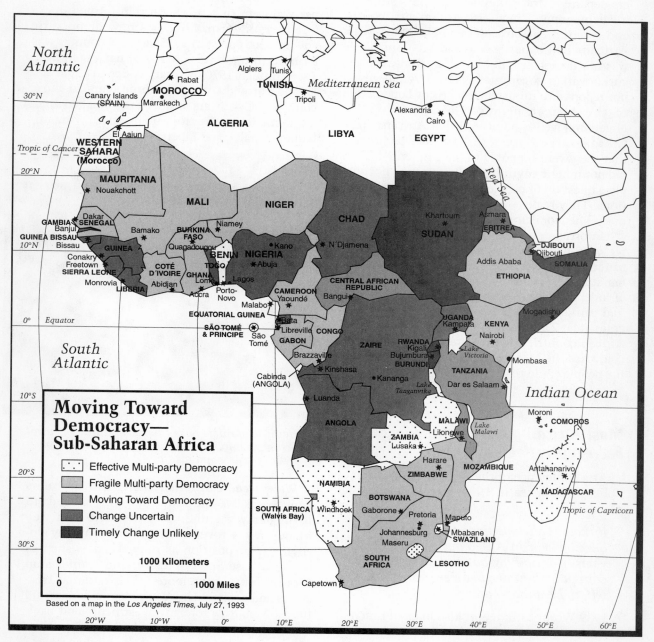

Moving Toward Democracy— Sub-Saharan Africa

- Effective Multi-party Democracy
- Fragile Multi-party Democracy
- Moving Toward Democracy
- Change Uncertain
- Timely Change Unlikely

0 — 1000 Kilometers
0 — 1000 Miles

Based on a map in the *Los Angeles Times*, July 27, 1993

Map Study

Sub-Saharan Africa is moving erratically toward democracy. As this map illustrates, several countries already have successful democracies while others have more fragile democratic governments. The map also illustrates the regions where there is a trend toward democracy. According to the map, in which countries is the movement toward democracy uncertain or unlikely?

No democratic model When the colonial powers departed Africa, they left behind a structure for democracy. They left parliaments, courts, and government bureaucracy. However, what Africans had experienced under colonial rule was not democracy, but rather a strong, central, authoritarian government. The colonial governor reported to ministers in Paris or London, not to the African people. Chinua Achebe, a Nigerian novelist, points out that Africans "really had no experience of this so-called democracy that they were supposed to have inherited. They did not inherit anything of the sort. It is not simply a question of people not living up to expectations. They really were not prepared. They were not trained for democracy."

Unfortunately, there were also very few people who had enough training to take over the functions of government. There were only a handful of university trained people at the time of independence. About a dozen people in Zaire had university degrees. With 100 university graduates, Zambia had more than most other African countries. Literacy rates were low in all countries; in Mozambique, only 10 percent of the people could read or write.

Most African governments have been repressive.

At a conference of the African Association of Political Sciences in 1991, one African leader noted:

If there is any one thing that has retarded development in Africa during the last 30 years, it is nothing but bad, irresponsible, corrupt and unimaginative government of left, right, military and civilian types.

A 1989 World Bank report also blamed much of Africa's poverty and debt on bad government.

Regardless of the political system they inherited or chose, most African leaders have preferred to rule with unlimited power. The majority of African nations are now ruled by single-party or military governments. There are countries with democratic governments, such as Namibia, Zambia, and Mali, but only Botswana has remained a democracy since its independence.

Ghana, under Kwame Nkrumah, and Kenya, under Jomo Kenyatta, started out with a multi-party system that was soon transformed into a one-party system. Nigeria's new democratic government ended in 1965, and the country was plunged into a bitter civil war that lasted from 1966 through 1970. Military coups in Chad and Uganda brought violent ethnic wars to those countries. Civil wars followed the breakdown of democratic institutions in Angola, Mozambique, Somalia, and Liberia.

Many African rulers have exercised military control. For example, Mobutu's military government took over the treasury and media.

Widespread corruption Many African rulers kept themselves in power by giving rewards to loyal party members, by installing trusted friends in key government positions, and by glorifying their position as ruler. Leaders such as Mobutu Sese Seko of Zaire, and Daniel arap Moi of Kenya have looted their national treasuries and pocketed huge amounts of foreign aid funds. Mobutu's foreign investments and bank accounts total an estimated $3 to $7 billion. Moi is often listed as one of the world's richest men. As some observers have pointed out, the wealth of some African leaders equals their country's national debt.

Corruption at all levels of government has contributed to the devastation of African economies. In 1964, Zambia, with its great copper reserves, showed high income levels. Despite this mineral wealth and large amounts of foreign aid, Zambia's rate of economic growth from 1965 to 1988 was minus 2.1 percent. While his citizens were getting poorer, Kenneth Kaunda continued to live in luxury at his presidential estate, complete with private zoo.

Military takeovers Typically in Africa, government mismanagement and corruption leads to unrest. Before too long, the military comes to the rescue. Soldiers erupt from their barracks and seize power. They vow to clean up corruption, to restore national morale, and to pursue policies that will encourage economic growth and political unity. African citizens, hoping that things will improve, often welcome the military regimes. However, once installed, military governments suspend democratic constitutions and eliminate all political parties completely.

Military coups have occurred in Nigeria, Ghana, Togo, Benin, Burkina Faso, Niger, Chad, Zaire, Uganda, Ethiopia, Somalia, the Sudan, Liberia, and Egypt. Since 1960, there have been 74 successful military coups in sub-Saharan Africa. Some countries have experienced six or more successful coups since gaining their independence.

Cold War policies During the early years of turmoil and political instability in Africa, the United States and the Soviet Union were engaged in Cold War policies. The two superpowers struggled for strategic positions in Africa and directly supported whichever country was crucial to their cause.

Dictators in Zaire, Liberia, Ethiopia, Uganda, and other African countries were able to remain in power partly because of military support and foreign aid from the United States, Europe, and the Soviet Union. Idi Amin of Uganda, Mobutu Sese Seko of Zaire, Samuel Doe of Liberia, and Siad Barre of Somalia, among others, used this military aid against their own citizens, causing frequent wars and famine.

No opposition parties During the years that followed independence, most African rulers refused to allow opposition parties. Claiming that opposition parties would undermine national unity and disrupt political stability, they consolidated their power into one official party.

While it is true that ethnic conflict has caused violent upheavals in African nations, many observers both inside and outside Africa believe that African rulers often have used this view

A bloody military coup occurred in Liberia in 1980 when soldiers, led by Samuel Doe, killed the then-president William Tolbert, Jr. Samuel Doe's years as president ended in 1990 with a coup that resulted in his death. Charles Taylor, whose soldiers are shown above, continued vying for power with Prince Yormie Johnson and interim-president Amos Sawyer. A civil war following the coup claimed millions of lives.

to hold on to power. Although African leaders have tended to promise that human rights and democratic principles would be observed in their one-party governments, the record shows something different.

In many modern African nations, dissenters have routinely been beaten, jailed, or forced to flee their country. As governments became obsessed with national security or self-preservation, the basic rights of their citizens were sacrificed.

Opposition leaders force multi-party elections in Kenya.

Once considered the most likely place for democracy to succeed, Kenya has had only two presidents since winning its independence in 1963. Jomo Kenyatta ruled from 1964 until his death in 1978. He was succeeded by his vice president, Daniel arap Moi.

Entrance to Nairobi Park in Kenya

Unlike most other African nations, this East African country enjoyed steady economic growth in the 1980's and generous amounts of foreign aid. (Kenya received a total of $1.1 billion in 1989.) A large part of Kenya's revenue also comes from tourism. More than 6,000 tourists visit Kenya's famous game parks and beaches each year. Kenyans have been recognized for good schools and the high value they place on education.

Despite its past achievements, the country began a downhill slide in the late 1980's. Corruption at all levels of government caused many investors to pull out of the country. Foreign donors cut assistance due to government corruption and mismanagement. Poor people in Kenya were eating less; almost 30 percent of the population was malnourished and the number was increasing. Less money was available for schools and health care. Slum dwellers, 60 percent of the people living in Nairobi, seemed to have been forgotten.

Critics not tolerated Under Moi's increasingly repressive government, democratic reform has moved slowly in Kenya. Many who have dared to criticize the government have been arrested and held without charges, sometimes for years at a time. In addition to intimidating opposition leaders, the government has repeatedly censored the press.

Alarmed at Moi's increasing violations of human rights, the World Bank suspended aid in 1991 for six months. It insisted on social and economic reforms before resuming aid. International pressure continued to build until, finally, President Moi agreed to elections in 1992.

The 1992 and 1997 elections During the months preceding the 1992 election, President Moi's government forces arrested opposition leaders, banned political gatherings, and disrupted prodemocracy rallies. Nevertheless, three candidates ran against Moi in Kenya's first multiparty election since independence in 1963. President Moi was declared the winner with 36 percent of the vote. Opposition leaders, accusing the ruling party of stuffing ballot boxes and other irregularities, contested the results, but without success.

Kenya's next election is scheduled for 1997. A new political party called Safina, led by the archaeologist Richard Leakey, has been formed to oppose President Moi. Safina leaders pledge to fight corruption, rebuild Kenya's crumbling

A voter in Kenya puts her ballot in a ballot box while another woman casts her ballot in a voting booth.

infrastructure, and provide more food to the people. Yet Moi's Kenya African National Union party remains the dominant force in Kenya.

Africans plan for a second chance at democracy.

Winds of change in Africa ushered in the decade of the 1990's. Activists, students, and farmers across the continent of Africa have become increasingly unhappy with their governments. Promises have not been kept, economies have declined, people have become poorer, and ethnic conflicts have grown worse.

Strong pro-democracy movements are blossoming all over Africa. Africans are calling the pro-democracy movement that is spreading across the continent their **Second Liberation.** Their first liberation was to free themselves from colonial rule. The Second Liberation is to free themselves from repressive rulers.

In just one year, from 1990 to 1991, Africans in 32 nations forced substantial democratic changes. Benin, for example, moved from a repressive government to a multi-party democracy. Namibia adopted a democratic constitution with a strong bill of rights after winning its independence in 1990. Riots in several cities forced Zambia's Kenneth Kaunda to allow multi-party elections in 1991. The results: President Kaunda was soundly defeated by Frederick Chiluba.

Dissenters in Sierra Leone, Central African Republic, Chad, and Cameroon have forced their governments to work toward accepting a multi-party system. Opposition parties helped the governments of Benin and Congo design new democratic constitutions. Military governments of more than 20 years were overthrown in Togo and Mali. Rebel forces in Ethiopia overthrew dictator Mengistu Haile Mariam and adopted a two-year plan for democracy.

Africa's newest nation The rebel victory in Ethiopia paved the way for an end to the fighting between Ethiopia and its annexed neighbor, Eritrea. After fighting a 30-year war of independence, Eritrea became independent in 1993. Its ruling party, the People's Front for Democracy and Justice (PFDJ), is the successor to the organization that won Eritrea's independence and governed Eritrea during the long war. Though elections have been promised, the PFDJ is likely to continue ruling Eritrea into the next century.

Africans are demanding that governments be more responsive to all the people, not just those in cities, or those related by ethnic ties to leaders. It may be too early to determine whether Africa's wave of democratization will succeed. Ethnic rivalries, low food production, drought, economic problems, and more troubles will continue to challenge these new governments. Additionally, leaders of the pro-democracy movement worry that Western democratic nations may have abandoned Africa at its most critical time of need.

With the Cold War over now, Africa has lost its strategic importance. Foreign aid has decreased, and interest in helping to solve Africa's many problems seems to have declined as well. Maina Kiai, an African political writer, urges Western governments to "get serious about democracy in Africa and prove our commitment to a new world order based on the rule of law and the protection of human rights." Most agree that one way foreign nations can support the democratization of Africa is by making democratic reforms a requirement for foreign aid.

Democracy's African face African writer Ali Mazuri believes that Africans must invent their own way, their own African democracy. He explains that "Africans are caught up between rebellion against the West and imitation of the West." Mazuri emphasizes that Africans are not rooted in their own traditions or experiences. He worries that they have learned from Americans and Europeans how to consume rather than how to produce.

Jerry J. Rawlings

Ghana's head of state, Jerry J. Rawlings, is Africa's most determined reformer and experimenter. His ambitious and very successful program saved Ghana from the brink of disaster. First, he attacked corruption at all levels and slashed prices for city workers. When drought threatened to destroy the farmers, his government expected urban dwellers to tighten their belts so farmers could get higher prices for their crops. He also shifted large quantities of consumer goods to the rural areas. The plan worked, and crop yields went up. His economic reforms have often been harsh and not always popular, but the government has been flexible and free of corruption. More importantly, Ghana's leader seems determined to do what will work, whether that be foreign advice or African creativity, or a combination of both.

Nigerian statesman Olusagen Obasanjo sums up this new spirit by asking Africans to be the architects of their future, "as we have been the architects of our misfortune by and large for the past quarter of a century."

Lesson Review 1

Define: (a) refugee, (b) Second Liberation
Identify: (a) Wangari Maathai, (b) Idi Amin, (c) Daniel arap Moi, (d) Mobutu Sese Seko, (e) Eritrea, (f) Jerry J. Rawlings
Answer:
1. What resources did Africa have in the 1960's?
2. What troubles befell Africa in the 1970's?
3. What problems did colonialism leave in Africa?
4. Explain or give an example of each of these problems in African governments (a) corruption, (b) military regimes, and (c) one-party systems.
5. Trace the major events in Kenyan government from 1964 to 1992.
6. Give two examples of the Second Liberation at work.

Critical Thinking
7. Ghana's Rawlings emphasizes "whatever works" to help African nations—whether assistance comes from within or outside of the country. Do you feel Africa needs more foreign aid or internal reform? Explain your position.

Refugees receive food rations in Belet Huen in Somalia following United States airlifts.

Leaders favor cash crops over food crops.

2

Listless children, their eyes appearing too large for the shrunken bodies that support them, their hair turned red from malnutrition, reach forward to get food. Famine has again hit sub-Saharan Africa. This time the place is Somalia, a country of 6 million people in the so-called Horn of Africa.

The dictatorial ruler of Somalia, Mahammad Siad Barre, was overthrown in January of 1991. Since then, outside relief agencies have delivered food to try to head off famine. By fall 1992, the Red Cross each day fed about 1.5 million hungry Somalians at 900 kitchens throughout the country. Other relief agencies helped at hospitals trying to revive those near death. But the task of saving Somalia's starving people ran into a shocking problem: Somalis themselves were hijacking relief trucks. They either used the food themselves or sold it across the borders to merchants in Kenya or Ethiopia.

In the absence of government or police, two warlords—General Mahammad Farrah Aidid and the self-proclaimed "president" Ali Mahdi Mahammad—struggled for control of the country. The small UN peacekeeping force could not stand up to them. Half the youth of the country seemed to have machine guns. Half the food aid pouring into the country never reached those who were starving.

In December 1992, President Bush sent United States troops to Somalia to restore order and protect relief efforts. These troops, and the UN forces that replaced them, helped Somalia deal with the immediate famine. But neither the United States nor the UN was able to unite Somalia's warring clans or lay the groundwork for long-term stability. In fact, Somalia's problems were compounded when Somaliland, in northwestern Somalia, declared independence. Somalia's lack of central authority seemed to promise continued misery, including future famines, for its people.

The problem of hunger does not stop with one country or one famine. In the civil wars that have raged for years in such countries as Mozambique, Sudan, and Sierra Leone, food supplies are always a target and famine a constant threat. As much as 70 percent of the population of sub-Saharan Africa lives on the edge of poverty.

Most discouraging is the fact that the problem of hunger has been growing steadily worse. Today, Africans struggle with the lowest average incomes in the world—from $59 to $115 per year. Only one of every four Africans has access to clean water. Food production since independence has declined by 20 percent. This means that in a continent whose main industry is agriculture, most countries have to import food to get by. Africa spends more than $18 billion yearly on food.

In short, even aside from extreme breakdowns like Somalia's, the countries of sub-Saharan Africa are not now producing the food their people need. If new shocks—drought or war—invade the countries now barely getting by, or if the population of Africa doubles in 20 years as the latest figures predict, it is hard to see how famine can be avoided.

The question almost asks itself. Africa is a massive continent, with enormous natural resources. Africans themselves now control those resources. Why do so many African nations have a problem feeding their people?

Resources were once sufficient.

Africa has vast grasslands, huge rainforests, an area equal to Europe, China, and the United States combined—all growing under a tropic sun. The continent would seem to be the ideal place for a "green revolution" of a kind that has tripled food production in India. Yet a closer look reveals that though parts of Kenya, Mozambique, and Uganda contain lush growing areas, two-thirds of Africa consists of arid or semi-arid grassland. Half the continent receives less than 16 inches of rainfall per year, and even that is irregular. Farmers may count on rains arriving, but rarely at the right time. Every decade or so, the rains don't come at all.

Traditional agriculture Africa's traditional cultures—the groups who occupied the continent for millenia before Europeans invaded—adapted to these conditions. Farmers learned to plant crops that matured at different rates, thus preparing for possible late rains. With this system, they might lose a yam crop, but the millet would survive. Equally important, without strict land ownership, farmers could move their fields often, letting the unused plots lie fallow for as many as 20 years. In this way, the soil renewed itself and families survived.

Equally adapted were the nomadic groups. By moving skillfully in anticipation of fresh grass, nomads could count on their camel and goat herds to provide them with milk, meat, and other products. So valuable were such herds that for people such as the Turkana of Kenya, a man could not be initiated into the group, or marry, without them.

The change to colonial economies For millions of Africans today, the traditional ways of using land have been made impossible. Europeans started this trend by taking the most fertile lands to grow the crops they valued. In Kenya, huge tea plantations displaced native farms. The farmers were forced to labor on the tea crop, and so had to neglect their own crops. To the colonial governments, Africa existed not for its people, but to provide England, France, or Portugal with cheap commodities—crops such as tea, cocoa, or coffee and minerals such as gold, copper, and platinum.

Semi-arid grassland

What attitudes about exporting food are expressed in this cartoon?

Although advances have taken place since the African nations gained their independence, post-colonial Africa has continued the trend away from traditional ways. Most western countries call this "development," and have used their money and influence to foster it. Increasingly, however, Africans themselves have called this **neo-colonialism**. They mean that development in Africa has continued to concentrate on exports at the expense of the African people. Such **export-led development** benefits mainly trading nations whose interests are served by an Africa that remains a source of cheap raw materials.

Therefore, since independence, virtually all African nations have kept their emphasis on exports. In some cases, these exports are minerals—copper in Zambia, uranium and cobalt in Zaire. In other cases, they are crops. The crops, such as cotton from Sudan or cocoa from Ghana, are known as cash crops because they are sold outside the country for much-needed cash. In nearly all cases, each new nation remains what it had been under colonialism—a one-product economy. The success or failure of that one product means life or death for its people. In other words, if the product fails so does the economy.

Nations need exports.

Why would Africa's new leaders allow their nations to develop in such narrow ways? The answer has to do with money. New nations need cash to buy manufactured goods they cannot yet make for themselves: radios, computers, chemical fertilizers, replacement parts for industrial machines, modern weapons. To get cash for these purchases, a country needs a sellable product. The main products Africa had to offer on world markets were its tried-and-true commodities: gold, platinum, copper, cocoa, coffee, tea, and cotton.

Aid for exports When foreign countries gave Africa aid, they earmarked much of it to develop commodities. When the World Bank lent money to African governments, it earmarked the money in the same way. A look at a recent report on agriculture in Africa demonstrates what happened. From the 1960's to the early 1980's, the production of food grains in 24 sub-Saharan countries dropped steadily each year. Yet the same countries produced a record cotton crop, even in the first year of a drought. Why? Because their governments gave more help to producers of cotton—a cash crop—than to grain farmers.

Another example concerns Botswana. Since the 1980's, the World Bank has financed a cattle project in the fragile Kalahari Desert and the Okavango Delta. Ten million dollars helped finance a beef-producing operation run in part by a wealthy landowner from South Africa. All the beef was exported, earning millions for the private owners. At the same time, Botswana was producing barely 5 percent of its own food, and importing the rest. The fragile desert area lost its native herds, and turned into a wasteland.

Not even famine changes the situation. From 1984 to 1986, while nearly 2 million of its people starved, the Ethiopian government continued to export green beans to England for cash. The government's need for weapons to carry on its civil war outweighed its need to feed its people. Fantu Cheru, an African scholar, puts it this way:

> In short, ordinary Africans [are] vulnerable to famine not because of the intensity and frequency of drought, but because of the rape and pillage of the peasantry and the environment in the name of export-led development.

Favoring the large and the urban
Aside from their interest in cash crops, most African leaders have made it clear that they favored the development of urban over rural areas. For one thing, most government jobs are located in cities. Government money flowed into the building of universities and grand government buildings and highways, all located in cities. To do all this development, and to staff government agencies, Africa's new leaders often employed far more people than necessary, beginning with members of their own ethnic groups. These were the people they could count on for support. Increasingly, these were the people they chose to keep happy with benefits, inflated salaries, and controls to keep food prices low. These were also the people who wanted imported goods such as Japanese cars and TV's, European clothes and foods, American films and recordings, and so on. If such people could be kept

happy, then the government leaders such as Mobutu Sese Seko of Zaire could stay in power and build enormous personal wealth.

When they did attempt to help rural areas, Africa's leaders often favored huge, Western-style projects. Foreign aid money helped to confirm this bias. In Ghana, for example, President Kwame Nkrumah sank enormous time and resources into the Akosombo Dam project. Aided by United States money, the dam was meant to provide hydroelectric power to factories such as the Volta Meat Canning plant and to supply water for irrigation and tourist facilities on the Volta River. As planned, the Valco Aluminum Works, owned by the American Kaiser Corporation, would use Ghana's bauxite to make aluminum. In return, it would get cheap electricity.

Akosombo Dam

But problems soon arose. Even in normal times, the Volta River delivered too little water to power all the turbines. When drought began, the dam sputtered, generating little power. Valco Aluminum refused to use Ghana's bauxite because it could import cheaper bauxite from Jamaica. The Volta Meat Canning plant faltered, too. Nearby herders refused to sell what planners thought was "surplus" cattle because their traditions made cattle too valuable to sell. Eventually the factory had to import beef from Argentina. Furthermore, the plant could not use the cans made from Valco aluminum. These cans lacked an important alloy, so different cans had to be imported from Germany. Far from helping Ghana to develop, the dam, according to African professor Ali Mazuri, became "a relatively empty technological monument."

A frozen fish factory in Kenya where people do not eat fish, a tomato paste factory in the Sudan where no tomatoes grow—such projects multiplied in independent Africa for many of the same reasons. First, foreign aid donors were impressed with high-tech projects and were eager to fund them. Second, African leaders could control such projects, staff them with friends, and get kickbacks for their own bank accounts. Third, such projects gave the impression that the country building them was becoming a modern, industrial state.

In the meantime, little or no funds went to traditional farmers. The funds that did reach rural areas tended to favor farms that would produce cash crops that outside nations wanted. Traditional farmers stayed too poor to buy fertilizer or equipment. Because their governments kept prices artificially low to please their urban supporters, the prices most farmers could get for their products hardly paid for their labor.

More and more farmers gave up their farms and moved to the cities. As a result, Africa's cities have grown into huge metropolises since independence. But along with populations in the cities, unemployment has grown. Too many city people depend either on government jobs or on the welfare supplied by the state.

Africa goes into debt.

Even had the world demand for Africa's cash crops stayed constant, the growth in its population would have strained Africa's ability to feed itself. But prices on world markets changed. Zambia, for example, had been one of Africa's success stories. The high price its copper commanded on world markets helped bring in piles of cash. The cash fueled a growth rate of 13 percent a year, and brought great prosperity.

Schools, hospitals, roads, health care, and education all thrived. When more of its farmers moved to its cities, Zambia simply used its copper money to import food. Four out of ten people in Zambia worked for the government.

Then in the mid-1970's, the price of copper collapsed. Zambia's leader, President Kenneth Kaunda, was encouraged by foreign banks to borrow what he needed. The debt to foreign governments, banks, and agencies reached $6 billion. The interest payments on this debt rapidly became too great for Zambia to pay. Soon, the World Bank and the International Monetary Fund halted further loans. Before Zambia could get more loans, it would have to agree to undergo **structural adjustment.**

Structural adjustment hit almost every African country in the 1980's. It means that a country must try to structure its economy on free-market principles. Generally this means the country must increase exports. It also means the country must cut its spending on government and on expensive social welfare services for its people. Zambia made these cuts. Its spending on education fell 62 percent in ten years. Spending on drugs for hospitals fell 75 percent in four years. The government had almost no money for roads, hospitals, schools, or transportation. Food prices could not be subsidized, so prices for such important staples as cornmeal rose 100 percent.

In Zambia the rise in cornmeal prices caused riots in 1986. President Kaunda called out the army, and 15 people were killed. Kaunda then gave in and lowered prices on cornmeal. This caused loan agencies to refuse Zambia any more money. The country had no choice but to let prices rise—and to use force as needed to control its population.

This scenario has been repeated in almost every African country. With the collapse of cash-crop prices, governments borrow. They then find that just paying the interest on their debt takes most of their export earnings. Sudan, for example, had borrowed $8 billion by 1983; it had to pay $1 billion in interest each year just to stay current. Little is left to buy manufactured goods or replacement parts. With money rushing out faster than it comes in, a country must take measures to stem the flow. Spending on health, education, roads, and so on must be cut.

Eventually, the people rebel as they did in Zambia. Spending on military equipment to control events or people increases. This leaves even less for social programs to relieve the people who get poorer. It leaves less for farmers, who abandon their farms. It leaves less for food imports that could help keep people from becoming malnourished. It makes more likely the riots to which desperate people often resort.

The result is increasing conflict between the different ethnic groups that make up African countries. This strife leads to civil war, and war in Africa is the chief cause of famine. War produces increasing numbers of refugees, people whose homes have been so ravaged by armies that they flee to another section or to another country entirely. Africa has more refugees than any other continent in the world. Without homes, or jobs, or a network of support, these are the people most at risk when famine strikes. This is the vicious cycle that leaves many people wondering if Africa can ever get out of its crisis.

Can Africans help themselves?

Many people in Africa are calling for cooperation among African nations on a continental scale. Rather than depending on the international commodities markets, African nations are seeking ways to trade their commodities among themselves. The result might be something like the European Common Market. The economic crises of the 1980's have made many African leaders realize how urgent this is. "I think right now there is a real sense of recognition on the continent that economic integration is not an option; it is the only option in town," says Salim Ahmed Salim, head of the Organization of African Unity.

Salim has another goal: to organize an African peacekeeping force that will be able to end the disputes and civil wars that have caused so much suffering. American intervention in Somalia, he says, has caused Africans to realize how important a peacekeeping force is because nothing else could have saved the situation.

A refugee camp at Kebre Beyah in Ethiopia in June 1991

Rwandan refugees streaming into Zaire. At times as many as 20,000 refugees crossed the border at this point alone. Their prospects were bleak at the severely overcrowded refugee camps.

Now, African nations must agree to support their own peacekeeping force. In the event of war or famine, this force could do what United States troops did in Somalia.

Many people agree with Salim. African specialist Alex de Waal, for example, points out that famines are often due to factors other than drought or overpopulation. "Famines," says De Waal, "are human rights disasters." He means that respect for human rights must be honored, even during war. Africa's civil wars have flagrantly violated these rights. In the Sudan in 1988 and in Ethiopia in 1984 through 1985, civil wars became anti-population wars. Crops were deliberately destroyed. Aid from outside countries was kept from reaching starving villages. Whole areas were cleared of their inhabitants, who were forced to resettle in refugee camps in unfamiliar territory.

In Africa, war has been a major cause of virtually every recent famine. If African nations can cooperate to control wars and market their products, they can advance their continent a long way toward solving its problem of feeding itself.

Lesson Review 2

Define: (a) neo-colonialism, (b) export-led development, (c) structural adjustment
Identify: (a) Somalia, (b) Botswana, (c) Akosombo Dam Project (a) Kenneth Kaunda, (e) Salim Ahmed Salim
Answer:
1. Why did U.S. forces go to Somalia in 1992?
2. Which crops are valued in Africa and why?
3. Why have urban areas in Africa often been recipients of the most foreign funds for development?
4. How can war be viewed as a cause of famine?
5. Describe Salim's solution to Africa's economic crisis.

Critical Thinking
6. African nations need sources of money other than cash crops so that farming lands can grow food for Africans. Suggest some other products Africans could produce and sell, and explain how countries such as the United States could assist in this development.

99

Africans organize to help themselves. 3

Like people in every corner of the planet, Africans suffer from the destruction of their environment and the loss of natural resources. **Deforestation**, or loss of forests, is most likely the ecologist's gravest concern. As trees are cut down, many events follow: soil becomes eroded, plants and wildlife vanish, watersheds are ruined, crops fail, people go hungry.

Forests in Africa are dwindling rapidly. In West Africa, more than half of the coastal forests have been destroyed since 1950. For every tree that is planted in Africa, ten are cut down. As the land becomes more barren and dry, it is taken by the expanding deserts. Kenya, for example, continues to lose land to the Sahara as the desert moves in from the northwestern corner.

For the people who live off the land, a loss of trees means a scarcity of firewood, and firewood is their main source of energy. As population increases, there is more demand for fuel, so more trees are cut, more soil is depleted, less food is produced, more people go hungry, and the cycle continues.

The primary victims of the degradation of the African landscape are the people who live in the rural areas, or 70 percent of all Africans. They are the backbone of the African economy, yet they have been ignored by most African governments. Many have left the land for the crowded cities. Many who remain are barely surviving. Today, nongovernmental organizations and grass-roots groups are leading the efforts to help African farmers not only to survive, but also to grow prosperous.

Deforestation begins a chain of events resulting in total destruction of the environment of an affected region. Wangari Maathai (inset, left) has been instrumental in establishing tree nurseries.

Wangari Maathai starts the Green Belt Movement in Africa.

Wangari Maathai grew up in the town of Nyeri, a very green and beautiful part of Kenya near the Great Rift Valley. Where she lived there were many trees, but her favorite was a giant wild fig that grew by a spring. The tree was so magnificent that her mother would not allow anyone to cut even a small branch.

In 1960, Maathai received a scholarship to study at a university in the United States. Six years later, when she returned, the fig tree was gone and the spring had dried up. In its place was a tea plantation. People were growing tea for money instead of planting food for themselves. Now that the trees were gone, there was very little firewood. Without the firewood to cook with, women couldn't cook their traditional diets of vegetables and roots. With their money from selling tea, they bought less nourishing foods, and even these foods were not always available. In the fertile valley Maathai remembered, there now was poverty and hunger.

The Green Belt Movement Wangari Maathai went on to become the first woman in Kenya to receive a doctorate. As she became more aware of the connection between poverty and a damaged environment, she was determined to do something positive. She began by planting trees. From this small beginning, the Green Belt Movement grew. Maathai urged farmers to plant "green belts" of trees. She talked to children in the schools, involving them in planting trees as windbreaks and then caring for them until graduation from school.

Soon some mothers got involved, and Maathai helped them establish tree nurseries. The women grew the seedlings and then distributed them to local farmers. For each tree that was still alive at the end of three months, the women received 50 Kenya cents (about 4 United States cents) from the Green Belt organization. For many poor women who were barely growing enough to eat, this small amount was their only income.

10 million trees All over Kenya, but mostly in the rural areas, groups of women planted fruit trees or the fast-growing native trees that had begun to disappear after the arrival of the Europeans. Within three or four years, the acacias,

Women tree planters celebrate World Environment Day.

thorn trees, crotons, cedars, and baobabs had branches big enough to cut for firewood. By 1990, 50,000 women of the Green Belt Movement had planted 10 million trees. What's more, many other African nations began Green Belt movements of their own.

What started out as an environmental movement had turned into much more. The Green Belt Movement had provided more than firewood and fruit and income. It offered hope to thousands of women who succeeded in doing one small thing to change their lives. Many of the women changed, too. They felt better about themselves. By succeeding, by having made a difference, the women of the Green Belt Movement had become empowered.

International support With so many women working part-time in the nurseries, Maathai had to seek funding. First, she convinced the Kenya branch of Mobil Oil to fund her growing organization. Later, Scandanavian groups, the Windstar Foundation in the United States, and other international donors contributed to Green Belt.

101

The majority of farmers throughout Africa are women, who work long and hard to achieve success.

In 1988, the United Nations presented Maathai with their Environmental Program Global 500 award. She has received many other international awards as well, including the prestigious Goldman Environmental Prize, called the "Nobel Prize for environmentalists." This prize is awarded to individuals who have the vision to take action at the grass-roots level to protect the environment.

Dishonored at home Although Maathai has been internationally honored, the government of her own country considers her activities destructive. Maathai's battles to save the environment have brought her into conflict with a government that does not allow dissent. And any organized group is a threat to a government determined to stay in power.

The ruling party of Kenya has attacked her for going against African tradition. It has said that women should submit to men and not question their authority or decisions. According to the party, Maathai, a former professor at the University of Nairobi, is no exception.

The Kenyan government has arrested Maathai more than a dozen times for protesting government policy. Largely through the intervention of her many international friends, Maathai so far has avoided long prison sentences. However, she continues to put her life at risk by speaking out for human rights and by trying to empower Kenyan women.

Women farmers organize to help themselves.

African women living in the rural areas are what a World Bank report calls "the most neglected" of all African people. Women grow 70 percent of the food in Africa, but they do not own land. Women farmers generally work 10 to 15 hours each day. They may rise as early as 3:00 A.M. to grind flour, and end the day walking for miles in search of firewood and water. Often without transportation to markets, women must carry their produce on their heads for long distances several days a week.

In traditional African society, women did not have equality with men. However, under the cash crop economy installed by colonial rulers, women lost even more control over their lives. Colonial administrators refused to acknowledge that African women did most of the farming; they conducted all farming business with the men. Most African governments, farming advisers, lenders, and aid adminstrators continued to ignore women farmers and dealt exclusively with the men. This attitude is slowly beginning to change. African governments and foreign aid donors are recognizing that, given the opportunity, African women are a powerful source for change. African leader General Olesegun Obasanjo of Nigeria believes that African women have not been given enough recognition, "not just as farmers, but in all aspects of society." He urges Africans to "fight and struggle to get more education for women and get them into the mainstream of national life."

Jennifer Whitaker, a specialist on land development in Africa, observed one group of women rice farmers in Gambia who decided to change the way things were done. Most of the rice farmers along the Gambia River are women. Using primitive tools, they have worked hard to make this swampy land suitable for cultivating rice.

However, they received only 16 percent of the government credits to improve the land even though they were doing most of the work. The rest were given to the men in the community. With each new program to improve productivity, the men won more control of the land and its crops.

Finally, the women rebelled when a new United Nations project to improve the land was about to be launched. This time they wanted equal opportunity and held firmly to their position, even though the men resisted any attempts to change the old system. Many meetings and discussions followed, and eventually the women's complaints were heard. The land was drained and irrigated, and this time, both groups received the same credit to buy seeds, fertilizers, and machines.

Africans rely on their own expertise.

Burkina Faso is a tiny country in the Sahel region of western Africa. Formerly called Upper Volta, Burkina is subject to long droughts that have made it one of the poorest places in Africa. A study recently released notes that one third of the children die before the age of four. Adults rarely live beyond the age of fifty.

In 1980, Andre Eugene Ilboudo, a university student from Burkina Faso, began talking to workers in his village about how they might improve their lives. The meetings eventually evolved into a grass-roots organization of 1,000 members in 42 villages called *Vive le Paysan* (Long live the peasant). Its purpose, according to Ilboudo, was to make peasants aware and confident of their own strengths.

Vive le Paysan soon attracted attention and received grants from aid organizations around the world. With this help, the group has built reservoirs, nurseries for fruit trees, community centers to train medical workers, and resource centers so farmers can trade new techniques with their neighbors. It has provided women with credit to start their own cooperative restaurants and a soap factory. It has started schools and health centers.

Naam groups grow Grass-roots organizations, now known as **Naam**, have continued to spread throughout Burkina Faso into neighboring Senegal and beyond. Made up of farmers, these groups all have one purpose: to take control of their own development. They do not wish to be seen as victims. They do not wish to be told by outside relief agencies, banks, or governments how to run their affairs. They insist on being partners in their own development.

Naam groups have worked out soil conservation strategies. They have developed methods for using organic fertilizers. They have increased their use of different vegetables, which paid off when the millet crop failed in the drought year of 1984. The 54 Naam groups around Ouahiguoya produced 300 tons of vegetables, saving many lives. In some cases, Naam groups have gone back to traditional methods; in some cases, they have used modern methods. In every case, they use their long experience to develop strategies suited to the lands they know so well. Most participants, like Mamadou Cissokho, are confident that they can end hunger in their time:

If rainfall is adequate, we can end hunger in the coming ten years, not only in our village, but in all the regions of Senegal that work with us. You see, we share the same philosophy: 50 percent of the harvest of communal fields is automatically stored (as buffer stocks), and past food aid is also added to food reserves....

Such grass-roots movements are spreading in Africa, especially rural Africa. Although most of the groups are led by men, the members are usually women and they do most of the work. They dig wells, create communal farms, practice conservation, and improve food production. Some women's co-ops pool their income for things their communities need, such as medical supplies or tools.

103

After years of depending on imported solutions, Africans are now determined to try their own. Many African experts feel that this is the only movement that can make a difference in Africa. Already, they say, people are producing in ways the governments cannot measure. Farmers are dropping out of the formal economy and marketing crops on their own.

The traditional caravan routes, routes that existed long before modern borders chopped up Africa into states, have been revived to take food across borders. One scholar, Fantu Cheru, calls this "the silent revolution."

Alimata Doumbia of Mali Not all women farmers are relying on co-ops and self-help projects to improve their lives. Take Alimata Doumbia from the African nation of Mali in northwestern Africa. She lives in Kourouba, a village on a dusty plain near the Niger River.

Against the advice of the other villagers, Doumbia decided to plant her own banana and mango orchard. Because she does not grow cotton or tobacco, she was denied credit from the rural aid organization in her region. With the money she saved from harvesting her other crops, Doumbia bought fertilizers and fruit plants. She has no water pump, and must water each of the trees by hand during the dry season.

While she waits for her new fruit trees to mature, she continues to tend her traditional crops of maize, beans, millet, and squash. Doumbia is confident that her risky venture will succeed. She is already considered the most enterprising and resourceful person in her village. And unlike the other women in the village, she makes more money than her husband. The other

Despite having to water her orchard by hand, Alimata Doumbia has increased her income and improved her life-style by planting non-traditional crops.

women are watching her progress carefully. If her plan works, they will try growing bananas and mangoes, too.

Africans battle the AIDS crisis.

In 1993, the World Health Organization estimated that more than 8 million Africans were infected with the AIDS virus. This number accounts for more than 60 percent of the total number of AIDS cases worldwide. By the year 2000, some 25 million Africans could be infected.

Why the disease has spread so quickly in Africa is unclear. What is clear is the growing threat that AIDS poses to Africa's population. In the country of Uganda for example, more than 1 million people, out of a total population of 16 million, have tested HIV positive. Unlike many of its neighbors, the government of Uganda has recognized the severity of the epidemic and asked for help in establishing testing and counseling services. This has not always been the case.

Despite the dimensions of the crisis, African nations were initially slow in taking action against the disease. Like many nations worldwide, Africans for a time tried to ignore the epidemic. In the 1980's when news of the disease was just becoming public, there was a widespread belief that AIDS had originated in Africa. Whether AIDS did originate in Africa is uncertain, but this perception put many African leaders on the defensive and caused them to downplay the crisis. Even the international medical community was slow to involve African doctors and researchers in developing ways to halt the spread of AIDS. African doctors and researchers

Publicity campaigns provide the public with factual information about AIDS.

were often left out of important conferences, even when the subject was AIDS on the African continent.

At the same time, Africans in foreign countries were being subjected to discriminatory AIDS testing. In the country of Belgium for example, African students were required to be tested for AIDS, and positive results meant expulsion from school. On the other hand, Belgian students who traveled back and forth frequently from the former Belgian colony of Zaire were not required to take an AIDS test.

Assessing the AIDS crisis in Africa or making accurate projections for the future is difficult. Many African nations refuse to gather data on AIDS or make information available. For the time being, Africa's best hope for halting the spread of the disease is education. In several countries publicity campaigns use vivid posters, radio announcements, and information pamphlets to distribute information widely. Some AIDS activists hope that Africa will take the lead in the fight against a serious international health problem.

Lesson Review 3

Define: (a) deforestation, (b) Naam
Identify: (a) Green Belt Movement,
(b) Burkina Faso, (c) Alimata Doumbia
Answer:
1. How has Wangari Maathai helped African women?
2. Why has Maathai had troubles in her home country of Kenya?
3. (a) What changes for women does Obasanjo of Nigeria encourage? (b) Give two examples of such progress.
4. What changes did Ilboudo of Burkina Faso originate in his country?
5. Describe "the silent revolution," as named by Fantu Cheru.
6. What is the impact of AIDS on Africa?

Critical Thinking
7. Compare the undertaking of Mali's Doumbia with the early efforts of Maathai. How are they similar? Predict some possible outcomes of Doumbia's work if she proves successful.

A *new South Africa is born.* 4

There will really be no peace as long as apartheid exists because apartheid divides people into races. If you are black, you do not qualify for higher wages. You do not qualify for a decent house. You do not qualify to own the land. You do not qualify to own property. As long as apartheid continues, the government will have to continue to use force to contain those who are oppressed, because we cannot keep quiet. We cannot die there in the quiet when we are starving without jobs, we are starving in the homelands. We cannot keep quiet. We must speak out. When one puts his foot on a red hot iron, he is not expected [not] to say, I am feeling the pain. We will say so. We are feeling the pain. We cannot keep quiet.

In 1985, Popo Molefe spoke these words in a courtroom in South Africa. Along with 22 other black South Africans, he was on trial for treason. He and his co-defendants were leaders of an organization called the United Democratic Front (UDF). Formed in 1983, the UDF had worked to coordinate all black South African groups in their protests against the South African government's newest apartheid policies. In response, the government grew increasingly brutal. When the protests continued, the government arrested all the UDF leaders for treason. The government said they were the cause of the violence and terrorism ripping South Africa apart.

Molefe and co-leader Patrick Lekota challenged the government's accusations. In their view, it was the national government and its apartheid policy that had deprived black South Africans of their rights. In their view, it was the government that was using terrorism against its own people:

Here we are in Cape Town. . . . In winter, when these people did not have houses, police would come in there, in the middle of winter, and smash down these shacks, plastic shacks that they had. . . . In the eyes of the people watching these things, it was terrorising them. . . . Women sit there in the open with little kids in their arms, they do not know what they are going to do when night comes—people say, This is terrorism. . . .

Not everyone agreed about terrorism, but it was clear that South Africa was suffering through the worst period of violence it had ever seen. Just in the months between September of 1984 and March of 1985, 217 people were killed, 700 more were injured, and 10,000 were arrested. On March 21, 1985, police fired on an unarmed crowd of marchers, killing 20 and wounding 37. The violence continued until the end of the trial in November 1988.

South Africans in the township of Soweto take cover as police fire at protesters.

Children in a desperately poor township

Apartheid tries to reform itself.

The events that led to such widespread strife might have seemed puzzling to an outsider. The Nationalist government, led by P.W. Botha, appeared in the 1980's to be implementing reforms that would lead to more democracy. It had drawn up a new constitution that called for three chambers of the formerly all-white Parliament: a House of Assembly for whites, a House of Representatives for "coloureds" to be elected by "coloureds," and a House of Delegates for Indians elected by Indians. For the first time, the Nationalist government was including non-white South Africans in the political process.

The government also passed a series of bills known as the Koornhof Bills, named after the Minister of Cooperation and Development. The bills provided for the election of black councils that would run the "affairs" of the black townships around major cities.

The government claimed its new laws constituted serious reforms. White South Africans seemed to agree, and in November 1983 approved of the new constitution by a two-thirds majority. To black South Africans like Popo Molefe, however, the constitution was "a clever way of denying the black people, the African people, the right to participate in the government of the country at a time when the 'coloured' and Indian people were offered a vote in the tricameral system. Our reaction was one of anger."

In other words, the constitution took another step in freezing 75 percent of South Africans—the blacks—out of power and out of the country. To the black majority, this had been going on since white Europeans had settled South Africa in the 1600's. But its pace had dramatically increased in 1948 when the National party, the party of the white Afrikaners who had originally emigrated from Holland, came to power. At that time, the separation of the races, or apartheid, was formalized by law.

Black South Africans were assigned homelands. This meant that 75 percent of South Africans could legally live only in poor areas that made up 13 percent of the land. To work in "white" South Africa, they had to get government permission. They had to show passes proving they were temporary workers only. They could not vote or own land or homes. They could live only in the townships that sprawled for miles outside cities such as Johannesburg. Often constructed of cheap metal or plastic, the homes in these townships lacked the most basic necessities, such as heat, electricity, or running water. Streets had no names.

By giving power in 1983, however limited, to "coloureds" (people of mixed white and black parentage) and Indians, the new constitution dramatized black powerlessness even more. As for the Koornhof Bills, they tended in the same direction. Now the townships had to raise all their own funds. The new councillors had one major way to do this: raise rents. Poor people in the townships would be made even poorer. The councillors did not help the situation by helping themselves to businesses in the townships and building themselves new houses. Most township residents regarded them as collaborators with the oppressive government.

The resistance To challenge these changes, the newly formed United Democratic Front announced a campaign of resistance. Composed of more than 1,000 church, professional, sports, workers', students', and women's organizations, it held meetings to urge people to boycott the August elections. The result was that only 18 percent of eligible "coloureds" and 12 percent of eligible Indians voted. UDF also organized marches, meetings, and rallies to protest the new rent increases. Many people boycotted the election of councillors. The new councillors became objects of scorn.

In one township outside Johannesburg, church leaders organized work and business boycotts to protest the new council. A nervous government called out police and set up barricades nearby. The night of September 2, police fired a shot and killed Reuben Twala, the popular captain of a local soccer team. Rioting began, and built to a mob that attacked the homes of several councillors, killing three of them. The rest fled. Then, as protest marchers moved toward the council offices, police met them, and opened fire with shotguns and tear gas. This sparked two days of street battles in which 30 people were shot and killed. Riots flared across the country, engulfing townships and some of the homelands as well.

The protests that followed lasted three years, claimed more than 3,000 lives, and resulted in the imprisonment of 30,000 people. Trade union members, clergy, educators, students and politicians—black and white—all took part. Increasingly harsh measures adopted by the police forces led to a grim pattern. Black South Africans, often children, were killed by police gunfire. The funerals for the slain protestors became huge stadium rallies that usually ended with a march to the cemetery. Onlooking police in their armored vehicles would see something threatening and open fire. Those killed would be honored at the next funeral.

Botha makes promises The violence increased on all sides. The government called out the army to supplement the police. It declared three states of emergency, which allowed the government to conduct a virtual war against the South African people. When world opinion—stirred up by revolting video images of police using whips and bullets on unarmed protesters—began to hamper its efforts, the government offered some concessions. In January of 1985, Prime Minister Botha announced he would release jailed black leader Nelson Mandela if Mandela would renounce violence. Mandela said he would renounce violence if the government would.

Mandela stayed in jail, but people began to see the revolutionary leader and his African National Congress (ANC) as more reasonable than the government. South African business leaders began to visit Mandela and other ANC leaders. They began to ask the government to change its policy. In July of 1986, the prime minister announced that he was repealing the hated pass laws—laws requiring black South Africans to show a pass allowing them to enter certain areas in their own country.

Basic policy did not change, however. Instead, the government had decided to wage total warfare against the townships. It forbade any coverage by news media. Then it proceeded to destroy certain townships and some shantytowns growing near them. The people living there, such as those at Crossroads, a township outside Cape Town, were forced to move elsewhere. Those who resisted were shot or detained in prison without charges. Police detained every leader they could find, often without charges. Arrested for treason were Popo Molefe and Patrick Lekota. Their rebellion, said the government, was financed and led by outside Communists.

Not everyone believed this. Most could see that black South Africans were fighting for basic human rights. Banks, such as Chase Manhattan Bank of New York, stopped all operations in South Africa. International businesses began to close their South African offices, and institutions canceled South African investments. These **sanctions** created a crisis for the government, but the leaders remained defiant.

The trial of Popo Molefe, Patrick Lekota, and others ended in 1988 with their conviction and imprisonment. By that time, an ominous quiet had set in. The government had put down the rebellion, and its troops controlled the townships. Most black leaders were either dead or in prison. But the struggle was far from over. Black South Africans were not giving up, and they knew time was on their side.

South Africa's actions had made it an outcast. Its athletes could not compete in the Olympics or travel to most countries for other contests. Entertainers stopped touring South Africa. The United Nations each year condemned South African policies and violations of human rights. An arms embargo kept South Africa from buying weapons legally. Its economy was being badly hurt by sanctions from countries that refused to do business with a country that denied the most basic human rights to three-quarters of its people.

A *new president dismantles apartheid.*

No one expected the National party to compromise, given its bulldog hold on power. But the year 1989 brought about sweeping changes both inside and outside South Africa. In January, President Botha suffered a heart attack and his minister of education, F.W. De Klerk, became the new president of South Africa.

President De Klerk saw trouble ahead for a South Africa unwilling to change. The numbers were unmistakable: the proportion of black to white South Africans was changing at a rate that would give blacks a five to one majority by the year 2000. Their share of jobs and wealth was similarly increasing. Labor unions had helped black workers gain wages that now amounted to 70 percent of white wages. Black graduates from universities now exceeded 8,000 a year. For whites, on the other hand, the government's huge debt payments, inflation, and sanctions were causing decreased buying power and demands for relief.

Outside the country, the changes in the Soviet Union marked an end to the Cold War. This meant that Western countries, especially the United States, no longer had to support South Africa as part of a strategy to stop communism. The aid South Africa had always counted on could easily evaporate.

President De Klerk wasted little time. Announcing his plan to make reforms, he released eight political prisoners in October. Most were members of the long-banned African National Congress. Then in January 1990, he made his most stunning move by releasing ANC leader Nelson Mandela. A prisoner for 27 years, Mandela was the greatest hero in black South African history. The formerly banned ANC was not only a legal political party; it was now the majority party.

In the next months, De Klerk successively repealed one after another of the apartheid laws, including the Population Registration Control Act. This act had legally separated people into white, black, coloured, or Asian groups. The signs that once segregated theaters, restaurants, hotels, and other facilities soon vanished.

ANOTHER WALL

In what ways was apartheid a wall against black South Africans?

Many South Africans have strong feelings about their ethnic roots.

Apartheid had officially ended and Nelson Mandela was free to act as a political leader. Expectations soared for a "new South Africa" with equal rights for all. As ANC deputy president Walter Sisulu said, "We have reached the last mile of our struggle." But the last mile soon proved to be long indeed. While everyone agreed that Nelson Mandela could easily win an election for president, the blacks required to elect him still could not vote. Worse, few leaders could agree on how to establish the conditions that would even allow an election.

The problem was that the many factions that made up South Africa continued to jockey for power. The National party still in power wanted to make sure that any new constitution would guarantee whites a permanent hold on that power. The blacks who made up 75 percent of the country wanted simple majority rule. In December of 1991, nineteen organizations sent 200 delegates to the Convention for a Democratic South Africa. The purpose was to draw up a new, nonracial constitution giving everyone the same rights. Hopes ran high, but after months of tense negotiations, the talks collapsed in June 1992. Violence in the townships was blamed. South Africans had resumed killing one another at a rate that would leave 3,000 people dead from political causes in 1992 alone.

Each side accused the others of promoting the violence. Whites said ethnic rivalries among blacks were to blame. The Inkatha party, headed by Mangosuthu Buthelezi, and made up of South Africans of the Zulu ethnic group, had long been a rival of the ANC, which is mainly made up of the Xhosa ethnic group. Many Zulu men were migrant workers who worked in mines or factories. Unable to find houses in the townships, they lived in all-male hostels. Much of the violence aimed at ANC supporters came out of these hostels. Townspeople loyal to the ANC would retaliate and the killing would escalate.

Black South Africans, such as Archbishop Desmond Tutu, winner of the Nobel Peace Prize, denied that ethnic rivalries, or tribalism, caused violence: "In Soweto we have lived harmoniously. I am Xhosa. I have a Zulu family on one side. A Swazi family there. A Mopedi family over there. . . . If we quarrel, it is because you have a new suit and I am jealous. We have never quarreled in Soweto because of tribalism."

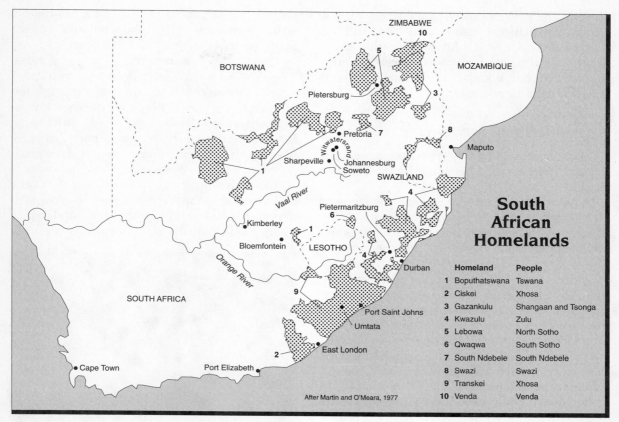

After Martin and O'Meara, 1977

South African Homelands

	Homeland	People
1	Boputhatswana	Tswana
2	Ciskei	Xhosa
3	Gazankulu	Shangaan and Tsonga
4	Kwazulu	Zulu
5	Lebowa	North Sotho
6	Qwaqwa	South Sotho
7	South Ndebele	South Ndebele
8	Swazi	Swazi
9	Transkei	Xhosa
10	Venda	Venda

Map Study

White South Africans have set up ethnically separate homelands in specified areas that are underdeveloped and overpopulated. Each area has been designated as being the homeland of a particular ethnic group. The map shows the location of the homelands, and the chart shows which ethnic group lives in each homeland. How might these ethnically separate homelands contribute to tensions among South Africa's ethnic groups?

Nelson Mandela made public appearances soon after his release from prison.

Allen Boesak, an ANC leader in Cape Town, said that the blame rested with the violent legacy of apartheid. Others went further, blaming the white government, which they saw allowing, and even encouraging, the violence. Violence among black South Africans, they argued, played into white hands because it implied that peace was possible only if whites continued to govern.

Still, the violence continued and no one knew what to do about it. In September of 1992, the killing became so bad that it brought the parties back together again. All agreed that talks had to go on and violence had to stop. Nelson Mandela of the ANC and Chief Buthelezi, the leader of Inkatha, agreed to keep meeting. But in the townships, millions of migrant workers still lived in the squalid hostels, sometimes 15 to a room. Township residents still lived in fear. Their belief that South African security forces were supplying automatic weapons and grenades to their Inkatha enemies led mainly to renewed calls for revenge.

After apartheid comes hope.

"I am oppressed by this government, yes, but I am not oppressed. I have life; I have hope for better."

A black street vendor in Soweto, the group of 32 townships outside Johannesburg, made this remark recently. It expresses both a sense of the troubled past and a knowledge that the future of South Africa lies here. In 1976, Soweto exploded in protest over the law making Afrikaans the official language in schools. In the riots and police actions that followed, nearly 600 South Africans died. Today, Soweto's more than 3 million people make up South Africa's largest metropolis. Post-apartheid South Africa will have to build itself on both the promise and the problems of such places.

Soweto's people need jobs. Unemployment runs as high as 40 percent, with two out of three black South Africans living below the poverty line. Its children need education—schools struggle with a shortage of teachers, books, and even chalk. More than anything, perhaps, its people need to feel secure. So far, that security has proved elusive. Hostel violence continues. More troubling, in April of 1993, one of the top leaders of the ANC, Chris Hani, was assassinated. A prominent pro-apartheid politician, Clive Derby-Lewis, was charged with planning the murder of Hani as well other top black leaders, including Nelson Mandela.

Yet one sign of the new spirit in black South Africa may lie in the fact that Soweto did not explode this time. Nelson Mandela was able to go on television and counsel calm. Most people complied, perhaps because they knew that Mandela was responsible for the agreements that continue to move South Africa toward fully representative government. In November of 1992, President De Klerk called for open elections by April of 1994. In February, Mandela and the African National Congress agreed to this plan. The 400-person assembly thus elected would

include representatives from all races, would write a new constitution, and would serve as the South African parliament for five years.

This plan was a compromise for both sides. The ANC agreed that the new government would guarantee white minority participation at least until 1999. Black demands for pure majority rule have been set aside until then. F.W. de Klerk and the National party, in turn, gave up their demand for a constitution guaranteeing whites a permanent share of power.

To be sure, not everyone was happy with the compromise. Many white conservatives still insisted on a separate white homeland, while many black radicals still demanded a purely

An ANC member protests the death of Chris Hani.

Nelson Mandela casts his vote in South Africa's first universal election. His party, the ANC, won more than half the seats in the National Assembly, and he became the nation's first black president.

black government. The elections themselves, held in April 1994, were troubled by long lines, rumors of fraud, threats of violence, and a near-boycott by several parties.

Yet by and large, the elections were remarkably peaceful, free, and fair. The ANC scored a decisive victory with 62.7 percent of the vote. The National party, which dominated white-ruled South Africa, gained 20.4 percent and received four cabinet seats in the government headed by new president Nelson Mandela. The Inkatha Freedom party received two cabinet seats.

Now one of the biggest challenges is keeping the peace, not merely between blacks and whites, but also between the Xhosa and Zulu black African groups. Another challenge is dealing with the plight of South Africa's many desperately poor blacks, who have high expectations now that majority rule has arrived. To fulfill these expectations, the government has taken steps to improve education, health, housing, and other services aimed at South Africa's long-neglected people.

Lesson Review 4

Define: sanctions
Identify: (a) United Democratic Front, (b) P.W. Botha, (c) National party, (d) Nelson Mandela, (e) F.W. De Klerk, (f) Population Registration Control Act, (g) Inkatha party, (h) Soweto
Answer:
1. Why were black South Africans angered by the National party's new constitution of 1983?
2. How did the UDF resist the changes of 1983?
3. How did Botha's death affect South Africa?
4. Why didn't the end of apartheid bring peace to South Africa?
5. How did the agreements reached in 1992 represent compromise?

Critical Thinking
6. Consider this statement: "In the modern world, violence is often a symbol of people's dissatisfaction with their condition in life." If this generalization is true, what needs to happen in South Africa to eradicate violence?

Chapter 6 Review

Summary

1. African democracy struggles to take hold.
Although hopes were high that an Africa free from colonialism would be a prosperous continent of democratic nations, the years since independence have brought widespread problems in economics, government, and health. Violent civil wars, a drop in prices for exported goods, and repeated droughts all took their toll, causing millions of Africans to become refugees.

Some of Africa's problems can be traced back to colonialism. European boundaries in Africa did not respect the existence of different ethnic groups, and caused deep-rooted problems. Additionally, colonialism left behind no models for democratic government. Africa's problems also stem from its own bad governments. Corruption, military dominance, and one-party systems are the rule rather than the exception. However, ambitious reformers will continue to employ different methods to turn Africans' long-lasting dreams of prosperity into reality.

2. Leaders favor cash crops over food crops.
Many sub-Saharan countries are constantly poised on the brink of disaster because they are not producing the food their people need. Famine is a constant threat that often becomes reality because of drought or war. These problems began when Africa became an attractive source of cash crops for colonial governments. Agricultural and mining efforts, once undertaken to meet the needs of Africans, became geared for the export market. This trend continues today, with Africans needing the cash from exports to buy manufactured goods, and foreign aid often linked directly to the continued export of the "tried-and-true" cash sources. However, since prices for these crops typically have dropped, African nations have found themselves heavily in debt and unable to provide their citizens with what they need. Often, unrest and violence follow, quickly escalating because of ethnic differences.

3. Africans organize to help themselves. As the natural environment in Africa has become damaged by deforestation, people have suffered, and a mass migration to cities has occurred. Recognizing the link between poverty and a damaged environment, individuals have organized Africans to employ strategies designed to revive and nurture green belts and farmlands. Farmers have also organized themselves to demand equity in government credits and to grow crops that are good for Africans rather than cash crops.

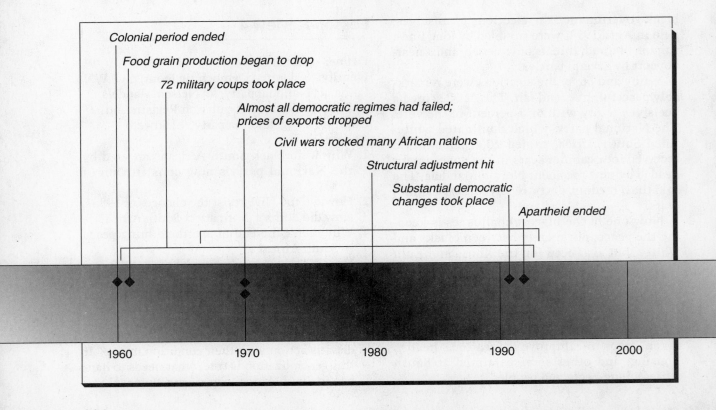

Colonial period ended

Food grain production began to drop

72 military coups took place

Almost all democratic regimes had failed; prices of exports dropped

Civil wars rocked many African nations

Structural adjustment hit

Substantial democratic changes took place

Apartheid ended

1960 1970 1980 1990 2000

Another crisis facing Africa that must be dealt with is AIDS. Since 62 percent of the world's AIDS victims live in Africa, this crisis is expected to worsen before it gets better. African nations are looking for help in dealing with this crisis.

4. A new South Africa is born. After the white-dominated South African government passed a new constitution in 1983 that continued to ignore black South Africans, violence around the issue of apartheid escalated to an all-time high. Armed clashes between anti-apartheid protesters and the police and army claimed thousands of lives. In 1989, however, South Africa gained a new president, F. W. de Klerk. Recognizing the need for change, De Klerk released imprisoned opposition leaders and replaced apartheid laws. In 1994, the move toward reform resulted in South Africa's first all-race elections. The African National Congress, with Nelson Mandela at its head, won a majority of votes, and Mandela became the new South African president. The new government is struggling to maintain peace among South Africa's racial and ethnic groups, build a stable democracy, and improve the lives of its citizens.

Reviewing the Facts

1. Define the following terms:
   a. Second Liberation   d. Naam
   b. export-led development   e. sanctions
   c. structural adjustment
2. Explain the importance of each of the following names or terms:
   a. Wangari Maathai   e. Alimata Doumbia
   b. Eritrea   f. National party
   c. Akosombo Dam Project   g. Nelson Mandela
   d. Burkina Faso   h. Soweto
3. How do Kenya's problems with government reflect the problems of many African nations?
4. (a) How were traditional African agricultural methods altered by colonial governments? (b) What negative outcomes came from these changes?
5. What goals do Salim and others have for continent-wide cooperation?
6. Why has the deforestation been so devastating?
7. (a) How have women traditionally been viewed in Africa? (b) Give specific examples of the new empowerment of Africa women.
8. What has contributed to the alarming increase of AIDS in Africa?

9. (a) What was the purpose of sanctions against South Africa? How effective were they? (b) What was the actual catalyst of the end of apartheid?
10. What are the two main opposing groups in South Africa, and why do they disagree?

Basic Skills

1. **Building vocabulary** Consider names of organizations and movements discussed in the chapter: Second Liberation, neo-colonialism, Green Belt Movement, the silent revolution, United Democratic Front. Choose one and write a one-paragraph definition of it. How does the name itself indicate the organization's or movement's meaning?
2. **Reading strategically** Skim the heads in Lesson 2. Based on these heads, list possible reasons for the hunger problem in Africa. Improve the list based on what you learned from actually reading the lesson.

Critical Thinking

1. **Identifying cause and affect** Experts believe that the causes of famine lie in the social, political, and economic conditions of societies. (a) How could this be viewed as true in sub-Saharan Africa? (b) How have natural disasters contributed to famine there?
2. **Identifying bias and point of view** As you have read, the National Party and South African blacks disagree on who should participate in government. What guidelines would you use to moderate the debate on this issue? Explain your reasoning.

Perspectives on Past and Present

Other regions of the world besides Africa, including the Middle East, India, and eastern Europe, have been subjected to the imposition of artificial boundary lines. Find out how these boundaries have affected the nations involved. What common problems do all of these areas share? Speculate on how these problems might have been avoided if differences among ethnic groups had been respected.

Investigating History

1. Do library research to find the recorded hopes of Africans in the 1960's as they looked toward the end of colonialism. Could these same hopes be echoed as Africa prepares for a Second Liberation?
2. Research how much money the United States spent restoring order in Somalia in 1992–1993. If the money were used for aid rather than intervention, what might it buy for Africans?

Chapter 7   Nigeria: A Case Study

"Figures," by Nigerian artist Rufus Ogundele, is a linocut print.

Key Terms

secede
indigenization decree

Read and Understand
1. Nigeria is a land of contrast and change.
2. Foreign powers affected Nigeria's development.
3. Nigeria struggles with nationhood.

The excerpt below is from a book called *Things Fall Apart*, written by the Nigerian author, Chinua Achebe. A great deal of Nigerian literature explores the effect of the European presence on Nigeria. In this passage two Nigerians discuss how white missionaries changed their society at the turn of this century.

"Does the white man understand our custom about land?"
"How can he when he doesn't even speak our tongue? But he says that our customs are bad; and our own brothers who have taken up his religion also say that our customs are bad. How do you think we can fight when our own brothers have turned against us? The white man is very clever. He came quietly and peaceably with his religion. We were amused at his foolishness and allowed him to stay. Now he has won our brothers, and our clan can no longer act like one. He has put a knife on the things that held us together and we have fallen apart."

There have been many moments in Nigerian history when it seemed that things were falling apart. For centuries, Nigerian society has been torn, both by forces from outside Nigeria, and by regional differences among its own people. Today, Nigeria continues to search for unity within its borders. To help in this search, Nigerians have a number of tools, including diverse and rich cultures and a treasure store of natural resources. Nigerians also possess a shared inheritance that includes a history of resisting foreign invaders. Though it is true that many forces divide Nigeria, its people are also discovering the "things that hold them together." This quest for unity is part of Nigeria's fascinating and ongoing history.

Traditional village (above), Lagos (right)

Nigeria is a land of contrast and change.

1

The 373,000 square miles that make up Nigeria offer a breathtaking panorama of people and places. From the cool peaks of the Jos Plateau, to the mangrove swamp forests of the coastline, to the rain forests of the west, Nigeria is a celebration of contrast and diversity. Cities such as Lagos bustle with construction, traffic, and people. Lagos, the former capital, is a sharp contrast to some northern cities with their cool, hushed, Muslim mosques and tranquil streets. Such variety is understandable considering that Nigeria is about the size of California, Nevada, and Arizona combined. Roughly 110 to 120 million people live there in 30 states. Today, about one of every six Africans is a Nigerian. As you will read, this diversity of land and people gives Nigeria a vibrancy that is reflected in its rich culture and history.

Map Study

How might the rivers in Nigeria have affected where people settled?

Nigeria contains many ethnic groups.

One of the most remarkable features of West Africa and Nigeria is the variety of languages spoken by the people there. English is the official language; however, researchers have recently catalogued 395 different languages spoken in Nigeria. Perhaps even more amazing for Nigeria is that of those languages, only two have origins beyond Nigeria's borders.

Although Nigeria contains hundreds of ethnic groups, most Nigerians belong to one of three dominant groups. These three groups are

117

the Hausa-Fulani in the north, the Yoruba in the west, and the Igbo in the east. Though much of this chapter will study the friction between these three groups, it is important to remember that Nigeria's history is also about the bonds and shared inheritance that bring these groups together.

Hausa-Fulani Northern Nigeria is home to more than half of Nigeria's population: the Hausa-Fulani, who are predominantly Muslim people. The Hausa were converted to Islam centuries ago. Early on, Hausa society developed a complex, sophisticated political system. Its people were literate in Arabic script and were influenced by Islamic political and social ideas.

Fulani society, which spread eastward throughout the savanna areas of West Africa, was based mainly on cattle raising. Some of the Fulani settled in Hausa towns and villages and intermarried with the Hausa. Many of these Fulani became educated in Islamic beliefs and took positions in the courts of the Hausa kings.

Igbo and Yoruba Southern Nigeria is divided into two regions, both predominantly Christian. In the eastern region most of the population is Igbo. For centuries, Igbo society was ruled by elders who interpreted traditional laws and guided the practices of their people. Society elders were the judges and rulers and gave counsel to Igbo villages.

In the western region, the Yoruba are the dominant people. In Chapter 1, you read about the cultural contributions made by the Yoruba living in Ile Ife. The Yoruba have a rich political history as well. While Ile Ife was an important religious, cultural, and artistic center of the Yoruba, the neighboring city of Oyo was an important political center that ruled the region with a highly advanced constitutional monarchy.

To divide Nigeria into these three groups does not do justice to the rich and ever changing cultural alliances and themes that are a part of Nigerian society and politics. The Edo, Ibibio, Kanuri, Nupe, Tiv, Chamba, Ekoi, and

Kano, a traditional mud-walled city in northern Nigeria

Ijaw are smaller, but still important ethnic groups. Furthermore, the distinctions between Nigerian ethnic groups is not always clear. For example, Fulani families who speak Hausa, (and not Fulfulde), still retain a strong sense of their Fulani identity.

Before Europeans established a colony in Nigeria, ethnic groups did not identify themselves with political units as they do today. The colonial government in Nigeria often classified groups according to language, therefore reinforcing ethnic divisions. One way to understand how these groups are different is not to examine their languages, but rather their different religious practices.

Nigeria has a number of religions.

Religion has an important and special place in Nigerian society and often enters into Nigerian political, social, and economic matters. Present-day political disputes in Nigeria often center around religious divisions.

Islam Islamic missionaries are believed to have first reached the Nigerian province of Borno around 1150. The missionaries converted a leader of the region and thus began the Islamic tradition in Nigeria. In the centuries that followed, Islamic missionaries made converts throughout Nigeria.

In fact, the key to the growth of Islam in Nigeria is the fervent work done by Islamic missionaries. One account from the late 1800's explains how devoted Nigerian Muslims worked to spread their religion.

African or Yoruba Mohammedans [Muslims] are more anxious than African or Yoruba Christians to spread their religion. . . . There is scarcely a single town, hamlet, and even farm village where Mohammedans have not represented themselves. . . . Wherever two or three are, there is a mosque; and, burnt down ever so many times, it is rebuilt. . . . Each tradesman, each farmer, each man and each woman, at home and abroad, considers himself or herself a missionary.

As more converts were made, Nigerian Muslims made pilgrimages to Islamic centers to study the teachings of their religion. So many pilgrims came from Nigeria that by the fourteenth century, some Nigerian pilgrims had their own homes in Cairo. An Egyptian writer wrote of the Nigerian visitors. "They follow the rite of Iman Malik. They dress simply and are fervent in their religion." One Nigerian family in the seventeenth century described their son's trip to Baghdad this way.

He went to Baghdad where he remained six months and enriched his own store of learning while enriching the learning of others. He performed the obligations of religion while learning the art of a cultivated life, and engaged in the science of analogical deduction and the study of the Hadith of the Prophet.

Today, nearly half of all Nigerians are Muslim. Their exact numbers, however, are difficult to gauge. In some regions, such as Borno, Kano, Nupe, Sokotos, and Zaria, Muslims are a majority, but in others they are a minority.

Christianity During the nineteenth century, Christian missionaries established schools and hospitals in Nigeria. Unfortunately, many of these same missionaries demanded that Nigerian converts abandon aspects of their own culture. As was true for other African Christians, many Nigerians established their own Christian churches to be free from the European cultural biases the missionaries brought with them. Today, about one third of Nigeria's population is Christian.

Traditional religions Traditional religions continue to thrive in Nigeria. These religions contain a rich tradition of local practices, customs, and beliefs. In many areas of Nigeria, people have combined Islam or Christianity with their own traditional religious beliefs. A good deal of Nigerian art has religious connotations as well. This mix of religion and art is an important part of Nigeria's cultural heritage.

Nigeria continues to make many cultural contributions.

In Chapters 1 and 5 you read about some of Nigeria's remarkable cultural achievements. Many of these, such as the bronze and terracotta sculptures, date back many centuries (see

Chapter 5). Nigeria's cultural achievements are not restricted to the past, however. Nigerian writers, artists, and musicians continue to influence Nigerians and the world community.

In 1977, people of African descent from 59 countries gathered in Lagos for the Second World Black and African Festival of Arts and Culture. The largest group of visitors from outside of Nigeria were African Americans. It was fitting that the festival was held in Nigeria. Art, music, and literature have flourished in this nation, despite the ebb and flow of political and economic fortunes. In many ways, Nigeria is a cultural center for all of Africa.

Today, Nigerian artists such as Bruce Onobrakpeya continue Nigeria's tradition of producing remarkable sculptures, often using traditional and contemporary motifs. Present-day Nigerian artists continue to expand art traditions in weaving, pottery, and architecture.

Nigeria also has internationally recognized musicians. Nigerian musicians often combine traditional folk music with contemporary instruments. For example, Nigerian musicians might play traditional instruments such as drums and flutes along with electric guitars and saxophones.

Soyinka (top), Ade

A number of performers such as Sunny Ade have brought Nigerian music to the rest of the world. Ade's music is based on Juju, a form of Nigerian folk music. Another popular Nigerian musician is Fela Anikulapo-Kuti. He is considered a social crusader because of the biting, often satirical lyrics he sets to music.

Perhaps Nigeria's greatest cultural achievements of this century have been in literature. In 1986, as you have read, the Nigerian writer Wole Soyinka was the first African writer to be awarded the Nobel Prize for Literature. For many Nigerians, Soyinka's award was the kind of international recognition Nigerian writers have long deserved. Other writers such as Chinua Achebe, John Pepper Clark, and Christopher Okigbo, have brought Nigerian culture, politics, and history to readers worldwide.

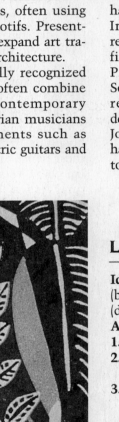
"Fulani Milk Woman" by Bruce Onobrakpeya

Lesson Review 1

Identify: (a) *Things Fall Apart,* (b) Chinua Achebe, (c) Bruce Onobrakpeya, (d) Sunny Ade

Answer:
1. In what ways is Nigeria diverse?
2. What is remarkable about the languages spoken in Nigeria?
3. (a) What are the three main ethnic groups in Nigeria? (b) Why is it difficult to divide Nigerians into these three groups?
4. What role does religion play in Nigeria?
5. How do Nigerians make cultural contributions to the international community?

Critical Thinking
6. Why is the title *Things Fall Apart* appropriate for the point that Chinua Achebe makes about Nigeria?

Foreign powers affected Nigeria's development. 2

The threat of domination by a foreign power has been with Nigerians for centuries. Saharan and Atlantic trade routes offered Nigerians more than goods—the routes also brought information. In this way, Nigerian leaders learned of the British and French colonial ventures in other parts of Africa, India, and the Americas. The stories Nigerians heard about European colonialists caused understandable alarm. From the early 1600's onward, it seemed to many Nigerians that the stories they heard were increasingly being played out in their own country.

The slave trade took a toll.

You have already read in Chapter 2 about the Atlantic slave trade. In the early 1600's, Europeans discovered that the leaders of Nigerian kingdoms such as Benin and Oyo could supply them with one of their greatest needs—a low-cost workforce. The development of this tragic trading relationship caused one of the greatest migrations in human history. For the next four centuries, the slave trade defined Nigeria's relationship with Europeans and people in the Americas. The volume of trade along Nigeria's coastline was so great that the region became known as the Slave Coast.

The slave trade took an oppressive toll on the cultures in Nigeria. In the 1700's, many Africans were forcibly removed from their homes to work on farms and plantations in Brazil, the West Indies, and mainland North America. As you read in Chapter 3, the slave trade diminished in the late 1800's, only to have a different kind of oppression rise to take its place: colonialism.

The British ruled Nigeria.

By the beginning of the twentieth century, all of Nigeria was under British colonial rule. British occupation began around 1866, when a number of British companies began trading on the Niger River. They eventually united into one entity called the Royal Niger Company. The company was led by Sir George Goldie who notified the Berlin Conference that he had effectively "occupied" the Niger River basin (see Chapter 3). Goldie was an overt racist who had no misgivings about using violence to obtain his economic goals. The company's headquarters were in the village of Asabga, where the local people were forced to endure inhuman hardships at the hands of Goldie and his men. For example, Goldie's men took local foodstuff at will. In one raid, the British even destroyed seedlings for the next year's harvest.

British merchants understood the value of the Niger River trade. The company's goal was to wrest control of this profitable enterprise from the African traders who had developed it. In the late 1800's, African merchants based in Lagos found that their trade routes were being increasingly overtaken by the Royal Niger Company—mainly by violence. In 1897, the company invaded Nupe and Ilorin, supposedly to stop slave trading, but in reality to establish their dominance in trading. The Royal Niger Company came to epitomize the British colonial attitude of using whatever means necessary to extract local resources for the good of the controlling country. The company used its resources to create a monopoly, thereby preventing African merchants from gaining any profit.

While the Royal Niger Company changed life drastically for the communities along the Niger River, it had little effect outside this area. Consolidating British power in areas beyond the river thus became the goal of the British government. In the late nineteenth century, the British tried to unify the many different groups in Nigeria into one nation. From 1901 to 1906, the British conquered states in northern Nigeria. By 1914, the rest of Nigeria was under the control of the British in a single unit called the Colony and Protectorate of Nigeria.

Though the British allowed Nigerians some degree of local control, the colonial system slowly but surely dragged the Nigerian people into economic, political, and social collapse. Besides extracting Nigerian natural resources, the British taxed Nigerians heavily. In this way, the economic resources of Nigeria were steadily drained by the British. As you will read, Nigerians soon sought ways to rid themselves of the British colonialists and regain control of their country.

Nigerians fought for independence.

By 1929, uprisings against the British were becoming increasingly common in colonial Nigeria. Sometimes the protests were peaceful, and Nigerians used their influence to effect change and reforms. At other times, the protests were violent. British firepower often made these violent protests deadly, as described in this account by a British soldier of an attack by the Ezza and Ikwo of northeastern Igboland.

The effect of the fire from the troops was a sad show, the Ikwos dropping down like flies . . . not minding the heavy casualties [they] kept on coming. . . . At this time we did not know that other parties of the Ikwos were also attacking the camp. Of course both attempts of the Ikwos failed disastrously. They appeared brave but foolish. . . . About 200 yards outside the camp we found scores of dead and wounded lying about the field.

The Women's War of 1929 In the 1920's, a number of the resistance efforts were led by Nigerian women in southeastern Nigeria. In one uprising, which came to be known as the Women's War of 1929, the conflict stemmed from British taxation policies in the eastern region. The revolt involved Igbo, Ibibio, and Opobo women from a large number of communities throughout Nigeria.

Understandably, British taxation policies had always irritated Nigerians. In the late 1920's, prices for palm oil, a major agricultural product, fell and Nigerian businesswomen found themselves earning less and less in the marketplace. Then in 1929, a tax official trying to get an accurate census met with a woman named Nwanyeruwa in the village of Oloko. Nwanyeruwa was insulted by his questions concerning children and possessions and the two scuffled. Nwanyeruwa ran to a local church meeting, where she enlisted the support of other women in her community against the tax collector. A British official sided with the women and imprisoned the tax collector. News of the victory spread throughout the region and sparked a small scale revolt against British officials and their Nigerian collaborators.

During the revolt, women attacked courts, local agencies, and European trading factories. It seemed as if all their pent up grievances exploded, causing the rebellion to grow. Like many Nigerian protests of the 1920's and 1930's, the uprising started as a demonstration against specific abuses, but grew into an overall rejection of colonialism. A number of women were killed during the fighting. Many took the rebellion as a sign that Nigerian desire for independence was growing and that even different ethnic groups were willing to unite for this cause.

Herbert Macaulay Nigerian's independence movement had other heroes as well. Herbert Macaulay, for one, has been called the Father of Nigerian nationalism. Throughout the 1930's and 1940's, Macaulay fought for Nigerian issues and against British abuses. He founded the Nigerian National Democratic party and used the party to fight for the rights of

Nigerian women continue to run businesses in the markets of Nigeria.

Nigerians. Macaulay became a chief spokesperson for Nigerians in political and economic matters. He demanded free compulsory education and the abolition of provincial courts, and he strove to abolish all forms of racial discrimination.

Nnamdi Azikiwe Another independence movement leader was Nnamdi Azikiwe, who came to the United States as a young man, after racial discrimination at the hands of British colonial officials forced him to leave his homeland. In the United States, Azikiwe overcame poverty and racial prejudice to earn three university degrees. Upon his return to Nigeria in 1937, he established a chain of newspapers, which he used to attack colonialism. His intelligent, insightful editorials spoke to the hearts of Nigerians and made him a hero in the eyes of many.

The efforts of people like Nwanyeruwa, Macaulay, and Azikiwe laid the foundation for Nigerian independence. As you will read in Lesson 3, however, gaining independence was only the first step toward creating a unified Nigeria.

Lesson Review 2

Identify: (a) Sir George Goldie, (b) Royal Niger Company, (c) The Women's War of 1929, (d) Nwanyeruwa, (e) Herbert Macaulay, (f) Nnamdi Azikiwe

Answer:
1. Why did the Nigerian coast become known as the Slave Coast?
2. Describe how Britain took colonial control of Nigeria.
3. What method did Nnamdi Azikiwe use to attack colonialism?
4. What were Herbert Macaulay's demands for Nigerians?
5. Why did Nnamdi Azikiwe come to the United States?

Critical Thinking
6. How did colonialism make it difficult for Nigerians to move toward independence?
7. Consider the ways Nwanyeruwa, Macaulay and Azikiwe rebelled against colonialism. Why were their methods especially effective?

Nigeria struggles with nationhood. 3

On October 1, 1960, Nigeria stepped onto the world stage as an independent nation. As the ties of colonialism fell from its shoulders, Nigeria confronted the difficult task of forming a unified government. In many ways, Nigeria's struggle to form a democratic government was a test case for all of Africa. It seemed to many that Nigeria, with its vast resources, had the potential to become a beacon for all African nations emerging from the colonial era. One news magazine even called Nigeria the first "black power" in the world. But there was much to be done and many groups to unite before that goal could be achieved. On that October day in 1960 the question remained: would Nigeria be able to bring together its diverse regions and people to undo the damage caused by decades of colonial rule?

Establishing a government was difficult for Nigeria.

For a number of reasons, many observers believed that Nigeria would adjust to independence better and more easily than most African countries. Nigerian political parties had existed since the 1920's. Even before World War II, Nigerian intellectuals were laying the foundation for an independence movement. As you read in Chapter 4, World War II played a part in helping Nigerians and other Africans break free. Nigerian soldiers returning home from foreign battles were filled with the desire to liberate their own country. Many also realized that the relative lack of white settlers in Nigeria would make it easier for Nigerian nationalists to organize openly. As Nigeria looked toward liberation, most people believed that independence could be achieved without a military struggle.

In the 1950's, three main political groups emerged in Nigeria. One party took root in northern Nigeria, dominated by the Hausa-Fulani. In western Nigeria, a party that represented the interests of the Yoruba emerged. In the east, a third party represented the interests of the Igbo. These three groups maneuvered for the best position in post-colonial Nigeria, and each was suspicious of the other. At times it seemed that the three groups could agree on nothing, including an exact date for Nigeria's independence. These differences often erupted in violence. For example, in 1953, a particularly heated debate in the legislature led to violent riots in the Kano region.

Unfortunately, these regional differences and outbursts of violence would become a pattern for Nigerian politics. When the Nigerian people finally did become independent in 1960, their country's new shape reflected the three regional powers that had brought it into being, but offered no solution for resolving their differences.

Nigeria's new constitution established three regional governments. Watching over them was the federal government at Lagos. (Today, the capital is Abuja.) The new government consisted of a council of ministers presided over by a prime minister, a senate, and a house of representatives. Executive powers were vested in the council of ministers; legislative powers, in the senate and the house. The prime minister was appointed by the president. The president chose someone who could win the support of a majority in the legislative branch.

Initially, independence and the new government brought hope to Nigeria. Nigerians believed that colonialism had thwarted their country's development. The people of Nigeria were now anxious to fulfill their nation's enormous potential. There was plenty to be done. Nigeria had to find jobs for its large ranks of unemployed workers. Agriculture had to be revived to provide food for Nigeria's people. Power and water supplies had to be put into place. A better health care system was urgently needed. Unfortunately, before these problems could be solved, Nigeria's government had to find some unity among its own leaders. This proved to be extremely difficult.

Regional differences plagued Nigeria's new government.

Even with their new government in place, the three sections of Nigeria disagreed constantly, and often violently, with one another. From the beginning, plots and conspiracies were common. Nigeria's first prime minister, Abubakar Tafawa Balewa, was a member of the Northern

People's Congress from northern Nigeria. His election alarmed many people in western Nigeria who feared being overtaken by Islamic forces in the north. Early in his rule, Balewa was forced to declare a state of emergency in the western region as violent clashes erupted between opposing political groups. Balewa himself was a victim of this violence. Five years after independence, Nigeria's first prime minister was killed by bullets from an assassin's gun.

A general feeling of instability was made worse by the growing discontent among Nigeria's voters. Nigerian elections were unpredictable, and the citizens often contested or ignored the results. One reason for this was Nigeria's inability to conduct an accurate census. A census is important for creating electoral districts. For example, in 1964, Nigerians were told that the population of their country had reached 55.6 million. According to the government, 22.6 million lived in the north. The remaining 23 million lived in the west, midwest, and east, as well as in Lagos. Southern Nigerians suspected that the numbers were shifted to give the north more electoral power. Suspicions about census taking continue to plague Nigerian elections even today. As Nigerians' faith in the election process declined, political campaigns became violent. Increasingly, elections were held against a backdrop of riots, bombings, and brutal killings of political opponents.

As the new government struggled to find stability, discontent among Nigeria's workers was also growing. The country drifted without direction, and the standard of living for workers declined. In 1964, workers went on a general strike that nearly shut the nation down. These problems were made worse by poor communication and transportation links between northern and southern Nigeria.

Instead of finding ways to unify Nigeria, the new government dabbled with dividing up the nation into smaller regions. Federal leaders believed that if Nigeria's regions were divided, sectional rivalries would be eliminated. The first division proposed by the new Nigerian government was to split the cocoa-rich western region in two. Westerners rebelled against the proposal. Led by Obafemi Awolowo, the western region resisted any attempts to weaken its power by breaking it apart. The Nigerian federal government responded to Awolowo's protests by imprisoning him and many of his followers.

Several coups erupted in Nigeria.

On January 15, 1966, tensions exploded and Nigeria's first republic was overthrown by a military coup. The new leaders tried to unify Nigeria by eliminating all regions and declaring Nigeria a single state. Nigeria was put under military rule, and all government officials were replaced by military leaders. In some regions of the country, the change to military rule was welcomed. Some people hoped that the soldiers would end the rampant corruption and be able to stamp out the regional differences that were tearing the new nation apart. Odumegwu Emeka Ojukwu, the governor of the eastern region, expressed his own hopes that the military would put an end to "years of planlessness, incompetence, inefficiency, greed, corruption, avarice and gross disregard for the interest of the common man."

Ojukwu

As would be the case again and again in Nigeria, regional differences proved to be stronger than any government, even a military one. Northerners distrusted the new military government, which was led mainly by Igbo officers. Northerners believed that the real purpose of the new government's unification plan was to take away the northern region's power. This resentment eventually burst into violence. Hundreds of Igbo in the north were killed. The bloodshed spread as northern troops killed southern soldiers and civilians.

In July 1966, a second coup shook Nigeria. From this confusion emerged a charismatic leader named Yakubu Gowon. For a time, it seemed as though Gowon might be able to unify the ravaged nation. He released Obafemi Awolowo from prison and worked to establish a power base that included all ethnic groups. Gowon created twelve regional states in the hope of providing better minority representation.

Before Gowon's ideas could be tested, however, Odumegwu Emeka Ojukwu declared his eastern region a separate nation called the Republic of Biafra. Nigeria's struggle to establish a unified government was about to face its greatest test.

Nigeria fought a costly civil war.

Ojukwu's decision to **secede**, or break apart, from Nigeria on May 30, 1967, was a calculated risk to establish a new nation based on the rich natural resources of the eastern region. Ojukwu shrewdly understood that a great deal of Nigeria's wealth came from eastern oil exports. Ojukwu reasoned that if he could hold out long enough, the Nigerian federal government would become bankrupt.

Ojukwu and his people gained considerable international support for their cause. A number of African nations including the Ivory Coast (Cote D'Ivoire), Gabon, Tanzania, and Zambia lent their support to Biafra. These nations might have hoped to break up Nigeria's considerable power with Biafra's secession.

Aware of the importance international opinion had for his movement, Ojukwu hired a multinational public relations company to present his fight in a favorable light. Ojukwu's tactic worked. Many people abroad came to identify the Biafrans as a beleaguered Christian minority fighting against an authoritarian, and mainly Muslim, federal government. Other African nations, however, painfully aware of their own fragile unity, supported the Nigerian federal government against the Biafran rebels.

Nigerians in pursuit of fleeing Biafran troops

The civil war lasted for an agonizing two and half years. It pitted two factions of Nigeria's best trained troops against each other. Initially, the Biafran forces penetrated deep into Nigeria, coming within miles of Lagos. The Nigerian federal government regrouped, however, and began a counterattack. With British and Soviet aid, the Nigerian federal government eventually turned the rebels back. As the government tightened its hold around the rebels, the toll in human life grew. An estimated 1 million people died during the conflict. Many of the deaths were the result of famine.

On January 12, 1970, the leaders of the secessionist movement called a halt to the fighting, and the civil war ended. Nigeria's civil war had a number of consequences. As painful as the lesson was, it built unity among Nigerians and increased awareness of their country as whole. The civil war also affected other African nations with diverse cultural groups. These nations viewed the Nigerian civil war as a lesson on the importance of keeping their own boundaries intact. There was another unexpected result of the civil war. The conflict put in place a number of international charities that continue to play a part in the African community.

After the war, General Gowon, who was still head of the federal government, tried to bring his war-torn nation back together. The 35-year-old leader showed maturity in his decision to offer amnesty to all the rebels. The rebel leader Ojukwu, however, escaped to the Ivory Coast. Gowon promised to work for Nigeria's development and for a return to civilian rule. In many ways, Nigeria did a remarkable job of mending the damage caused by the war. The nation quickly went to work repairing its roads and industries. There was something new on Nigeria's horizon that would give a much needed boost to the rebuilding: increasing revenue from oil exports. Oil was a benefit that Nigerians were only then beginning to realize fully. It would soon change Nigeria's place in the world drastically.

Nigeria experienced an oil boom.

Oil exports had been leaving Nigeria since 1958, but it was not until the 1970's that this valuable export began to play a major role in the fledgling nation's economy. By 1972, Nigeria was the world's ninth largest oil producer. Before this time, Nigeria received as much money from peanuts and other agricultural exports as it did from oil. Nigeria was also heavily dependent on foreign aid, much of it from the United States. The newfound revenues from oil enabled Nigeria to pay off war debts and plan large-scale public works projects.

Money from oil also made it possible for more Nigerians to become active in Nigeria's commercial economy. The government helped involve Nigerians in their economy in 1972 when it issued an **indigenization decree**. This decree forced foreign companies to yield large percentages of their business to Nigerians. For the first time, many Nigerians were taking their rightful place in their country's economy.

As Nigeria's economy expanded, its role in international affairs also grew. In 1973, this growing importance in world affairs came into sharp focus. During this time, much of the western world was scrambling to find oil supplies because of an oil embargo led by the Organization of Petroleum Exporting Countries (OPEC). Though Nigeria was a member of OPEC, it did not join the boycott. At the time of the embargo, Nigeria was quickly becoming the second largest supplier of oil to the United States. Nigeria's decision to ignore the OPEC

An oil refinery near Warri, Nigeria

126

boycott helped make it possible for the United States to ride out OPEC's ban on oil exports. Besides forming a closer alliance with the United States, the event taught Nigerians an important lesson about the value of their oil resource and how to use it.

The oil boom transformed Nigeria in many ways, but the changes were not always predictable. Nigerians hoped that money from oil would magically transform their developing country almost overnight. As with most large changes, however, the boom caused a number of growing pains for Nigeria. In many ways the city of Lagos epitomized the double-edged sword that oil brought to Nigeria.

From 1965 to 1980, the population of Lagos increased tenfold. Much of this growth can be attributed to the oil boom, which lured workers from the countryside to the city. Today, ten million people or more are living in the Lagos metropolitan area. Along with this astonishing growth came a number of problems common to many large cities worldwide.

The oil boom created new neighborhoods filled with luxury apartments. Alongside the luxury apartments, however, crime-ridden slums also sprang up. Large-scale building projects were planned though not all were successful. Public works projects were often poorly planned, or became bogged down in disputes or government incompetence. At times, traffic was so bad in Lagos that the government ordered people with cars with odd-numbered license plates to drive only on odd-numbered days, while those with even-numbered plates could drive only on even-numbered days. As money from oil poured into Nigeria, the cost of living skyrocketed dramatically. And as more and more Nigerians came to Lagos, jobs became scarce and crime rates soared.

Even today, oil is both a benefit and a problem for Nigeria. Being overly dependent on one export causes problems when oil prices plummet, as they did in the 1980's. In many ways, Nigeria's success depends on the roller coaster price of oil on the world market. Even in the best of times, Nigeria needs a strong, decisive government to oversee oil exports. As you will read in the next section, finding this kind of government continues to be a problem for Nigeria.

New leaders tried to bring civilian rule to Nigeria.

Four years after the civil war ended in 1970, Nigeria was still under Yakubu Gowon's military regime. Regional governments were run by military governors, who had a reputation for corruption and incompetence. Nigerians were impatient to regain control of their country and hold national elections. Though Gowon continued to promise a return to civilian rule, the date was continually pushed further back. In 1974, Nigeria once again attempted to take a census of its people so that honest elections could be held. Once again, the results were contested by southerners who distrusted the results, which gave northern Nigeria twice as many people as the south.

In July 1975, another coup toppled Gowon's government. It was led by a northern war hero named Murtala Muhammed. The new leader quickly set to work on a plan to hold elections in Nigeria. Muhammed also retired thousands of government employees to end the rampant government corruption. Before these ideas could take hold, however, violence ended his rule. Just as quickly, Muhammed's chief of staff, Olusegun Obasanjo, took power and eventually fulfilled Muhammed's dream of returning Nigeria to civilian rule.

Unlike some of his predecessors, Obasanjo truly worked to end military rule in Nigeria. He reduced Nigeria's large army nearly by half. He also lifted the ban on political parties. His next step was to create a constitutional drafting committee with the purpose of forming a new civilian government. Nigerians took hope in their new leader's activity and entered the political activity with vigor. Nigerians watched as their leaders debated, often heatedly, each action taken by the constitutional committee. The active and outspoken Nigerian press debated each action of the committee on their front pages. Many Nigerians who had left their nation during the years of turmoil came home to help build the new civilian government.

The constitutional committee agreed to recognize only political parties that were truly national. They hoped that this would put an end to the regional differences and fighting that had caused so many governments in the past to topple. By 1978, national elections were underway. Unfortunately, many of the political parties that emerged looked just like the old ones and seemed to represent regional more than national interests. There was one exception, though. The National Party of Nigeria tried to build a power base that included many segments of Nigerian society. The party selected Alhaji Shehu Shagari as its presidential candidate for the 1979 election. Shagari was the first person from his ancestral Fulani village to obtain a secular (non-religious) education. He became a well-known poet in the Hausa language. The popular leader won the presidential election in 1979, and on October 1, Nigeria's Second Republic was in place. For the time being, Nigeria's people were once again in control of their nation.

Shagari

Shagari's rule (1979–1983) offered some successes for Nigerians. In some ways, his rule was the freest in Nigerian modern history. The new leader was popular with the people, and he worked to bring disparate political groups together. Shagari even asked some of his political opponents to participate in his government. In a letter to his former opponents, Shagari expressed his desire to form a "broad based government."

There were also disappointments under Shagari's rule. Hunger was a recurring problem in Nigeria. In 1979, Shagari announced a plan for a crash program to boost food production. These hopes soon came up against some hard economic realities, however. Also, Shagari's administration, like many before it, was rampant with corruption and seemed incapable of getting Nigeria on a healthy economic foundation. Despite Nigeria's economic promise, the nation's finances continued to plummet. Nigeria's foreign debt skyrocketed. Increasingly, Nigeria was forced to import food, and under Shagari's regime there was less and less money with which to buy it.

As the economy weakened, Nigerians used their newly won freedoms of speech and the press to attack Shagari's administration. Nowhere was this right exercised more freely than on the pages of Nigeria's vibrant and outspoken newspapers. Much of the press aimed their criticism at corruption in Shagari's government and the deteriorating economy. Eventually, the criticism became too much for the Nigerian president. In 1981, he arrested two editors of the *Nigerian Tribune*, which had printed a front-page story accusing him of bribery. Increasingly, Shagari turned to authoritarian tactics to silence his enemies.

Nigeria returned to military rule.

In 1983, the debate over Shagari's leadership ended. In an all too familiar pattern, Shagari's civilian regime was overthrown by a group led by military officers. The brief period of civilian rule was over. The generals who seized power claimed that Shagari had lost touch with the Nigerian people and their problems. For the next two years, the new government, led by General Mohammed Buhari, used authoritarian tactics to clean up government corruption and get Nigeria's economy back on track. Federal spending was cut by 40 percent. Despite his strong-arm tactics, many Nigerians supported Buhari's efforts to end the pervasive corruption that was strangling Nigeria. Buhari did so, however, at great cost to the personal freedoms of Nigerians.

It was not surprising that in 1985, a counter-coup led by General Ibrahim Babangida overthrew the Buhari regime. When General Babangida took power in Nigeria in 1985, it was the fifth time Nigeria's government had been toppled since gaining independence in 1960. Though Babangida took power by military force, he initially offered Nigerians hope for change.

Babangida promised to straighten out Nigeria's economy, which was still in a tailspin. Many states in Nigeria did not have enough money to run even the most basic services, such as schools and health clinics. At this time, most of Nigeria's economy was run by the government. Babangida abolished a number of inefficient government agencies and tried to put businesses back in the hands of Nigerian citizens. By cutting government spending,

Babangida did have some success in lessening Nigeria's national debt. Though these measures won Nigeria the support of the international banking community, they also caused widespread discontent because of rising unemployment and increases in the price of food. As the voices of discontent grew, Nigeria's impatience with Babangida's military regime increased. The nation clamored for the promised return to civilian rule.

Once again, however, the people's hopes were frustrated. In June 1993, what many international observers called the most honest election in Nigeria's history took place. Yet Babangida, unhappy at the results, voided the election. A year later another coup brought to power another general, Sani Abacha. Abacha unleashed a reign of terror against anyone considered a threat to his regime. M.K.O. Abiola, a Yoruba Muslim businessman who apparently won the 1993 election, was jailed. Many other prominent Nigerians were arrested and sentenced to death.

The repressive measures of Abacha's regime stifled public debate on the future of Nigeria. Nigerians lived in fear that Abacha's secret, military-run courts would declare them enemies of the state and sentence them to prison or even death. Other nations, meanwhile, threatened economic sanctions if the government failed to restore civilian rule. In response, Abacha promised a return to civilian rule in 1999. Nigerians hoped that this promise, unlike previous ones, would be fulfilled.

Lesson Review 3

Define: (a) secede, (b) indigenization decree
Identify: (a) Abubakar Tafawa Balewa, (b) Odumegwu Emeka Ojukwu, (c) Yakubu Gowon, (d) Biafra, (e) Murtala Muhammed, (f) Olusegun Obasanjo, (g) Alhaji Shehu Shagari, (h) Ibrahim Babangida, (i) Sani Abacha
Answer:
1. Why did many people think that Nigeria would adjust to independence more easily than other African countries?
2. How did regional differences affect the Nigerian government?
3. Why did Ojukwu think his secession would be successful?
4. How did the oil boom affect Nigeria?
5. Why did the military overthrow Shagari?
6. What did Abacha promise to the Nigerian people?

Critical Thinking
7. Ojukwu knew that international opinion was important. Why does what the world thinks about one country matter?

As Nigerians look to the future, they continue to observe the traditional ways of the past.

Chapter 7 Review

Summary

1. Nigeria is a land of contrast and change. Nigeria is a country of diverse land and peoples. Hundreds of ethnic groups and nearly 400 different languages can be found in Nigeria. However, the three dominant groups are the Hausa-Fulani, the Yoruba, and the Igbo. Religion—including Islam, Christianity, and traditional Nigerian religions—is important throughout Nigerian society. Often political disputes arise from religious differences. Nigeria's cultural contributions are many and ongoing. Remarkable historical achievements in the arts are being matched by the accomplishments of Nigerian artists, writers, and musicians today.

2. Foreign powers affected Nigeria's development. Since the beginning of the Atlantic slave trade, Nigeria has been threatened by foreign domination. The oppression brought about by that trade continued during colonial rule. By the 1920's, Nigerians regularly began to resist their foreign rulers. From these resistance efforts arose nationalism, spearheaded by Herbert Macaulay.

3. Nigeria struggles with nationhood. In 1960, Nigeria became an independent nation. However, the transition to self-rule was not an easy one. Regional differences and outbursts of violence plagued Nigeria throughout the 1960's, proving stronger than any government. In 1966 alone, two coups shook Nigeria. From May 1967 to January 1970, a terrible civil war tore the country apart. When it ended, Nigerians were remarkably successful in rebuilding their nation. An oil boom helped. Nigeria's economy improved and the country gained power on the international scene. However, the type of strong, decisive government that would make Nigeria predictably stable has not surfaced. A pattern seems to be in place: civilian rule followed by military rule, followed by a return to civilian rule, and so on. Yet, Nigerians remain firm in their attempts to fulfill the many promises of their nation.

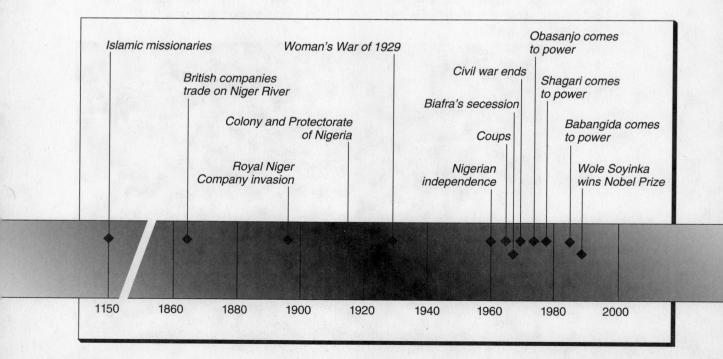

Islamic missionaries

Woman's War of 1929

Obasanjo comes to power

British companies trade on Niger River

Civil war ends

Shagari comes to power

Colony and Protectorate of Nigeria

Biafra's secession

Babangida comes to power

Coups

Royal Niger Company invasion

Nigerian independence

Wole Soyinka wins Nobel Prize

1150   1860   1880   1900   1920   1940   1960   1980   2000

Reviewing the Facts

1. Define the following terms:
   a. secede
   b. indigenization decree
2. Explain the importance of each of the following names or terms:
   a. Lagos
   b. Oyo
   c. Juju
   d. Yakubu Gowon
   e. Nnamdi Azikiwe
   f. Herbert Macaulay
   g. Women's War of 1929
   h. Abubakar Tafawa Balewa
   i. Sir George Goldie
   j. Odumegwu Emeka Ojukwu
   k. Olusegun Obasanjo
   l. Alhaji Shehu Shagari
3. Give two reasons why trying to divide Nigerians into a certain number of ethnic groups is a flawed approach to understanding the nation's culture.
4. Why did Islam gain so many Nigerian followers?
5. How did many Nigerians who practiced traditional religious beliefs treat Christianity and Islam?
6. Give one example of a contemporary Nigerian for each category, briefly describing his or her work: (a) sculpture, (b) music, (c) literature.
7. How big was the impact of the Atlantic slave trade on Nigeria?
8. What British attitude did the Royal Niger Company come to represent?
9. What victory did a Nigerian woman named Nwanyeruwa win in 1929?
10. Why is Herbert Macaulay known as the Father of Nigerian nationalism?
11. Why did many people believe that Nigeria would find it easy to make the transition to independence?
12. Describe the structure of Nigeria's first independent government.
13. Why has the census been such an important issue in Nigeria?
14. Why did Ojukwu and his followers decide to secede from Nigeria?
15. What important lessons were learned from the civil war in Nigeria?
16. What important decision did Nigeria make regarding OPEC?
17. How can oil be problematic for Nigeria?
18. (a) How did Obasanjo and then Shagari give Nigerians new hope in the government? (b) How were these hopes eventually shattered by Shagari's regime?
19. What happened following the 1993 elections?

Basic Skills

1. **Making a chart** Create a chart that summarizes the facts about Nigeria's three dominant ethnic groups. The columns of the chart should be labeled: *Location, Main Religion,* and *Importance in History*.
2. **Summarizing** Summarize the several unjust attitudes of the Royal Niger Company. Use your own words in completing the summary.
3. **Making a time line** Create a time line titled *Nigerian Government Since 1960.* On the time line indicate the date of each change of power and the person who took control.

Critical Thinking

1. **Evaluating sources** Read the quotation from *Things Fall Apart* on page 116. Remembering that this book is a novel, answer the following questions. (a) Does the passage express fact or opinion? (b) Based on this excerpt, how would you say the character who is speaking feels about the white missionaries?
2. **Contrasting events** You have read about the pattern of Nigerian government, which seems to alternate between civilian and military rule. Yet, each system of rule has been different. Contrast the military regimes of Gowon, Obasanjo, and Babangida. Look for differences in their promises, emphases, and tactics.
3. **Predicting outcomes** What sort of government do you think will emerge in Nigeria that will have the lasting stability the nation needs?

Perspectives on Past and Present

What gains would you say Nigeria has made since independence? What has the country lost? Make two lists that you can compare. Then write a conclusion about your findings.

Investigating History

1. The text states that the Nigerian civil war put into place several international charities that are still important to Africa. Do research to find out more specific information about these charities.
2. In *Things Fall Apart,* Chinua Achebe describes traditional Igbo life at the time of the missionary and colonization movements. Read this novel to find out how one Nigerian views the changes brought about by these movements.

131

Atlas

Algeria

Capital: Algiers
Area: 919,595 sq mi (2,381,741 sq km)
Population: 28,539,000
Official Language: Arabic
Industries and Products: barley, wheat, potatoes, tomatoes, grapes, dates; sheep, goats, cattle; timber; fish; iron, phosphates, silver; cement, flour and semolina, bricks; petroleum, natural gas

Angola

Capital: Luanda
Area: 481,354 sq mi (1,246,700 sq km)
Population: 10,070,000
Official Language: Portuguese
Industries and Products: cassava, sugarcane, corn; cattle, goats, chickens; timber; fish; diamonds; bread, corn and wheat flour, laundry soap, sugar, pasta, shoes, matches, beverages; natural gas

Benin

Capital: Porto-Novo
Area: 43,450 sq mi (112,600 sq km)
Population: 5,523,000
Official Language: French
Industries and Products: yams, cassava, corn, seed cotton, sorghum, tomatoes, peanuts, dry beans, sweet potatoes; goats, sheep, cattle, chickens; timber; fish; salt; cement, sugar, cotton fiber, palm oil

Botswana

Capital: Gaborone
Area: 224,607 sq mi (581,730 sq km)
Population: 1,392,000
Official Language: English (Tswana is the national language.)
Industries and Products: cereals, vegetables, melons, fruits, roots and tubers, cotton, peanuts; cattle, goats; timber; diamonds; food products, textiles, chemicals, wood products, paper products

Burkina Faso

Capital: Ouagadougou
Area: 105,946 sq mi (274,400 sq km)
Population: 10,423,000
Official Language: French
Industries and Products: sorghum, millet, sugarcane, corn, cotton, peanuts, rice; goats, sheep, cattle, chickens; gold; flour, soap, cotton yarn, tires, motorcycles and bicycles, footwear, beverages

Burundi

Capital: Bujumbura
Area: 10,740 sq mi (27,816 sq km)
Population: 6,262,000
Official Languages: Rundi; French
Industries and Products: bananas, cassava, sweet potatoes, dry beans, corn, yams and taros, sorghum, peanuts, rice, coffee; goats; timber; fish; peat; beverages, tobacco products, blankets, footwear

Cameroon

Capital: Yaoundé
Area: 179,714 sq mi (465,458 sq km)
Population: 13,521,000
Official Languages: French; English
Industries and Products: sugarcane, cassava, plantains, bananas, melons, corn, peanuts; cattle, goats, sheep, pigs; timber; fish; marble; cement, palm oil, flour, soap, shoes, beverages; petroleum

Cape Verde

Capital: Praia
Area: 1,557 sq mi (4,033 sq km)
Population: 436,000
Official Language: Portuguese
Industries and Products: sugarcane, coconuts, sweet potatoes, melons, bananas, cassava, potatoes, dates; goats; fish; tobacco products, flour, cocoa powder, bread, beverages

Central African Republic

Capital: Bangui
Area: 240,324 sq mi (622,436 sq km)
Population: 3,210,000
Official Languages: French; Sango
Industries and Products: cassava, yams, peanuts; cattle, goats, chickens; timber; fish; diamonds, gold; food, beverages, tobacco products, wood and metal products, textiles, apparel, chemicals

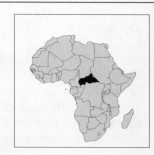

Chad
Capital: N'Djamena
Area: 495,755 sq mi (1,284,000 sq km)
Population: 5,587,000
Official Languages: Arabic; French
Industries and Products: sugarcane, cassava, millet, cotton; cattle, goats, sheep, camels, chickens; timber; fish; clay, gold; refined sugar, cattle hides, woven cotton fabrics, tobacco products

Comoros
Capital: Moroni
Area: 719 sq mi (1,862 sq km)
Population: 549,000
Official Languages: Arabic; French
Industries and Products: bananas, coconuts, cassava, corn, rice, cloves, vanilla, copra, spices; goats, cattle, sheep; fish; processed vanilla, cement, handicrafts, soaps, woodwork, clothing

Congo
Capital: Brazzaville
Area: 132,047 sq mi (342,000 sq km)
Population: 2,505,000
Official Language: French
Industries and Products: cassava, sugarcane, pineapples; goats; timber; gold; raw sugar, wheat flour, cement, jet fuel, soap, tobacco products, beverages, veneer sheets, footwear; petroleum

Coté d'Ivoire
Capital: Abidjan
Area: 123,847 sq mi (320,763 sq km)
Population: 14,791,000
Official Language: French
Industries and Products: yams, sugarcane, cassava, plantains, cocoa beans, rice, coconuts, corn, coffee; sheep, cattle, goats; timber; fish; diamonds; cement, beverages, synthetic fibers; petroleum

Djibouti
Capital: Djibouti
Area: 8,950 sq mi (23,200 sq km)
Population: 421,000
Official Languages: Arabic; French
Industries and Products: tomatoes, eggplant, melons; goats, sheep, cattle, camels; fish; salt; furniture, beverages, meat and hides, electromechanical goods

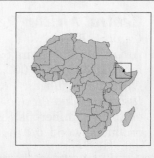

Egypt

Capital: Cairo
Area: 385,229 sq mi (997,739 sq km)
Population: 62,360,000
Official Language: Arabic
Industries and Products: sugarcane, corn, wheat, rice, oranges, tomatoes; sheep, goats, cattle, buffalo, camels, chickens; timber; fish; cement, fertilizer, sugar, appliances; petroleum, natural gas

Equatorial Guinea

Capital: Malabo
Area: 10,831 sq mi (28,051 sq km)
Population: 420,000
Official Language: Spanish
Industries and Products: cassava, sweet potatoes, bananas, coconuts, cocoa beans, coffee, palm oil and kernels; sheep, goats, pigs, cattle; timber; fish; veneer sheets

Eritrea

Capital: Asmara
Area: 45,405 sq mi (117,598 sq km)
Population: 3,579,000
Languages: Tigrinya, Tigre, Arabic, others (no official language yet)
Industries and Products: sesame seeds, lentils; salt; food products, textiles, leather goods

Ethiopia

Capital: Addis Ababa
Area: 426,372 sq mi (1,104,304 sq km)
Population: 55,980,000
Official Language: Amharic
Industries and Products: wheat, corn, sugarcane, barley; cattle, sheep, goats, horses, camels; timber; gold, platinum; food, beverages, leather, shoes, tobacco products; petroleum, natural gas

Gabon

Capital: Libreville
Area: 103,347 sq mi (267,667 sq km)
Population: 1,156,000
Official Language: French
Industries and Products: cassava, plantains, sugarcane; sheep, chickens; timber; manganese; cement, flour, refined sugar, beverages, tobacco products, textiles; petroleum, natural gas, fuel wood

Gambia

Capital: Banjul
Area: 4,127 sq mi (10,689 sq km)
Population: 989,000
Official Language: English
Industries and Products: peanuts, millet, rice, corn, cassava, palm oil and kernels, cotton; cattle, goats, sheep; fish; processed food, beverages, textiles, chemicals, printing and publishing

Ghana

Capital: Accra
Area: 92,098 sq mi (238,533 sq km)
Population: 17,763,000
Official Language: English
Industries and Products: roots and tubers, cereal, bananas, cocoa, coconuts, peppers, peanuts; goats, sheep, cattle, pigs, chickens; timber; fish; gold, diamonds; cement, flour, soap, toothpaste; fuels

Guinea

Capital: Conakry
Area: 42,042 sq mi (108,889 sq km)
Population: 6,549,000
Official Language: French
Industries and Products: sugarcane, corn, bananas, coffee, tomatoes; cattle, pigs, sheep; timber; fish; iron ore; food products, beverages, clothing, footwear, textiles, metal products

Guinea-Bissau

Capital: Bissau
Area: 13,948 sq mi (36,125 sq km)
Population: 1,125,000
Official Language: Portuguese
Industries and Products: rice, fruits, sweet potatoes, cassava, plantains, coconuts, peanuts, millet; cattle, pigs, sheep, goats, chickens; timber; fish; beverages, clothing, peanut and palm oil

Kenya

Capital: Nairobi
Area: 224,961 sq mi (582,646 sq km)
Population: 28,817,000
Official Languages: Swahili, English
Industries and Products: sugarcane, corn, cassava, sweet potatoes, plantains, potatoes, pineapple; cattle, goats, sheep; timber; fish; soda ash, salt, garnets; cement, sugar, wheat flour, beverages

Lesotho

Capital: Maseru
Area: 11,720 sq mi (30,355 sq km)
Population: 1,993,000
Official Languages: Sotho; English
Industries and Products: corn, fruit, sorghum, roots and tubers, peas, beans; sheep, goats, cattle, horses, pigs, chickens; timber; food, beverages, textiles, apparel, chemicals, printing, publishing

Liberia

Capital: Monrovia
Area: 38,250 sq mi (99,067 sq km)
Population: 3,073,000
Official Language: English
Industries and Products: cassava, sugarcane, rice, fruit, sweet potatoes, yams, rubber; sheep, goats, pigs, cattle, chickens; timber; fish; diamonds, gold; cement, palm oil, tobacco products

Libya

Capital: Tripoli
Area: 678,400 sq mi (1,757,000 sq km)
Population: 5,248,000
Official Language: Arabic
Industries and Products: watermelons, tomatoes, wheat, potatoes, barley, oranges, onions; sheep, goats, cattle, camels, chickens; timber; fish; lime, gypsum, salt, cement; petroleum, natural gas

Madagascar

Capital: Antananarivo
Area: 226,658 sq mi (587,041 sq km)
Population: 13,862,000
Official Languages: Malagasy, French
Industries and Products: cassava, rice, sugarcane, sweet potatoes, potatoes; cattle, pigs, goats, sheep, chickens; timber; fish; salt, graphite, gold; raw sugar, cement, soap, vegetable oils

Malawi

Capital: Lilongwe
Area: 45,747 sq mi (118,484 sq km)
Population: 9,808,000
Official Language: English (Chewa is the national language.)
Industries and Products: sugarcane, corn, potatoes, cassava, plantains, tobacco; cattle, goats, pigs, sheep; timber; fish; limestone; cement, chemicals, textiles, food products, beverages

Mali

Capital: Bamako
Area: 482,077 sq mi (1,248,574 sq km)
Population: 9,375,000
Official Language: French
Industries and Products: cereals, cotton, corn, peanuts, wheat; goats, sheep, cattle, camels, horses, pigs; timber; fish; limestone, gold; cotton fibers, sugar, cement, beverage, shoes

Mauritania

Capital: Nouakchott
Area: 398,000 sq mi (1,030,700 sq km)
Population: 2,263,000
Official Language: Arabic
Industries and Products: sorghum, rice, dates, melons, sweet potatoes, yams; sheep, goats, cattle, camels, horses, chickens; timber; fish; iron, gypsum; dairy products, hides

Mauritius

Capital: Port Louis
Area: 788 sq mi (2,040 sq km)
Population: 1,127,000
Official Language: English
Industries and Products: sugarcane, tea, potatoes, tomatoes, cabbages, onions, corn, peanuts, pineapples; goats, cattle, pigs, sheep; timber; fish; clothing, raw sugar, molasses, beverages

Morocco

Capital: Rabat
Area: 177,117 sq mi (458,730 sq km)
Population: 29,169,000
Official Language: Arabic
Industries and Products: wheat, sugar beets, barley, sugarcane, tomatoes; sheep, goats, cattle, chickens; timber; fish; phosphate, iron; cement, refined sugar, carpets; petroleum, natural gas

Mozambique

Capital: Maputo
Area: 313,661 sq mi (812,379 sq km)
Population: 18,115,000
Official Language: Portuguese
Industries and Products: cassava, coconut, sugarcane, corn, sorghum, peanuts; cattle, goats, sheep, pigs, chickens; timber; fish; salt, bauxite, garnets; cement, wheat flour, raw sugar, soap

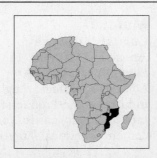

Namibia
Capital: Windhoek
Area: 318,580 sq mi (825,580 sq km)
Population: 1,652,000
Official Language: English
Industries and Products: roots and tubers, corn, millet, fruits, vegetables, wool; cattle, sheep, goats, karakul; fish; diamonds, zinc, lead, copper; processed foods, textiles, carved wood products

Niger
Capital: Niamey
Area: 458,075 sq mi (1,186,408 sq km)
Population: 9,280,000
Official Language: French
Industries and Products: millet, sorghum, roots and tubers, vegetables and melons, sugarcane; goats, sheep, cattle, camels, horses; fish; uranium; cement, cheese, beverages, cotton textiles

Nigeria
Capital: Abuja
Area: 356,669 sq mi (923,768 sq km)
Population: 101,232,000
Official Language: English
Industries and Products: roots, cereals, rice, corn; goats, sheep, cattle; timber; fish; limestone, marble; food products, beverages, textiles, chemicals, metal products, machinery; petroleum, natural gas

Rwanda
Capital: Kigali
Area: 9,757 sq mi (25,271 sq km)
Population: 8,605,000
Official Languages: Rwanda; French
Industries and Products: plantains, sweet potatoes, cassava, potatoes, cereals; goats, cattle, sheep, pigs; timber; fish; tin, tungsten, gold; cement, soap, sugar, beverages, shoes; natural gas

São Tomé and Príncipe
Capital: São Tomé
Area: 386 sq mi (1,001 sq km)
Population: 140,000
Official Language: Portuguese
Industries and Products: coconuts, cassava, fruits, cocoa, copra, bananas, palmetto, vegetables, cereals, taro; goats, cattle, pigs, sheep; timber; fish; bread, soap, coconut and palm oil, ice

Senegal
Capital: Dakar
Area: 75,951 sq mi (196,712 sq km)
Population: 9,007,000
Official Language: French
Industries and Products: sugarcane, peanuts, millet, rice, corn, sorghum, cotton; sheep, cattle, goats, pigs; timber; fish; peanut oil, wheat flour, fertilizers, soap, sugar, cotton fiber, beverages

Seychelles
Capital: Victoria
Area: 175 sq mi (453 sq km)
Population: 73,000
Official Languages: Creole; English; French
Industries and Products: coconuts, copra, bananas, tea; pigs, goats, cattle, chicken; fish; guano; canned tuna, beverages, tobacco products

Sierra Leone
Capital: Freetown
Area: 27,699 sq mi (71,740 sq km)
Population: 4,753,000
Official Language: English
Industries and Products: rice, cassava, sugarcane, palm oil and kernels, plantains; cattle, sheep, goats, pigs, chickens; timber; fish; bauxite, titanium, diamonds, gold; nails, beverages, paint

Somalia
Capital: Mogadishu
Area: 246,000 sq mi (637,000 sq km)
Population: 7,348,000
Official Languages: Somali; Arabic
Industries and Products: sugarcane, sorghum, bananas, corn, vegetables; goats, sheep, camels, cattle; timber; fish; salt; food, tobacco products, paper, printing, plastics, chemicals, beverages

South Africa
Capitals: Pretoria (admin.); Cape Town (leg.); Bloemfontein (jud.)
Area: 433,680 sq mi (1,123,226 sq km)
Population: 45,095,000
Official Languages: Afrikaans; English
Industries and Products: corn, fruits, sugar, wheat, wool; poultry, eggs, cattle, sheep, goats; timber; fish; gold, coal, platinum, diamonds; food, beverages, chemicals, metals, transport equipment

Sudan

Capital: Khartoum
Area: 966,757 sq mi (2,503,890 sq km)
Population: 30,120,000
Official Language: Arabic
Industries and Products: sugarcane, sorghum, wheat, millet, cotton, peanuts; cattle, sheep, goats, camels; timber; fish; salt, gold; flour, refined sugar, cement, plastics, yarn, perfume, textiles

Swaziland

Capital: Mbabane
Area: 6,704 sq mi (17,364 sq km)
Population: 967,000
Official Languages: Swazi; English
Industries and Products: sugarcane, corn, citrus fruits, cotton; cattle, goats, sheep, pigs, chickens; timber; fish; asbestos, diamonds; beverages, paper, textiles, wood products, machinery

Tanzania

Capital: Dar es Salaam
Area: 364,017 sq mi (942,799 sq km)
Population: 28,701,000
Official Languages: Swahili; English
Industries and Products: cassava, corn, sugarcane, bananas, plantains, rice, sorghum; cattle, goats, sheep, pigs, chicken; timber; fish; salt, diamonds; cement, hides, soap, fertilizer

Togo

Capital: Lomé
Area: 21,925 sq mi (56,785 sq km)
Population: 4,410,000
Official Language: French
Industries and Products: cassava, yams, corn, sorghum, millet, cottonseed, rice, peanuts, bananas, coconuts; timber; fish; phosphate, salt, marble; cement, wheat flour, beverages, footwear

Tunisia

Capital: Tunis
Area: 59,664 sq mi (154,530 sq km)
Population: 8,880,000
Official Language: Arabic
Industries and Products: wheat, barley, tomatoes, watermelon, olives, sugar beets, potatoes, oranges; sheep, goats, cattle; timber; fish; phosphate, iron ore; cement, flour, steel, beverages

Uganda

Capital: Kampala
Area: 93,070 sq mi (241,040 sq km)
Population: 19,573,000
Official Languages: English; Swahili
Industries and Products: bananas, plantains, cassava, sweet potatoes, sugarcane; cattle, goats, sheep; timber; fish; tungsten, tin, gold; soap, sugar, cement, animal feed, metal products, shoes

Zaire

Capital: Kinshasa
Area: 905,446 sq mi (2,345,095 sq km)
Population: 44,061,000
Official Language: French
Industries and Products: cassava, sugarcane, corn, bananas, peanuts; goats, cattle, sheep, chickens; timber; fish; copper, diamonds; cement, palm oil, flour, feed, explosives; petroleum

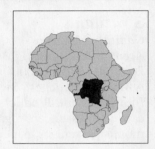

Zambia

Capital: Lusaka
Area: 290,586 sq mi (752,614 sq km)
Population: 9,446,000
Official Language: English
Industries and Products: corn, sugarcane, cassava, onions, tomatoes, oranges, cotton, wheat; cattle, goats, pigs, sheep, chickens; timber; fish; copper, gold; cement, sulfuric acid, sugar

Zimbabwe

Capital: Harare
Area: 150,873 sq mi (390,759 sq km)
Population: 11,140,000
Official Language: English
Industries and Products: sugarcane, wheat, tobacco, vegetables, cottonseed, peanuts; cattle, goats, sheep, chickens; timber; fish; gold, nickel, asbestos; chemicals, beverages, textiles, shoes

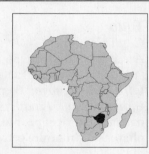

Glossary

— a —

abolition: A movement beginning in the late 1700's to end the slave trade and later to entirely do away with slavery itself. (p. 29)

apartheid: A policy of forced separation of races under white control, used in South Africa. (p. 64)

archaeology: The study of ancient societies through remains such as fossils, artifacts, buildings. (p. 3)

asiento: A license to import slaves into the Spanish colonies. (p. 23)

assimilation: The process of becoming absorbed into another culture rather than remaining distinctly different. (p. 42)

— b —

botany: The scientific study of plants. (p. 3)

— c —

colonialism: The process of acquiring and maintaining colonies. (p. 37)

— d —

deforestation: The loss of forests through logging operations or overuse. (p. 100)

desertification: The development of desert over a period of time in an area that was previously green land, due to climate changes or human use. (p. 4)

direct rule: A means of governing a colony through a centralized administrative system, with laws and regulations coming from the imperialist country. (p. 42)

divine kingship: A system in which the ruling king serves as both the political and spiritual head of state. (p. 17)

— e —

export-led development: A concentration on the production of goods for export rather than on the internal development of a nation's people. (p. 95)

— g —

griot: A professional African storyteller, trained in the oral tradition. (p. 1)

— h —

hadj: The Islamic pilgrimage to the Arabian city of Mecca. (p. 75)

hieroglyph: A character used in the picture-writing system of ancient Egypt. (p. 9)

— i —

imperialism: A policy of conquering and then ruling other lands as colonies. (p. 37)

indigenization decree: An economic policy that forces foreign companies to yield large percentages of their business to native citizens. (p. 126)

indirect rule: A means of governing a colony through councils of native authorities, who are in turn supervised by officers of the imperialist country. (p. 42)

— l —

legitimate trade: An economy based on products rather than on slave trade. (p. 38)

linguistics: The study of languages. (p. 3)

— m —

Middle Passage: The voyage across the Atlantic Ocean of people captured in Africa and sent to the Americas to be sold as slaves. (p. 21)

— n —

Naam: A grass-roots farmers' organization whose purpose is to take control of the farmers' own development. (p. 103)

nationalism: A feeling of loyalty for one's own land and people. (p. 49)

neo-colonialism: The current trend away from traditional African ways and toward a focus on exports at the expense of African people. (p. 95)

— o —

oasis: A green area in a desert where underground water comes to the surface in a spring or well. (p. 5)

oral tradition: A system of passing history down from one generation to the next through storytelling and other forms of oral language. (p. 1)

orisha: The officially recognized gods and goddesses of the Yoruba people. (p. 74)

— p —

pan-Africanism: A movement celebrating the kinship of all those of African descent and aiming to improve their lives. (p. 52)

patina: A special surface texture, achieved through age or use, that enhances the appearance of an artwork. (p. 80)

pharaohs: Rulers of ancient Egypt. (p. 9)

polyrhythm: A combination of contrasting rhythms commonly used in African music. (p. 78)

protectorate: The position of greater authority that a governing country assumes over a dependent one. (p. 54)

— r —

refugee: A person left homeless because of famine, drought, or political instability. (p. 86)

— s —

sanctions: An economic policy adopted by one or more nations to try to force another nation to change a disliked practice or custom. (p. 108)

savanna: A tropical grassland with scattered trees and bushes. (p. 4)

secede: To withdraw from a nation for the purpose of forming an independent nation. (p. 125)

Second Liberation: The pro-democracy movement currently spreading across Africa. (p. 91)

sedentary: Of a society that settles in one place. (p. 8)

structural adjustment: A method of controlling government debt by restructuring the economy on free-market principles, which often means increasing exports and decreasing spending on government and welfare services. (p. 97)

syncretism: The blending of two beliefs in such a way that neither is completely abandoned or altered. (p. 12)

— t —

trade language: A language used by a large number of people that may be either a combination of two or more languages, or a simplification of one language. (p. 6)

Triangular Trade: The trade between Africa, Europe, and the Americas during the time of the Atlantic slave trade, consisting of goods shipped from Europe to Africa in exchange for slaves, who were then sent by Europeans to the Americas in exchange for produce, cash, or promissory notes. (p. 24)

Minerals, 4, 5

Mining: in Africa, 12, 37, 43, 46; exports and, 12, 95, 97, 114; slavery and, 29, 32–34

Missionary work: in Africa, 39, 44, 46, 55–57, 116, 119, 130; and spread of culture, 78

Mobutu Sese Seko (President of Zaire), 88, 89, 96

Mogadishu, 12

Moi, Daniel arap (President of Kenya), 85, 88, 90

Mojimba, 36, 37

Molefe, Popo, 106–108

Mopedi people, 110

Moroccan leather, 74

Morocco, 59

Mosques, in North Africa, 74, 82

Mozambique, 81, 88, 94; civil war in, 88, 93; colonization of, 39; independence of, 62

Muhammad (Prophet), 11

Muhammed, Murtala, 127

Music: African, 69, 77–82, 120, 130; instruments, 79; slaves and, 78

Muslims, 14, 15, 50, 54–56, 66, 75, 117–119, 125. See also Islam.

Naam groups, 103

Nairobi, 84, 90; Park, 90

Namibia, 88, 91

Napata, 10, 71, 72

National party, 107, 109, 110, 112; Nigerian, 128

Nationalist movements, 45, 49–66, 122, 123

Native Americans, slavery and, 22

Native authorities, 42

Nbande, Nzinga, 23

Négritude, 52, 54

Neo-colonialism, 95

New Kingdom (Egypt), 10

Ngwenya, Malangatana Valente, 81

Niger, 89

Nigeria, 1, 17, 88, 102; archaeology in, 72; art of, 73, 74, 81, 82, 119, 120, 130; civil war in, 125–127, 130; colonialism in, 119, 121–124, 130; ethnic groups of, 117–119, 130; exports of, 43, 126, 127, 130; government, 88, 89, 92, 123–130; independence of, 122, 123; mining in, 43; nationalist movement in, 55, 56, 122, 123; natural resources of, 117, 123, 125; oil resources, 125–127; religions of, 119; Second Republic, 128; slave trade and, 21

Nigerian National Democratic party, 122

Niger River, 5, 6, 15, 16, 121, 130

Nile River, 5, 6, 9–11, 18, 69–71, 82

Nilo-Saharan languages, 6

Nkrumah, Kwame, 59–61, 85, 88, 96

Nobel Prize winners, African, 81, 110, 120, 130

Nok culture, 72, 73, 82

North Africa: architecture of, 74; colonization in, 39, 59; invasions by, 14; languages of, 6; slavery and, 21; struggle for independence in, 54–56, 61, 62. See also names of individual countries.

Northern People's Congress, 124

Nupe people, 118

Nwanyeruwa, 122, 123

Nyasaland, 45. See also Malawi.

Oasis, 5

Oba, 17

Obasanjo, Olusegen, 92, 102, 127, 130

Oil exports, 125–127, 130

Ojukwu, Odumegwu Emeka, 125, 126

Okigbo, Christopher, 120

Olowe of Ise, 74

Olympics, 109

Oni, 73, 74

Onobrakpeya, Burce, 120

OPEC (Organization of Petroleum Exporting Countries), 126

Opobo people, 122

Oral tradition, 1–3, 14, 15, 17, 18

Organization of African Unity, 60, 62, 66, 98

Orisha, 74

Ottoman Empire, 56

Oyo (Nigeria), 25, 118, 121

Pacification, and colonialism, 40, 41, 46

Pan-Africanism, 52; conferences, 52

Pan-Africanist Congress (PAC), 59, 64, 66, 113

Partition, of Africa, 38, 39, 46

Pastoral Period, 69

Patina, 80

Peca de India, 23

People's Front for Democracy and Justice (PFDJ), 91

Pemba, 12

Persia, African trade with, 12

Pharaohs, 9, 10

Piankhi, 71

Picasso, Pablo, 79

Piula, Trigo, 81

Plantations, African, 43, 94; slavery on American, 22, 29, 32–34. See also Agriculture; Farming.

Polyrhythm, 78, 79

Population: concerns, in Africa, 85, 94, 97, 99, 100, 126; growth, in ancient Africa, 8, 10

Population Registration Control Act, 109

Portugal: colonization by, 39, 42–44, 62, 94; slave trade and, 22, 23, 31; trade with, 17

Poverty, in Africa, 61, 85, 86, 88, 91, 93, 112, 114, 126

Profiteers, 76, 82

Prosser, Gabriel, 30

Protectorate, British, 54

Ptolemy IV (Greek Pharaoh), 71

Punch cartoons, 37, 38

Queen Mother, 70, 82

Quilting, African, 78, 79

Racism: colonial rule and, 42, 46, 50, 55, 62, 66, 121, 123; perceptions of African art and, 79; slavery and, 32, 34. See also Apartheid.

Rawlings, Jerry J., 92

Red Cross, 93

Refugees, 86, 93, 98, 99, 114

Religion: in ancient Africa, 12, 50, 69, 70, 73, 74, 80, 82; in ancient Egypt, 9–11; conflict and, 15, 130; colonization and, 44, 46, 119; slaves and, 32, 33, 78. See also Churches; Missionary work.

Renaissance, 77

Reparations, 33

Resources, natural, 94

Rhodes, Cecil, 37

Rhodesia, 45

Rioting/violence: in Nigeria, 124; in South Africa, 64, 108, 110–115. See also Civil war.

Rivers, 5. See also names of specific rivers.

Rock drawings, 69, 70, 82

Roman dynasty, in Egypt, 10, 72

Roundhead Period, 69

Royal Niger Company, 121, 130

Rwanda, 86, 99

Saar, Betye, 80

Safina party, 90–91

Sahara, 4, 5, 100; rock drawings in, 69, 70; slave trade and, 22; trade across, 14–16, 121

Saheli, el, 75

Salim Ahmed Salim, 98, 99

Samba, Cheri, 81

San people, 6, 8

Sanctions, against South Africa, 65, 108, 109

Weapons: in ancient Africa, 75; and colonialism, 41, 42, 46; in modern Africa, 96, 109, 112; and the slave trade, 23, 25, 26, 31, 32

West Africa, 5, 14–18, 50, 52, 55, 75; archaeology in, 72; colonialism in, 41, 42, 56; deforestation in, 100; independence movements in, 61, 62, 66; languages of, 6, 117; oral tradition in, 1, 15; slave trade and, 22

West Indies: pan-Africanism and, 52; slavery in, 21, 26, 121

Whitaker, Jennifer, 103

"White Man's Burden," 39

Wissman, Hermann von, 41

Women: empowerment of, 101–103; farmers, 102–104; in Green Belt Movement, 101; Islam and, 11; in prehistory, 8, 10

Women's War of 1929, 122, 130

World Bank, 88, 90, 95–97, 102

World Black and African Festival of Arts and Culture, 120

World Health Organization, 104

World War I, 54–56, 66

World War II, 50, 55, 56, 58, 64, 66, 123

Writing system: Arabic, 14, 118; Meroitic, 10; Kushite, 72. *See also* Hieroglyphs.

Xhosa people, 110, 113

Yemen, 10

Yoruba people, 1, 26, 50, 56, 73, 74, 78, 82, 118, 119, 123, 130

Young Kikuyu Association, 50, 57

Zaghlul, Saad, 56

Zaire, 8, 88, 105; art of, 81; climate of, 4; exports of, 95; government of, 88, 89, 96

Zaire River, 5, 16

Zambezi River, 5

Zambia, 43, 98, 125; colonization of, 43; exports of, 95, 97; government of, 88, 89, 91, 97, 98; mining in, 43, 95, 97; structural adjustment in, 97

Zanzibar, 12, 56

Zimbabwe, 12–14, 18, 39

Zong (slave ship), 28

Zulu people, 110, 113

Acknowledgments

Photo Credits

Cover: (tl) Ron Testa, photographer/Field Museum of Natural History. (tr) Doran H. Ross, photographer/Fowler Museum of Cultural History. (bl) Mike Yamashita/Woodfin Camp & Associates. (bm) H. Kanus/SuperStock. (br) Margaret Courtney-Clarks.

Contents: *iv* (t) © Tom Van Sant/The Stock Market. *iv* (cr) Brown Brothers. *iv* (br) UPI/Bettman. *iv* (bl) Werner Forman Archive/British Museum, London. *v* (t) © Jason Lauré. *v* (b) © Marc & Evelyne Bernheim/Woodfin Camp.

Introduction: *vi* © Wezelman/Elk Photo.

Chapter 1: *viii* © Tom Van Sant/The Stock Market. 3 © Marc & Evelyn Bernheim/Woodfin Camp. 4, 8, 13 © Jason Lauré. 5 © John Elk III. 9 Erich Lessing/Art Resource, NY. 11 © Werner Forman Archive. 15 Bibliothèque Nationale, Paris. 17 Photo © Don Carl Steffen/DCS Enterprises.

Chapter 2: 20 National Maritime Museum. 21 The Library Company of Philadelphia. 22 Photo © Michael Holford/Collection of British Museum. 25, 30 (b) Courtesy of the National Library of Jamaica. 26, 29 Bettmann/Hulton. 27 © John Elk III. 28 Wilberforce House Museum, Hull City Museums and Art Gallery. 30 (t) Mansell Collection. 33 © Wezelman/Elk Photo.

Chapter 3: 36 Harper & Brothers. 37, 38 Mary Evans Picture Library. 42 Culver Pictures. 43 The Bettmann Archive. 45 Brown Brothers.

Chapter 4: 48, 58, 59 UPI/Bettmann. 49, 61 (inset) The Bettmann Archive. 52 Culver Pictures. 53 National Archives. 55 Popperfoto. 60, 61 (r) AP/Wide World Photos. 62, 65 © Jason Lauré.

Chapter 5: 68 (l) Photograph by Anita J. Glaze, Dikodougou district, 1970, Côte d'Ivoire. 68 (r) The Paul and Ruth Tishman Collection of African Art loaned by the Walt Disney Company, photographed by Jerry L. Thompson. 70 (l), 71, 72, 75 © Werner Forman Archive. 70 (r) Bridgeman/Art Resource, NY. 73, 77, 78 Werner Forman Archive/British Museum, London. 74 Werner Forman Archive, National Museum, Lagos, Nigeria. 79 (t) Neg.No.2A10440. Photo: Logan. Courtesy Department of Library Services, American Museum of Natural History. 79 (b) STRING. Pieced by Rosie Lee Tompkins, Richmond, California, 1985. Restructured and quilted by Willia Ette Graham, Oakland, California. 1985 Photo by Geoffrey Johnson. Courtesy San Francisco Craft & Folk Art Museum. 80 William Nettles. 81 Museum of New Mexico Collections, Museum of International Folk Art, Santa Fe. Photographer, unknown.

Chapter 6: 84, 90, 91, 101, © Jason Lauré. 86 UPI/Bettmann. 88, © Sygma. 89 © Karim Daher/Gamma Liaison. 92 © Eli Reed/Magnum Photos. 93, 106 Reuters/Bettmann. 94 George Rodger/Magnum Photos. 96 © John Elk III. 98 © Les Stone/Sygma. 99 AP/Wide World Photos. 100 (b) © Michael Nichols/Magnum Photos. 100 (inset) © Wendy Stone/ Gamma Liaison. 102 © F. Mayer/Magnum Photos. 104 Carolyn Watson/Hunger Project. 105, 107 © W. Campbell/Sygma. 110 © Greg Marinovich/Sygma. 111 © Patrick Durand/Sygma. 112 © Patrick Robert/Sygma. 113 AP/Wide World Photos.

Chapter 7: 116, 120 (bl) National Archives. 117 (tr) © Wezelman/Elk Photo. 117 (cr), 129 © Bruno Barbey/Magnum Photos. 118 © Marc & Evelyne Bernheim/Woodfin Camp. 120 (tr), 120 (cr), 125 (cl), 125 (br) AP/Wide World Photos. 122 © Marc Riboud/Magnum Photos. 126 © Abbas/Magnum Photos. 128 UPI/Bettmann.